THE GRAND
CHESSBOARD

ZBIGNIEW BRZEZINSKI

THE GRAND CHESSBOARD

American Primacy and Its Geostrategic Imperatives

BASIC
BOOKS

A Member of the Perseus Books Group

Published by Basic Books, A Member of the Perseus Books
Group.

Designed by Elliott Beard.

Maps by Kenneth Velasquez.

Library of Congress Cataloging-in-Publication Data

Brzezinski, Zbigniew K., 1928–
    The grand chessboard : American primacy and its
geostrategic imperatives / Zbigniew Brzezinski.—1st ed.
        p.   cm.
    Includes index.
    ISBN-13 978-0-465-02725-5 ISBN-10 0-465-02725-3 (cloth)
    ISBN-13 978-0-465-02726-2 ISBN-10 0-465-02726-1 (paper)
    1. United States—Foreign relations—1989–   2. Geopol-
itics—United States—History—20th Century.   3. Geopolitics—History—20th century.   4. World politics—1989–
5. Eurasia—Strategic aspects.
I. Title.
E840.B785   1997   97-13812
327.73—dc20   CIP

        35 34 33 32 31 30 29 28 27

For my students—to help them shape tomorrow's world

CONTENTS

MAPS

LIST OF CHARTS AND TABLES

INTRODUCTION

Superpower Politics

EVER SINCE THE CONTINENTS started interacting politically, some five hundred years ago, Eurasia has been the center of world power. In different ways, at different times, the peoples inhabiting Eurasia—though mostly those from its Western European periphery—penetrated and dominated the world's other regions as individual Eurasian states attained the special status and enjoyed the privileges of being the world's premier powers.

The last decade of the twentieth century has witnessed a tectonic shift in world affairs. For the first time ever, a non-Eurasian power has emerged not only as the key arbiter of Eurasian power relations but also as the world's paramount power. The defeat and collapse of the Soviet Union was the final step in the rapid ascendance of a Western Hemisphere power, the United States, as the sole and, indeed, the first truly global power.

Eurasia, however, retains its geopolitical importance. Not only is its western periphery—Europe—still the location of much of the world's political and economic power, but its eastern region—Asia—has lately become a vital center of economic growth and rising political influence. Hence, the issue of how a globally engaged

America copes with the complex Eurasian power relationships—and particularly whether it prevents the emergence of a dominant and antagonistic Eurasian power—remains central to America's capacity to exercise global primacy.

It follows that—in addition to cultivating the various novel dimensions of power (technology, communications, information, as well as trade and finance)—American foreign policy must remain concerned with the geopolitical dimension and must employ its influence in Eurasia in a manner that creates a stable continental equilibrium, with the United States as the political arbiter.

Eurasia is thus the chessboard on which the struggle for global primacy continues to be played, and that struggle involves geostrategy—the strategic management of geopolitical interests. It is noteworthy that as recently as 1940 two aspirants to global power, Adolf Hitler and Joseph Stalin, agreed explicitly (in the secret negotiations of November of that year) that America should be excluded from Eurasia. Each realized that the injection of American power into Eurasia would preclude his ambitions regarding global domination. Each shared the assumption that Eurasia is the center of the world and that he who controls Eurasia controls the world. A half century later, the issue has been redefined: will America's primacy in Eurasia endure, and to what ends might it be applied?

The ultimate objective of American policy should be benign and visionary: to shape a truly cooperative global community, in keeping with long-range trends and with the fundamental interests of humankind. But in the meantime, it is imperative that no Eurasian challenger emerges, capable of dominating Eurasia and thus also of challenging America. *The formulation of a comprehensive and integrated Eurasian geostrategy is therefore the purpose of this book.*

Zbigniew Brzezinski
Washington, D.C.
April 1997

THE GRAND
CHESSBOARD

CHAPTER 1

Hegemony of a New Type

HEGEMONY IS AS OLD AS MANKIND. But America's current global supremacy is distinctive in the rapidity of its emergence, in its global scope, and in the manner of its exercise. In the course of a single century, America has transformed itself—and has also been transformed by international dynamics—from a country relatively isolated in the Western Hemisphere into a power of unprecedented worldwide reach and grasp.

THE SHORT ROAD TO GLOBAL SUPREMACY

The Spanish-American War in 1898 was America's first overseas war of conquest. It thrust American power far into the Pacific, beyond Hawaii to the Philippines. By the turn of the century, American strategists were already busy developing doctrines for a two-ocean naval supremacy, and the American navy had begun to challenge the notion that Britain "rules the waves." American claims of a special status as the sole guardian of the Western Hemisphere's security—proclaimed earlier in the century by the Monroe Doctrine and subsequently justified by America's alleged "manifest destiny"—were even further enhanced by the construction of the Panama Canal, which facilitated naval domination over both the Atlantic and Pacific Oceans.

The basis for America's expanding geopolitical ambitions was provided by the rapid industrialization of the country's economy. By the outbreak of World War I, America's growing economic might already accounted for about 33 percent of global GNP, which displaced Great Britain as the world's leading industrial power. This remarkable economic dynamism was fostered by a culture that favored experimentation and innovation. America's political institutions and free market economy created unprecedented opportunities for ambitious and iconoclastic inventors, who were not inhibited from pursuing their personal dreams by archaic privileges or rigid social hierarchies. In brief, national culture was uniquely congenial to economic growth, and by attracting and quickly assimilating the most talented individuals from abroad, the culture also facilitated the expansion of national power.

World War I provided the first occasion for the massive projection of American military force into Europe. A heretofore relatively isolated power promptly transported several hundred thousand of its troops across the Atlantic—a transoceanic military expedition unprecedented in its size and scope, which signaled the emergence of a new major player in the international arena. Just as important, the war also prompted the first major American diplomatic effort to apply American principles in seeking a solution to Europe's international problems. Woodrow Wilson's famous Fourteen Points represented the injection into European geopolitics of American idealism, reinforced by American might. (A decade and a half earlier, the United States had played a leading role in settling a Far Eastern conflict between Russia and Japan, thereby also asserting its growing international stature.) The fusion of American idealism and American power thus made itself fully felt on the world scene.

Strictly speaking, however, World War I was still predominantly a European war, not a global one. But its self-destructive character marked the beginning of the end of Europe's political, economic, and cultural preponderance over the rest of the world. In the course of the war, no single European power was able to prevail decisively—and the war's outcome was heavily influenced by the entrance into the conflict of the rising non-European power, America. Thereafter, Europe would become increasingly the object, rather than the subject, of global power politics.

However, this brief burst of American global leadership did not produce a continuing American engagement in world affairs. Instead, America quickly retreated into a self-gratifying combination of isolationism and idealism. Although by the mid-twenties and early thirties totalitarianism was gathering strength on the European continent, American power—by then including a powerful two-ocean fleet that clearly outmatched the British navy—remained disengaged. Americans preferred to be bystanders to global politics.

Consistent with that predisposition was the American concept of security, based on a view of America as a continental island. American strategy focused on sheltering its shores and was thus narrowly national in scope, with little thought given to international or global considerations. The critical international players were still the European powers and, increasingly, Japan.

The European era in world politics came to a final end in the course of World War II, the first truly global war. Fought on three continents simultaneously, with the Atlantic and the Pacific Oceans also heavily contested, its global dimension was symbolically demonstrated when British and Japanese soldiers—representing, respectively, a remote Western European island and a similarly remote East Asian island—collided thousands of miles from their homes on the Indian-Burmese frontier. Europe and Asia had become a single battlefield.

Had the war's outcome been a clear-cut victory for Nazi Germany, a single European power might then have emerged as globally preponderant. (Japan's victory in the Pacific would have gained for that nation the dominant Far Eastern role, but in all probability, Japan would still have remained only a regional hegemon.) Instead, Germany's defeat was sealed largely by the two extra-European victors, the United States and the Soviet Union, which became the successors to Europe's unfulfilled quest for global supremacy.

The next fifty years were dominated by the bipolar American-Soviet contest for global supremacy. In some respects, the contest between the United States and the Soviet Union represented the fulfillment of the geopoliticians' fondest theories: it pitted the world's leading maritime power, dominant over both the Atlantic and the Pacific Oceans, against the world's leading land power, paramount on the Eurasian heartland (with the Sino-Soviet bloc encompassing a space remarkably reminiscent of the scope of the Mongol Empire). The geopolitical dimension could not have been clearer: North America versus Eurasia, with the world at stake. The winner would truly dominate the globe. There was no one else to stand in the way, once victory was finally grasped.

Each rival projected worldwide an ideological appeal that was infused with historical optimism, that justified for each the necessary exertions while reinforcing its conviction in inevitable victory. Each rival was clearly dominant within its own space—unlike the imperial European aspirants to global hegemony, none of which ever quite succeeded in asserting decisive preponderance within Europe itself. And each used its ideology to reinforce its hold over its respective vassals and tributaries, in a manner somewhat reminiscent of the age of religious warfare.

The combination of global geopolitical scope and the proclaimed universality of the competing dogmas gave the contest unprecedented intensity. But an additional factor—also imbued with global implications—made the contest truly unique. The advent of nuclear weapons meant that a head-on war, of a classical type, between the two principal contestants would not only spell their mutual destruction but could unleash lethal consequences for a significant portion of humanity. The intensity of the conflict was thus simultaneously subjected to extraordinary self-restraint on the part of both rivals.

In the geopolitical realm, the conflict was waged largely on the peripheries of Eurasia itself. The Sino-Soviet bloc dominated most of Eurasia but did not control its peripheries. North America succeeded in entrenching itself on both the extreme western and extreme eastern shores of the great Eurasian continent. The defense of these continental bridgeheads (epitomized on the western "front" by the Berlin blockade and on the eastern by the Korean War) was thus the first strategic test of what came to be known as the Cold War.

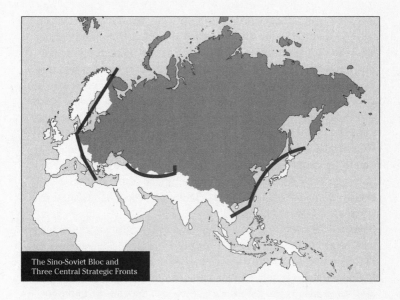

The Sino-Soviet Bloc and
Three Central Strategic Fronts

In the Cold War's final phase, a third defensive "front"—the southern—appeared on Eurasia's map (see map above). The Soviet invasion of Afghanistan precipitated a two-pronged American response: direct U.S. assistance to the native resistance in Afghanistan in order to bog down the Soviet army; and a large-scale buildup of the U.S. military presence in the Persian Gulf as a deterrent to any further southward projection of Soviet political or military power. The United States committed itself to the defense of the Persian Gulf region, on a par with its western and eastern Eurasian security interests.

The successful containment by North America of the Eurasian bloc's efforts to gain effective sway over all of Eurasia—with both sides deterred until the very end from a direct military collision for fear of a nuclear war—meant that the outcome of the contest was eventually decided by nonmilitary means. Political vitality, ideological flexibility, economic dynamism, and cultural appeal became the decisive dimensions.

The American-led coalition retained its unity, whereas the Sino-Soviet bloc split within less than two decades. In part, this was due to the democratic coalition's greater flexibility, in contrast to the hierarchical and dogmatic—but also brittle—character of the Communist camp. The former involved shared values, but without a formal doctrinal format. The latter emphasized dogmatic orthodoxy, with only one valid interpretative center. America's principal vassals were also significantly weaker than America, whereas the Soviet Union could not indefinitely treat China as a subordinate. The outcome was also due to the fact that the American side proved to be economically and technologically much more dynamic, whereas the Soviet Union gradually stagnated and could not effectively compete either in economic growth or in military technology. Economic decay in turn fostered ideological demoralization.

In fact, Soviet military power—and the fear it inspired among westerners—for a long time obscured the essential asymmetry between the two contestants. America was simply much richer, technologically much more advanced, militarily more resilient and innovative, socially more creative and appealing. Ideological constraints also sapped the creative potential of the Soviet Union, making its system increasingly rigid and its economy increasingly wasteful and technologically less competitive. As long as a mutually destructive war did not break out, in a protracted competition the scales had to tip eventually in America's favor.

The final outcome was also significantly influenced by cultural considerations. The American-led coalition, by and large, accepted as positive many attributes of America's political and social culture. America's two most important allies on the western and eastern peripheries of the Eurasian continent, Germany and Japan, both recovered their economic health in the context of almost unbridled admiration for all things American. America was widely perceived as representing the future, as a society worthy of admiration and deserving of emulation.

In contrast, Russia was held in cultural contempt by most of its Central European vassals and even more so by its principal and increasingly assertive eastern ally, China. For the Central Europeans, Russian domination meant isolation from what the Central Europeans considered their philosophical and cultural home: Western

Europe and its Christian religious traditions. Worse than that, it meant domination by a people whom the Central Europeans, often unjustly, considered their cultural inferior.

The Chinese, for whom the word "Russia" means "the hungry land," were even more openly contemptuous. Although initially the Chinese had only quietly contested Moscow's claims of universality for the Soviet model, within a decade following the Chinese Communist revolution they mounted an assertive challenge to Moscow's ideological primacy and even began to express openly their traditional contempt for the neighboring northern barbarians.

Finally, within the Soviet Union itself, the 50 percent of the population that was non-Russian eventually also rejected Moscow's domination. The gradual political awakening of the non-Russians meant that the Ukrainians, Georgians, Armenians, and Azeris began to view Soviet power as a form of alien imperial domination by a people to whom they did not feel culturally inferior. In Central Asia, national aspirations may have been weaker, but here these peoples were fueled in addition by a gradually rising sense of Islamic identity, intensified by the knowledge of the ongoing decolonization elsewhere.

Like so many empires before it, the Soviet Union eventually imploded and fragmented, falling victim not so much to a direct military defeat as to disintegration accelerated by economic and social strains. Its fate confirmed a scholar's apt observation that

> [e]mpires are inherently politically unstable because subordinate units almost always prefer greater autonomy, and counter-elites in such units almost always act, upon opportunity, to obtain greater autonomy. In this sense, empires do not *fall*; rather, they *fall apart*, usually very slowly, though sometimes remarkably quickly.[1]

[1]Donald Puchala. "The History of the Future of International Relations," *Ethics and International Affairs* 8 (1994):183.

THE FIRST GLOBAL POWER

The collapse of its rival left the United States in a unique position. It became simultaneously the first and the only truly global power. And yet America's global supremacy is reminiscent in some ways of earlier empires, notwithstanding their more confined regional scope. These empires based their power on a hierarchy of vassals, tributaries, protectorates, and colonies, with those on the outside generally viewed as barbarians. To some degree, that anachronistic terminology is not altogether inappropriate for some of the states currently within the American orbit. As in the past, the exercise of American "imperial" power is derived in large measure from superior organization, from the ability to mobilize vast economic and technological resources promptly for military purposes, from the vague but significant cultural appeal of the American way of life, and from the sheer dynamism and inherent competitiveness of the American social and political elites.

Earlier empires, too, partook of these attributes. Rome comes first to mind. Its empire was established over roughly two and a half centuries through sustained territorial expansion northward and then both westward and southeastward, as well as through the assertion of effective maritime control over the entire shoreline of the Mediterranean Sea. In geographic scope, it reached its high point around the year A.D. 211 (see map on page 11). Rome's was a centralized polity and a single self-sufficient economy. Its imperial power was exercised deliberately and purposefully through a complex system of political and economic organization. A strategically designed system of roads and naval routes, originating from the capital city, permitted the rapid redeployment and concentration—in the event of a major security threat—of the Roman legions stationed in the various vassal states and tributary provinces.

At the empire's apex, the Roman legions deployed abroad numbered no less than three hundred thousand men—a remarkable force, made all the more lethal by the Roman superiority in tactics and armaments as well as by the center's ability to direct relatively rapid redeployment. (It is striking to note that in 1996, the vastly more populous supreme power, America, was protecting the outer

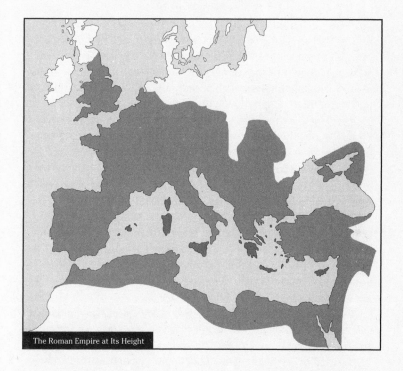

The Roman Empire at Its Height

reaches of its dominion by stationing 296,000 professional soldiers overseas.)

Rome's imperial power, however, was also derived from an important psychological reality. *Civis Romanus sum*—"I am a Roman citizen"—was the highest possible self-definition, a source of pride, and an aspiration for many. Eventually granted even to those not of Roman birth, the exalted status of the Roman citizen was an expression of cultural superiority that justified the imperial power's sense of mission. It not only legitimated Rome's rule, but it also inclined those subject to it to desire assimilation and inclusion in the imperial structure. Cultural superiority, taken for granted by the rulers and conceded by the subjugated, thus reinforced imperial power.

That supreme, and largely uncontested, imperial power lasted about three hundred years. With the exception of the challenge posed at one stage by nearby Carthage and on the eastern fringes by the Parthian Empire, the outside world was largely barbaric, not well organized, capable for most of the time only of sporadic attacks, and culturally patently inferior. As long as the empire was able to maintain internal vitality and unity, the outside world was noncompetitive.

Three major causes led to the eventual collapse of the Roman Empire. First, the empire became too large to be governed from a single center, but splitting it into western and eastern halves automatically destroyed the monopolistic character of its power. Second, at the same time, the prolonged period of imperial hubris generated a cultural hedonism that gradually sapped the political elite's will to greatness. Third, sustained inflation also undermined the capacity of the system to sustain itself without social sacrifice, which the citizens were no longer prepared to make. Cultural decay, political division, and financial inflation conspired to make Rome vulnerable even to the barbarians in its near abroad.

By contemporary standards, Rome was not truly a global power but a regional one. However, given the sense of isolation prevailing at the time between the various continents of the globe, its regional power was self-contained and isolated, with no immediate or even distant rival. The Roman Empire was thus a world unto itself, with its superior political organization and cultural superiority making it a precursor of later imperial systems of even greater geographic scope.

Even so, the Roman Empire was not unique. The Roman and the Chinese empires emerged almost contemporaneously, though neither was aware of the other. By the year 221 B.C. (the time of the Punic Wars between Rome and Carthage), the unification by Chin' of the existing seven states into the first Chinese empire had prompted the construction of the Great Wall in northern China, to seal off the inner kingdom from the barbarian world beyond. The subsequent Han Empire, which had started to emerge by 140 B.C., was even more impressive in scope and organization. By the onset of the Christian era, no fewer than 57 million people were subject to its authority. That huge number, itself unprecedented, testified to extraordinarily effective central control, exercised through a centralized and punitive bureaucracy. Imperial sway extended to today's Korea, parts of Mongolia, and most of today's coastal China. However, rather like Rome, the Han Empire also became afflicted by internal ills, and its eventual collapse was accelerated by its division in A.D. 220 into three independent realms.

China's further history involved cycles of reunification and expansion, followed by decay and fragmentation. More than once, China succeeded in establishing imperial systems that were self-contained, isolated, and unchallenged externally by any organized rivals. The tripartite division of the Han realm was reversed in A.D. 589, with something akin to an imperial system reemerging. But the period of China's greatest imperial self-assertion came under the Manchus, specifically during the early Ch'ing dynasty. By the eighteenth century, China was once again a full-fledged empire, with the imperial center surrounded by vassal and tributary states, including today's Korea, Indochina, Thailand, Burma, and Nepal. China's sway thus extended from today's Russian Far East all the way across southern Siberia to Lake Baikal and into contemporary Kazakstan, then southward toward the Indian Ocean, and then back east across Laos and northern Vietnam (see map on page 14).

As in the Roman case, the empire was a complex financial, economic, educational, and security organization. Control over the large territory and the more than 300 million people living within it was exercised through all these means, with a strong emphasis on centralized political authority, supported by a remarkably effective courier service. The entire empire was demarcated into four zones, radiating from Peking and delimiting areas that could be reached by courier within one week, two weeks, three weeks, and four weeks, respectively. A centralized bureaucracy, professionally trained and competitively selected, provided the sinews of unity.

That unity was reinforced, legitimated, and sustained—again, as in the case of Rome—by a strongly felt and deeply ingrained sense of cultural superiority that was augmented by Confucianism, an imperially expedient philosophy, with its stress on harmony, hierarchy, and discipline. China—the Celestial Empire—was seen as the center of the universe, with only barbarians on its peripheries

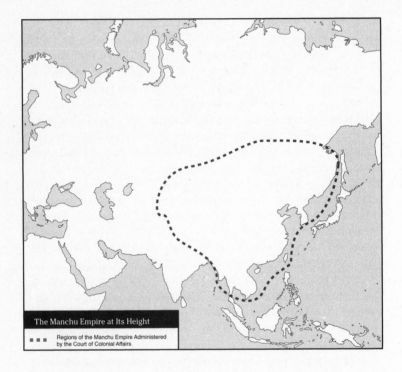

The Manchu Empire at Its Height

■ ■ ■   Regions of the Manchu Empire Administered
by the Court of Colonial Affairs

and beyond. To be Chinese meant to be cultured, and for that reason, the rest of the world owed China its due deference. That special sense of superiority permeated the response given by the
Chinese emperor—even in the phase of China's growing decline, in
the late eighteenth century—to King George III of Great Britain,
whose emissaries had attempted to inveigle China into a trading
relationship by offering some British industrial products as goodwill gifts:

> We, by the Grace of Heaven, Emperor, instruct the King of Eng-
> land to take note of our charge:
>   The Celestial Empire, ruling all within the four seas . . .
> does not value rare and precious things . . . nor do we have the
> slightest need of your country's manufactures. . . .
>   Hence we . . . have commanded your tribute envoys to re-
> turn safely home. You, O King, should simply act in conformity

with our wishes by strengthening your loyalty and swearing perpetual obedience.

The decline and fall of the several Chinese empires was also primarily due to internal factors. Mongol and later occidental "barbarians" prevailed because internal fatigue, decay, hedonism, and loss of economic as well as military creativity sapped and then accelerated the collapse of Chinese will. Outside powers exploited China's internal malaise—Britain in the Opium War of 1839–1842, Japan a century later—which, in turn, generated the profound sense of cultural humiliation that has motivated the Chinese throughout the twentieth century, a humiliation all the more intense because of the collision between their ingrained sense of cultural superiority and the demeaning political realities of postimperial China.

Much as in the case of Rome, imperial China would be classified today as a regional power. But in its heyday, China had no global peer, in the sense that no other power was capable of challenging its imperial status or even of resisting its further expansion if that had been the Chinese inclination. The Chinese system was self-contained and self-sustaining, based primarily on a shared ethnic identity, with relatively limited projection of central power over ethnically alien and geographically peripheral tributaries.

The large and dominant ethnic core made it possible for China to achieve periodic imperial restoration. In that respect, China was quite unlike other empires, in which numerically small but hegemonically motivated peoples were able for a time to impose and maintain domination over much larger ethnically alien populations. However, once the domination of such small-core empires was undermined, imperial restoration was out of the question.

To find a somewhat closer analogy to today's definition of a global power, we must turn to the remarkable phenomenon of the Mongol Empire. Its emergence was achieved through an intense struggle with major and well-organized opponents. Among those defeated were the kingdoms of Poland and Hungary, the forces of the Holy Roman Empire, several Russian and Rus' principalities, the Caliphate of Baghdad, and later, even the Sung dynasty of China.

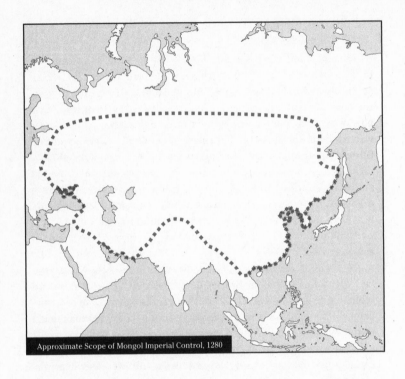

Approximate Scope of Mongol Imperial Control, 1280

Genghis Khan and his successors, by defeating their regional rivals, established centralized control over the territory that latter-
day scholars of geopolitics have identified as the global heartland,
or the pivot for world power. Their Eurasian continental empire
ranged from the shores of the China Sea to Anatolia in Asia Minor
and to Central Europe (see map). It was not until the heyday of the
Stalinist Sino-Soviet bloc that the Mongol Empire on the Eurasian
continent was finally matched, insofar as the scope of centralized
control over contiguous territory is concerned.

The Roman, Chinese, and Mongol empires were regional precursors of subsequent aspirants to global power. In the case of
Rome and China, as already noted, their imperial structures were
highly developed, both politically and economically, while the
widespread acceptance of the cultural superiority of the center exercised an important cementing role. In contrast, the Mongol Empire sustained political control by relying more directly on military

conquest followed by adaptation (and even assimilation) to local conditions.

Mongol imperial power was largely based on military domination. Achieved through the brilliant and ruthless application of superior military tactics that combined a remarkable capacity for rapid movement of forces with their timely concentration, Mongol rule entailed no organized economic or financial system, nor was Mongol authority derived from any assertive sense of cultural superiority. The Mongol rulers were too thin numerically to represent a self-regenerating ruling class, and in any case, the absence of a defined and self-conscious sense of cultural or even ethnic superiority deprived the imperial elite of the needed subjective confidence.

In fact, the Mongol rulers proved quite susceptible to gradual assimilation by the often culturally more advanced peoples they had conquered. Thus, one of the grandsons of Genghis Khan, who had become the emperor of the Chinese part of the great Khan's realm, became a fervent propagator of Confucianism; another became a devout Muslim in his capacity as the sultan of Persia; and a third became the culturally Persian ruler of Central Asia.

It was that factor—assimilation of the rulers by the ruled because of the absence of a dominant political culture—as well as unresolved problems of succession to the great Khan who had founded the empire, that caused the empire's eventual demise. The Mongol realm had become too big to be governed from a single center, but the solution attempted—dividing the empire into several self-contained parts—prompted still more rapid local assimilation and accelerated the imperial disintegration. After lasting two centuries, from 1206 to 1405, the world's largest land-based empire disappeared without a trace.

Thereafter, Europe became both the locus of global power and the focus of the main struggles for global power. Indeed, in the course of approximately three centuries, the small northwestern periphery of the Eurasian continent attained—through the projection of maritime power and for the first time ever—genuine global domination as European power reached, and asserted itself on, every continent of the globe. It is noteworthy that the Western European imperial hegemons were demographically not very numerous, especially when compared to the numbers effectively

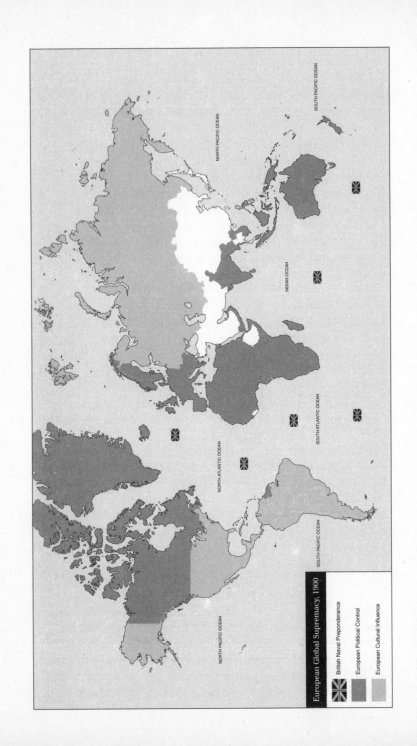

European Global Supremacy, 1900

British Naval Preponderance

European Political Control

European Cultural Influence

NORTH PACIFIC OCEAN

SOUTH PACIFIC OCEAN

INDIAN OCEAN

SOUTH ATLANTIC OCEAN

NORTH ATLANTIC OCEAN

SOUTH PACIFIC OCEAN

NORTH PACIFIC OCEAN

SOUTH OCEAN

subjugated. Yet by the beginning of the twentieth century, outside of the Western Hemisphere (which two centuries earlier had also been subject to Western European control and which was inhabited predominantly by European emigrants and their descendants), only China, Russia, the Ottoman Empire, and Ethiopia were free of Western Europe's domination (see map on page 18).

However, Western European domination was not tantamount to the attainment of global power by Western Europe. The essential reality was that of Europe's civilizational global supremacy and of fragmented European continental power. Unlike the land conquest of the Eurasian heartland by the Mongols or by the subsequent Russian Empire, European overseas imperialism was attained through ceaseless transoceanic exploration and the expansion of maritime trade. This process, however, also involved a continuous struggle among the leading European states not only for the overseas dominions but for hegemony within Europe itself. The geopolitically consequential fact was that Europe's global hegemony did not derive from hegemony in Europe by any single European power.

Broadly speaking, until the middle of the seventeenth century, Spain was the paramount European power. By the late fifteenth century, it had also emerged as a major overseas imperial power, entertaining global ambitions. Religion served as a unifying doctrine and as a source of imperial missionary zeal. Indeed, it took papal arbitration between Spain and its maritime rival, Portugal, to codify a formal division of the world into Spanish and Portuguese colonial spheres in the Treaties of Tordesilla (1494) and Saragossa (1529). Nonetheless, faced by English, French, and Dutch challenges, Spain was never able to assert genuine supremacy, either in Western Europe itself or across the oceans.

Spain's preeminence gradually gave way to that of France. Until 1815, France was the dominant European power, though continuously checked by its European rivals, both on the continent and overseas. Under Napoleon, France came close to establishing true hegemony over Europe. Had it succeeded, it might have also gained the status of the dominant global power. However, its defeat by a European coalition reestablished the continental balance of power.

For the next century, until World War I, Great Britain exercised

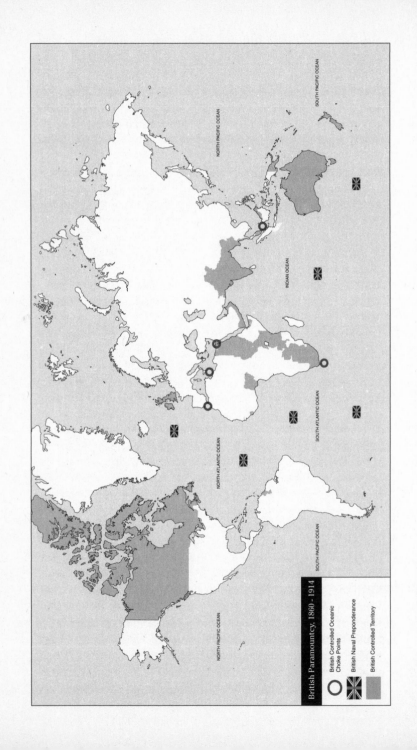

British Paramountcy, 1860 – 1914

British Controlled Oceanic Choke Points

British Naval Preponderance

British Controlled Territory

NORTH PACIFIC OCEAN

SOUTH PACIFIC OCEAN

INDIAN OCEAN

NORTH ATLANTIC OCEAN

SOUTH ATLANTIC OCEAN

NORTH PACIFIC OCEAN

SOUTH PACIFIC OCEAN

global maritime domination as London became the world's principal financial and trading center and the British navy "ruled the waves." Great Britain was clearly paramount overseas, but like the earlier European aspirants to global hegemony, the British Empire could not single-handedly dominate Europe. Instead, Britain relied on an intricate balance-of-power diplomacy and eventually on an Anglo-French entente to prevent continental domination by either Russia or Germany.

The overseas British Empire was initially acquired through a combination of exploration, trade, and conquest. But much like its Roman and Chinese predecessors or its French and Spanish rivals, it also derived a great deal of its staying power from the perception of British cultural superiority. That superiority was not only a matter of subjective arrogance on the part of the imperial ruling class but was a perspective shared by many of the non-British subjects. In the words of South Africa's first black president, Nelson Mandela: "I was brought up in a British school, and at the time Britain was the home of everything that was best in the world. I have not discarded the influence which Britain and British history and culture exercised on us." Cultural superiority, successfully asserted and quietly conceded, had the effect of reducing the need to rely on large military forces to maintain the power of the imperial center. By 1914, only a few thousand British military personnel and civil servants controlled about 11 million square miles and almost 400 million non-British peoples (see map on page 20).

In brief, Rome exercised its sway largely through superior military organization and cultural appeal. China relied heavily on an efficient bureaucracy to rule an empire based on shared ethnic identity, reinforcing its control through a highly developed sense of cultural superiority. The Mongol Empire combined advanced military tactics for conquest with an inclination toward assimilation as the basis for rule. The British (as well as the Spanish, Dutch, and French) gained preeminence as their flag followed their trade, their control likewise reinforced by superior military organization and cultural assertiveness. But none of these empires were truly global. Even Great Britain was not a truly global power. It did not control Europe but only balanced it. A stable Europe was crucial to British international preeminence, and Europe's self-destruction inevitably marked the end of British primacy.

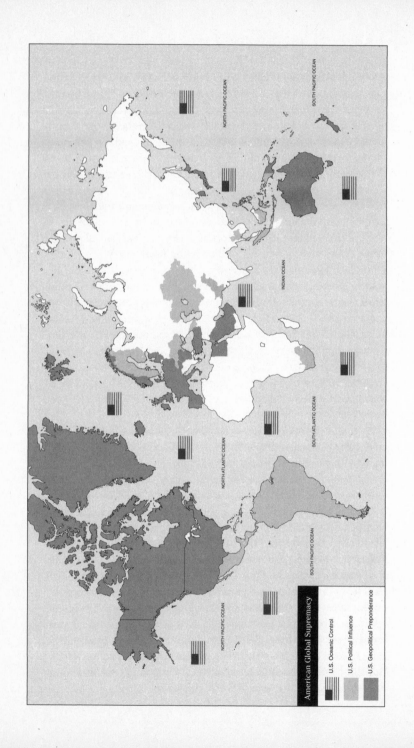

In contrast, the scope and pervasiveness of American global power today are unique. Not only does the United States control all of the world's oceans and seas, but it has developed an assertive military capability for amphibious shore control that enables it to project its power inland in politically significant ways. Its military legions are firmly perched on the western and eastern extremities of Eurasia, and they also control the Persian Gulf. American vassals and tributaries, some yearning to be embraced by even more formal ties to Washington, dot the entire Eurasian continent, as the map on page 22 shows.

America's economic dynamism provides the necessary precondition for the exercise of global primacy. Initially, immediately after World War II, America's economy stood apart from all others, accounting alone for more than 50 percent of the world's GNP. The economic recovery of Western Europe and Japan, followed by the wider phenomenon of Asia's economic dynamism, meant that the American share of global GNP eventually had to shrink from the disproportionately high levels of the immediate postwar era. Nonetheless, by the time the subsequent Cold War had ended, America's share of global GNP, and more specifically its share of the world's manufacturing output, had stabilized at about 30 percent, a level that had been the norm for most of this century, apart from those exceptional years immediately after World War II.

More important, America has maintained and has even widened its lead in exploiting the latest scientific breakthroughs for military purposes, thereby creating a technologically peerless military establishment, the only one with effective global reach. All the while, it has maintained its strong competitive advantage in the economically decisive information technologies. American mastery in the cutting-edge sectors of tomorrow's economy suggests that American technological domination is not likely to be undone soon, especially given that in the economically decisive fields, Americans are maintaining or even widening their advantage in productivity over their Western European and Japanese rivals.

To be sure, Russia and China are powers that resent this American hegemony. In early 1996, they jointly stated as much in the course of a visit to Beijing by Russia's President Boris Yeltsin. Moreover, they possess nuclear arsenals that could threaten vital U.S. interests. But the brutal fact is that for the time being, and for some time to come, although they can initiate a suicidal nuclear war, neither one of them can win it. Lacking the ability to project forces over long distances in order to impose their political will and being technologically much more backward than America, they do not have the means to exercise—nor soon attain—sustained political clout worldwide.

In brief, *America stands supreme in the four decisive domains of global power:* militarily, it has an unmatched global reach; economically, it remains the main locomotive of global growth, even if challenged in some aspects by Japan and Germany (neither of which enjoys the other attributes of global might); technologically, it retains the overall lead in the cutting-edge areas of innovation; and culturally, despite some crassness, it enjoys an appeal that is unrivaled, especially among the world's youth—all of which gives the United States a political clout that no other state comes close to matching. *It is the combination of all four that makes America the only comprehensive global superpower.*

THE AMERICAN GLOBAL SYSTEM

Although America's international preeminence unavoidably evokes similarities to earlier imperial systems, the differences are more essential. They go beyond the question of territorial scope. American global power is exercised through a global system of distinctively American design that mirrors the domestic American experience. Central to that domestic experience is the pluralistic character of both the American society and its political system.

The earlier empires were built by aristocratic political elites and were in most cases ruled by essentially authoritarian or absolutist regimes. The bulk of the populations of the imperial states were either politically indifferent or, in more recent times, infected by imperialist emotions and symbols. The quest for national glory, "the white man's burden," "la mission civilisatrice," not to speak of the opportunities for personal profit—all served to mobilize support for imperial adventures and to sustain essentially hierarchical imperial power pyramids.

The attitude of the American public toward the external projection of American power has been much more ambivalent. The public supported America's engagement in World War II largely because of the shock effect of the Japanese attack on Pearl Harbor. The engagement of the United States in the Cold War was initially endorsed more reluctantly, until the Berlin blockade and the subsequent Korean War. After the Cold War had ended, the emergence of the United States as the single global power did not evoke much public gloating but rather elicited an inclination toward a more limited definition of American responsibilities abroad. Public opinion polls conducted in 1995 and 1996 indicated a general public preference for "sharing" global power with others, rather than for its monopolistic exercise.

Because of these domestic factors, the American global system emphasizes the technique of co-optation (as in the case of defeated rivals—Germany, Japan, and lately even Russia) to a much greater extent than the earlier imperial systems did. It likewise relies heavily on the indirect exercise of influence on dependent foreign elites, while drawing much benefit from the appeal of its democratic principles and institutions. All of the foregoing are reinforced by the massive but intangible impact of the American domination of global communications, popular entertainment, and mass culture and by the potentially very tangible clout of America's technological edge and global military reach.

Cultural domination has been an underappreciated facet of American global power. Whatever one may think of its aesthetic values, America's mass culture exercises a magnetic appeal, especially on the world's youth. Its attraction may be derived from the hedonistic quality of the lifestyle it projects, but its global appeal is undeniable. American television programs and films account for about three-fourths of the global market. American popular music is equally dominant, while American fads, eating habits, and even clothing are increasingly imitated worldwide. The language of the Internet is English, and an overwhelming proportion of the global computer chatter also originates from America, influencing the content of global conversation. Lastly, America has become a Mecca for those seeking advanced education, with approximately half a million foreign students flocking to the United States, with many of the ablest never returning home. Graduates from American universities are to be found in almost every Cabinet on every continent.

The style of many foreign democratic politicians also increasingly emulates the American. Not only did John F. Kennedy find eager imitators abroad, but even more recent (and less glorified) American political leaders have become the object of careful study and political imitation. Politicians from cultures as disparate as the Japanese and the British (for example, the Japanese prime minister of the mid-1990s, Ryutaro Hashimoto, and the British prime minister, Tony Blair—and note the "Tony," imitative of "Jimmy" Carter, "Bill" Clinton, or "Bob" Dole) find it perfectly appropriate to copy Bill Clinton's homey mannerisms, populist common touch, and public relations techniques.

Democratic ideals, associated with the American political tradition, further reinforce what some perceive as America's "cultural imperialism." In the age of the most massive spread of the democratic form of government, the American political experience tends to serve as a standard for emulation. The spreading emphasis worldwide on the centrality of a written constitution and on the supremacy of law over political expediency, no matter how short-changed in practice, has drawn upon the strength of American constitutionalism. In recent times, the adoption by the former Communist countries of civilian supremacy over the military (especially as a precondition for NATO membership) has also been very heavily influenced by the U.S. system of civil-military relations.

The appeal and impact of the democratic American political system has also been accompanied by the growing attraction of the American entrepreneurial economic model, which stresses global free trade and uninhibited competition. As the Western welfare state, including its German emphasis on "codetermination" between entrepreneurs and trade unions, begins to lose its economic momentum, more Europeans are voicing the opinion that the more competitive and even ruthless American economic culture has to be emulated if Europe is not to fall further behind. Even in Japan, greater individualism in economic behavior is becoming recognized as a necessary concomitant of economic success.

The American emphasis on political democracy and economic development thus combines to convey a simple ideological message that appeals to many: the quest for individual success enhances freedom while generating wealth. The resulting blend of idealism and egoism is a potent combination. Individual self-fulfill-ment is said to be a God-given right that at the same time can ben-efit others by setting an example and by generating wealth. It is a doctrine that attracts the energetic, the ambitious, and the highly competitive.

As the imitation of American ways gradually pervades the world, it creates a more congenial setting for the exercise of the in-direct and seemingly consensual American hegemony. And as in the case of the domestic American system, that hegemony in-volves a complex structure of interlocking institutions and proce-dures, designed to generate consensus and obscure asymmetries in power and influence. American global supremacy is thus but-tressed by an elaborate system of alliances and coalitions that lit-erally span the globe.

The Atlantic alliance, epitomized institutionally by NATO, links the most productive and influential states of Europe to America, making the United States a key participant even in intra-European affairs. The bilateral political and military ties with Japan bind the most powerful Asian economy to the United States, with Japan re-maining (at least for the time being) essentially an American pro-tectorate. America also participates in such nascent trans-Pacific multilateral organizations as the Asia-Pacific Economic Coopera-tion Forum (APEC), making itself a key participant in that region's affairs. The Western Hemisphere is generally shielded from outside influences, enabling America to play the central role in existing hemispheric multilateral organizations. Special security arrange-ments in the Persian Gulf, especially after the brief punitive mis-sion in 1991 against Iraq, have made that economically vital region into an American military preserve. Even the former Soviet space is permeated by various American-sponsored arrangements for closer cooperation with NATO, such as the Partnership for Peace.

In addition, one must consider as part of the American system the global web of specialized organizations, especially the "inter-national" financial institutions. The International Monetary Fund (IMF) and the World Bank can be said to represent "global" inter-ests, and their constituency may be construed as the world. In re-ality, however, they are heavily American dominated and their origins are traceable to American initiative, particularly the Bret-ton Woods Conference of 1944.

Unlike earlier empires, this vast and complex global system is not a hierarchical pyramid. Rather, America stands at the center of an interlocking universe, one in which power is exercised through continuous bargaining, dialogue, diffusion, and quest for formal consensus, even though that power originates ultimately from a single source, namely, Washington, D.C. And that is where the power game has to be played, and played according to America's domestic rules. Perhaps the highest compliment that the world pays to the centrality of the democratic process in American global hegemony is the degree to which foreign countries are themselves drawn into the domestic American political bargaining. To the extent that they can, foreign governments strive to mobilize those Americans with whom they share a special ethnic or religious identity. Most foreign governments also employ American lobbyists to advance their case, especially in Congress, in addition to approximately one thousand special foreign interest groups registered as active in America's capital. American ethnic communities also strive to influence U.S. foreign policy, with the Jewish, Greek, and Armenian lobbies standing out as the most effectively organized.

American supremacy has thus produced a new international order that not only replicates but institutionalizes abroad many of the features of the American system itself. Its basic features include

- a collective security system, including integrated command and forces (NATO, the U.S.-Japan Security Treaty, and so forth);

- regional economic cooperation (APEC, NAFTA [North American Free Trade Agreement]) and specialized global cooperative institutions (the World Bank, IMF, WTO [World Trade Organization]);

- procedures that emphasize consensual decision making, even if dominated by the United States;

- a preference for democratic membership within key alliances;

- a rudimentary global constitutional and judicial structure (ranging from the World Court to a special tribunal to try Bosnian war crimes).

Most of that system emerged during the Cold War, as part of America's effort to contain its global rival, the Soviet Union. It was thus ready-made for global application, once that rival faltered and America emerged as the first and only global power. Its essence has been well encapsulated by the political scientist G. John Ikenberry:

> It was hegemonic in the sense that it was centered around the United States and reflected American-styled political mechanisms and organizing principles. It was a liberal order in that it was legitimate and marked by reciprocal interactions. Europeans [one may also add, the Japanese] were able to reconstruct and integrate their societies and economies in ways that were congenial with American hegemony but also with room to experiment with their own autonomous and semi-independent political systems ... The evolution of this complex system served to "domesticate" relations among the major Western states. There have been tense conflicts between these states from time to time, but the important point is that conflict has been contained within a deeply embedded, stable, and increasingly articulated political order. ... The threat of war is off the table.[2]

Currently, this unprecedented American global hegemony has no rival. But will it remain unchallenged in the years to come?

---

[2]From his paper "Creating Liberal Order: The Origins and Persistence of the Postwar Western Settlement," University of Pennsylvania, Philadelphia, November 1995.

CHAPTER 2

The Eurasian Chessboard

F OR AMERICA, THE CHIEF geopolitical prize is Eurasia. For half a millennium, world affairs were dominated by Eurasian powers and peoples who fought with one another for regional domination and reached out for global power. Now a non-Eurasian power is preeminent in Eurasia—and America's global primacy is directly dependent on how long and how effectively its preponderance on the Eurasian continent is sustained.

Obviously, that condition is temporary. But its duration, and what follows it, is of critical importance not only to America's well-being but more generally to international peace. The sudden emergence of the first and only global power has created a situation in which an equally quick end to its supremacy—either because of America's withdrawal from the world or because of the sudden emergence of a successful rival—would produce massive international instability. In effect, it would prompt global anarchy. The Harvard political scientist Samuel P. Huntington is right in boldly asserting:

A world without U.S. primacy will be a world with more violence and disorder and less democracy and economic growth than a world where the United States continues to have more influence than any other country in shaping global affairs. The sustained international primacy of the United States is central to the welfare and security of Americans and to the future of freedom, democracy, open economies, and international order in the world.[1]

In that context, how America "manages" Eurasia is critical. Eurasia is the globe's largest continent and is geopolitically axial. A power that dominates Eurasia would control two of the world's three most advanced and economically productive regions. A mere glance at the map also suggests that control over Eurasia would almost automatically entail Africa's subordination, rendering the Western Hemisphere and Oceania geopolitically peripheral to the world's central continent (see map on page 32). About 75 percent of the world's people live in Eurasia, and most of the world's physical wealth is there as well, both in its enterprises and underneath its soil. Eurasia accounts for about 60 percent of the world's GNP and about three-fourths of the world's known energy resources (see tables on page 33).

Eurasia is also the location of most of the world's politically assertive and dynamic states. After the United States, the next six largest economies and the next six biggest spenders on military weaponry are located in Eurasia. All but one of the world's overt nuclear powers and all but one of the covert ones are located in Eurasia. The world's two most populous aspirants to regional hegemony and global influence are Eurasian. All of the potential political and/or economic challengers to American primacy are Eurasian. Cumulatively, Eurasia's power vastly overshadows America's. Fortunately for America, Eurasia is too big to be politically one.

Eurasia is thus the chessboard on which the struggle for global primacy continues to be played. Although geostrategy—the strategic management of geopolitical interests—may be compared to

[1] Samuel P. Huntington. "Why International Primacy Matters," *International Security* (Spring 1993):83.

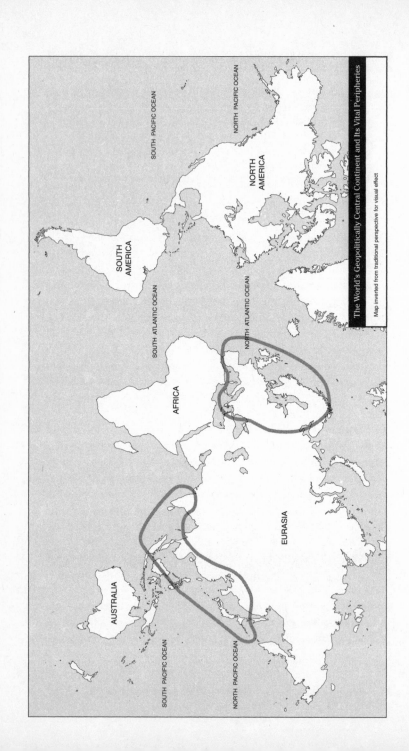

The World's Geopolitically Central Continent and Its Vital Peripheries

Map inverted from traditional perspective for visual effect

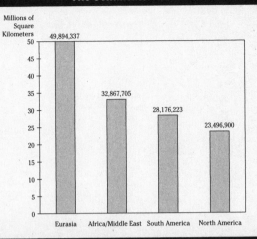

The Continents: Area

Millions of Square Kilometers

- Eurasia: 49,894,337
- Africa/Middle East: 32,867,705
- South America: 28,176,223
- North America: 23,496,900

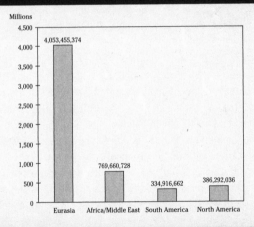

The Continents: Population

Millions

- Eurasia: 4,053,455,374
- Africa/Middle East: 769,660,728
- South America: 334,916,662
- North America: 386,292,036

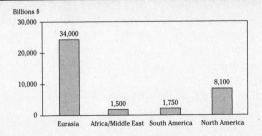

The Continents: GNP

Billions $

- Eurasia: 34,000
- Africa/Middle East: 1,500
- South America: 1,750
- North America: 8,100

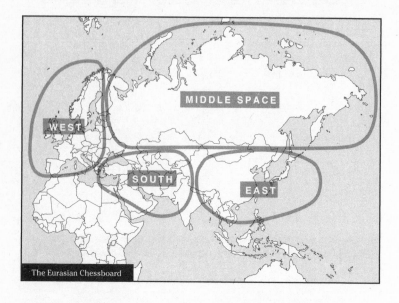

The Eurasian Chessboard

chess, the somewhat oval-shaped Eurasian chessboard engages not just two but several players, each possessing differing amounts of power. The key players are located on the chessboard's west, east, center, and south. Both the western and the eastern extremities of the chessboard contain densely populated regions, organized on relatively congested space into several powerful states. In the case of Eurasia's small western periphery, American power is deployed directly on it. The far eastern mainland is the seat of an increasingly powerful and independent player, controlling an enormous population, while the territory of its energetic rival—confined on several nearby islands—and half of a small far-eastern peninsula provide a perch for American power.

Stretching between the western and eastern extremities is a sparsely populated and currently politically fluid and organizationally fragmented vast middle space that was formerly occupied by a powerful rival to U.S. preeminence—a rival that was once committed to the goal of pushing America out of Eurasia. To the south of that large central Eurasian plateau lies a politically anarchic but energy-rich region of potentially great importance to both the western and the eastern Eurasian states, including in the southernmost area a highly populated aspirant to regional hegemony.

This huge, oddly shaped Eurasian chessboard—extending from Lisbon to Vladivostok—provides the setting for "the game." If the middle space can be drawn increasingly into the expanding orbit of the West (where America preponderates), if the southern region is not subjected to domination by a single player, and if the East is not unified in a manner that prompts the expulsion of America from its offshore bases, America can then be said to prevail. But if the middle space rebuffs the West, becomes an assertive single entity, and either gains control over the South or forms an alliance with the major Eastern actor, then America's primacy in Eurasia shrinks dramatically. The same would be the case if the two major Eastern players were somehow to unite. Finally, any ejection of America by its Western partners from its perch on the western periphery would automatically spell the end of America's participation in the game on the Eurasian chessboard, even though that would probably also mean the eventual subordination of the western extremity to a revived player occupying the middle space.

The scope of America's global hegemony is admittedly great, but its depth is shallow, limited by both domestic and external restraints. American hegemony involves the exercise of decisive influence but, unlike the empires of the past, not of direct control. The very scale and diversity of Eurasia, as well as the power of some of its states, limits the depth of American influence and the scope of control over the course of events. That megacontinent is just too large, too populous, culturally too varied, and composed of too many historically ambitious and politically energetic states to be compliant toward even the most economically successful and politically preeminent global power. This condition places a premium on geostrategic skill, on the careful, selective, and very deliberate deployment of America's resources on the huge Eurasian chessboard.

It is also a fact that America is too democratic at home to be autocratic abroad. This limits the use of America's power, especially its capacity for military intimidation. Never before has a populist democracy attained international supremacy. But the pursuit of power is not a goal that commands popular passion, except in conditions of a sudden threat or challenge to the public's sense of domestic well-being. The economic self-denial (that is, defense spending) and the human sacrifice (casualties even among professional soldiers) required in the effort are uncongenial to democratic instincts. Democracy is inimical to imperial mobilization.

Moreover, most Americans by and large do not derive any special gratification from their country's new status as the sole global superpower. Political "triumphalism" connected with America's victory in the Cold War has generally tended to receive a cold reception and has been the object of some derision on the part of the more liberal-minded commentators. If anything, two rather varying views of the implications for America of its historic success in the competition with the former Soviet Union have been politically more appealing: on the one hand, there is the view that the end of the Cold War justifies a significant reduction in America's global engagement, irrespective of the consequences for America's global standing; and on the other hand, there is the perspective that the time has come for genuine international multilateralism, to which America should even yield some of its sovereignty. Both schools of thought have commanded the loyalty of committed constituencies.

Compounding the dilemmas facing the American leadership are the changes in the character of the global situation itself: the direct use of power now tends to be more constrained than was the case in the past. Nuclear weapons have dramatically reduced the utility of war as a tool of policy or even as a threat. The growing economic interdependence among nations is making the political exploitation of economic blackmail less compelling. Thus maneuver, diplomacy, coalition building, co-optation, and the very deliberate deployment of one's political assets have become the key ingredients of the successful exercise of geostrategic power on the Eurasian chessboard.

GEOPOLITICS AND GEOSTRATEGY

The exercise of American global primacy must be sensitive to the fact that political geography remains a critical consideration in international affairs. Napoleon reportedly once said that to know a nation's geography was to know its foreign policy. Our understanding of the importance of political geography, however, must adapt to the new realities of power.

For most of the history of international affairs, territorial control was the focus of political conflict. Either national self-gratification over the acquisition of larger territory or the sense of national deprivation over the loss of "sacred" land has been the cause of most of the bloody wars fought since the rise of nationalism. It is no exaggeration to say that the territorial imperative has been the main impulse driving the aggressive behavior of nation-states. Empires were also built through the careful seizure and retention of vital geographic assets, such as Gibraltar or the Suez Canal or Singapore, which served as key choke points or linchpins in a system of imperial control.

The most extreme manifestation of the linkage between nationalism and territorial possession was provided by Nazi Germany and imperial Japan. The effort to build the "one-thousand-year Reich" went far beyond the goal of reuniting all German-speaking peoples under one political roof and focused also on the desire to control "the granaries" of Ukraine as well as other Slavic lands, whose populations were to provide cheap slave labor for the imperial domain. The Japanese were similarly fixated on the notion that direct territorial possession of Manchuria, and later of the important oil-producing Dutch East Indies, was essential to the fulfillment of the Japanese quest for national power and global status. In a similar vein, for centuries the definition of Russian national greatness was equated with the acquisition of territory, and even at the end of the twentieth century, the Russian insistence on retaining control over such non-Russian people as the Chechens, who live around a vital oil pipeline, has been justified by the claim that such control is essential to Russia's status as a great power.

Nation-states continue to be the basic units of the world system. Although the decline in big-power nationalism and the fading of ideology has reduced the emotional content of global politics—

while nuclear weapons have introduced major restraints on the use of force—competition based on territory still dominates world affairs, even if its forms currently tend to be more civil. In that competition, geographic location is still the point of departure for the definition of a nation-state's external priorities, and the size of national territory also remains one of the major criteria of status and power.

However, for most nation-states, the issue of territorial possession has lately been waning in salience. To the extent that territorial disputes are still important in shaping the foreign policy of some states, they are more a matter of resentment over the denial of self-determination to ethnic brethren said to be deprived of the right to join the "motherland" or a grievance over alleged mistreatment by a neighbor of ethnic minorities than they are a quest for enhanced national status through territorial enlargement.

Increasingly, the ruling national elites have come to recognize that factors other than territory are more crucial in determining the international status of a state or the degree of its international influence. Economic prowess, and its translation into technological innovation, can also be a key criterion of power. Japan provides the supreme example. Nonetheless, geographic location still tends to determine the immediate priorities of a state—and the greater its military, economic, and political power, the greater the radius, beyond its immediate neighbors, of that state's vital geopolitical interests, influence, and involvement.

Until recently, the leading analysts of geopolitics have debated whether land power was more significant than sea power and what specific region of Eurasia is vital to gain control over the entire continent. One of the most prominent, Harold Mackinder, pioneered the discussion early in this century with his successive concepts of the Eurasian "pivot area" (which was said to include all of Siberia and much of Central Asia) and, later, of the Central–East European "heartland" as the vital springboards for the attainment of continental domination. He popularized his heartland concept by the famous dictum:

> Who rules East Europe commands the Heartland;
> Who rules the Heartland commands the World-Island;
> Who rules the World-Island commands the world.

Geopolitics was also invoked by some leading German political geographers to justify their country's "Drang nach Osten," notably with Karl Haushofer adapting Mackinder's concept to Germany's strategic needs. Its much-vulgarized echo could also be heard in Adolf Hitler's emphasis on the German people's need for "Lebensraum." Other European thinkers of the first half of this century anticipated an eastward shift in the geopolitical center of gravity, with the Pacific region—and specifically America and Japan—becoming the likely inheritors of Europe's fading domination. To forestall such a shift, the French political geographer Paul Demangeon, as well as other French geopoliticians, advocated greater unity among the European states even before World War II.

Today, the geopolitical issue is no longer what geographic part of Eurasia is the point of departure for continental domination, nor whether land power is more significant than sea power. Geopolitics has moved from the regional to the global dimension, with preponderance over the entire Eurasian continent serving as the central basis for global primacy. The United States, a non-Eurasian power, now enjoys international primacy, with its power directly deployed on three peripheries of the Eurasian continent, from which it exercises a powerful influence on the states occupying the Eurasian hinterland. But it is on the globe's most important playing field—Eurasia—that a potential rival to America might at some point arise. Thus, focusing on the key players and properly assessing the terrain has to be the point of departure for the formulation of American geostrategy for the long-term management of America's Eurasian geopolitical interests.

Two basic steps are thus required:

- first, to identify the geostrategically dynamic Eurasian states that have the power to cause a potentially important shift in the international distribution of power and to decipher the central external goals of their respective political elites and the likely consequences of their seeking to attain them; and to pinpoint the geopolitically critical Eurasian states whose location and/or existence have catalytic effects either on the more active geostrategic players or on regional conditions;

- second, to formulate specific U.S. policies to offset, co-opt, and/or control the above, so as to preserve and promote vital U.S. interests, and to conceptualize a more comprehensive geostrategy that establishes on a global scale the interconnection between the more specific U.S. policies.

In brief, for the United States, Eurasian geostrategy involves the purposeful management of geostrategically dynamic states and the careful handling of geopolitically catalytic states, in keeping with the twin interests of America in the short-term preservation of its unique global power and in the long-run transformation of it into increasingly institutionalized global cooperation. To put it in a terminology that hearkens back to the more brutal age of ancient empires, the three grand imperatives of imperial geostrategy are to prevent collusion and maintain security dependence among the vassals, to keep tributaries pliant and protected, and to keep the barbarians from coming together.

GEOSTRATEGIC PLAYERS AND GEOPOLITICAL PIVOTS

Active geostrategic players are the states that have the capacity and the national will to exercise power or influence beyond their borders in order to alter—to a degree that affects America's interests—the existing geopolitical state of affairs. They have the potential and/or the predisposition to be geopolitically volatile. For whatever reason—the quest for national grandeur, ideological fulfillment, religious messianism, or economic aggrandizement—some states do seek to attain regional domination or global standing. They are driven by deeply rooted and complex motivations, best explained by Robert Browning's phrase: " . . . a man's reach should exceed his grasp, or what's a heaven for?" They thus take careful stock of America's power, determine the extent to which their interests overlap or collide with America, and shape their own more limited Eurasian objectives, sometimes in collusion but sometimes in conflict with America's policies. To the Eurasian states so driven, the United States must pay special attention.

Geopolitical pivots are the states whose importance is derived not from their power and motivation but rather from their sensitive location and from the consequences of their potentially vulnerable condition for the behavior of geostrategic players. Most often, geopolitical pivots are determined by their geography, which in some cases gives them a special role either in defining access to important areas or in denying resources to a significant player. In some cases, a geopolitical pivot may act as a defensive shield for a vital state or even a region. Sometimes, the very existence of a geopolitical pivot can be said to have very significant political and cultural consequences for a more active neighboring geostrategic player. The identification of the post–Cold War key Eurasian geopolitical pivots, and protecting them, is thus also a crucial aspect of America's global geostrategy.

It should also be noted at the outset that although all geostrategic players tend to be important and powerful countries, not all important and powerful countries are automatically geostrategic players. Thus, while the identification of the geostrategic players is thus relatively easy, the omission from the list that follows of some obviously important countries may require more justification.

In the current global circumstances, at least five key geostrategic players and five geopolitical pivots (with two of the latter perhaps also partially qualifying as players) can be identified on Eurasia's new political map. France, Germany, Russia, China, and India are major and active players, whereas Great Britain, Japan, and Indonesia, while admittedly very important countries, do not so qualify. Ukraine, Azerbaijan, South Korea, Turkey, and Iran play the role of critically important geopolitical pivots, though both Turkey and Iran are to some extent—within their more limited capabilities—also geostrategically active. More will be said about each in subsequent chapters.

At this stage, suffice it to say that in the western extremity of Eurasia the key and dynamic geostrategic players are France and Germany. Both of them are motivated by a vision of a united Europe, though they differ on how much and in what fashion such a Europe should remain linked to America. But both want to shape something ambitiously new in Europe, thus altering the status quo. France in particular has its own geostrategic concept of Europe, one that differs in some significant respects from that of the United States, and is inclined to engage in tactical maneuvers designed to play off Russia against America and Great Britain against Germany, even while relying on the Franco-German alliance to offset its own relative weakness.

Moreover, both France and Germany are powerful enough and assertive enough to exercise influence within a wider regional radius. France not only seeks a central political role in a unifying Europe but also sees itself as the nucleus of a Mediterranean–North African cluster of states that share common concerns. Germany is increasingly conscious of its special status as Europe's most important state—as the area's economic locomotive and the emerging leader of the European Union (EU). Germany feels it has a special responsibility for the newly emancipated Central Europe, in a manner vaguely reminiscent of earlier notions of a German-led Mitteleuropa. Moreover, both France and Germany consider themselves entitled to represent European interests in dealings with Russia, and Germany even retains, because of its geographic location, at least theoretically, the grand option of a special bilateral accommodation with Russia.

In contrast, Great Britain is not a geostrategic player. It has fewer major options, it entertains no ambitious vision of Europe's future, and its relative decline has also reduced its capacity to play the traditional role of the European balancer. Its ambivalence regarding European unification and its attachment to a waning special relationship with America have made Great Britain increasingly irrelevant insofar as the major choices confronting Europe's future are concerned. London has largely dealt itself out of the European game.

Sir Roy Denman, a former British senior official in the European Commission, recalls in his memoirs that as early as the 1955 conference in Messina, which previewed the formation of a European Union, the official spokesman for Britain flatly asserted to the assembled would-be architects of Europe:

The future treaty which you are discussing has no chance of being agreed; if it was agreed, it would have no chance of being applied. And if it was applied, it would be totally unacceptable to Britain. . . . au revoir et bonne chance.[2]

More than forty years later, the above dictum remains essentially the definition of the basic British attitude toward the construction of a genuinely united Europe. Britain's reluctance to participate in the Economic and Monetary Union, targeted for January 1999, reflects the country's unwillingness to identify British destiny with that of Europe. The substance of that attitude was well summarized in the early 1990s as follows:

- Britain rejects the goal of political unification.

- Britain favors a model of economic integration based on free trade.

- Britain prefers foreign policy, security, and defense coordination outside the EC [European Community] framework.

- Britain has rarely maximized its influence with the EC.[3]

Great Britain, to be sure, still remains important to America. It continues to wield some degree of global influence through the Commonwealth, but it is neither a restless major power nor is it motivated by an ambitious vision. It is America's key supporter, a very loyal ally, a vital military base, and a close partner in critically important intelligence activities. Its friendship needs to be nourished, but its policies do not call for sustained attention. It is a retired geostrategic player, resting on its splendid laurels, largely disengaged from the great European adventure in which France and Germany are the principal actors.

The other medium-sized European states, with most being

[2]Roy Denman, *Missed Chances* (London: Cassell, 1996).
[3]In Robert Skidelsky's contribution on "Great Britain and the New Europe," in *From the Atlantic to the Urals,* ed. David P. Calleo and Philip H. Gordon (Arlington, Va.: 1992), p. 145.

members of NATO and/or the European Union, either follow America's lead or quietly line up behind Germany or France. Their policies do not have a wider regional impact, and they are not in a position to alter their basic alignments. At this stage, they are neither geostrategic players nor geopolitical pivots. The same is true of the most important potential Central European member of NATO and the EU, namely, Poland. Poland is too weak to be a geostrategic player, and it has only one option: to become integrated into the West. Moreover, the disappearance of the old Russian Empire and Poland's deepening ties with both the Atlantic alliance and the emerging Europe increasingly give Poland historically unprecedented security, while confining its strategic choices.

Russia, it hardly needs saying, remains a major geostrategic player, in spite of its weakened state and probably prolonged malaise. Its very presence impacts massively on the newly independent states within the vast Eurasian space of the former Soviet Union. It entertains ambitious geopolitical objectives, which it increasingly proclaims openly. Once it has recovered its strength, it will also impact significantly on its western and eastern neighbors. Moreover, Russia has still to make its fundamental geostrategic choice regarding its relationship with America: is it a friend or foe? It may well feel that it has major options on the Eurasian continent in that regard. Much depends on how its internal politics evolve and especially on whether Russia becomes a European democracy or a Eurasian empire again. In any case, it clearly remains a player, even though it has lost some of its "pieces," as well as some key spaces on the Eurasian chessboard.

Similarly, it hardly needs arguing that China is a major player. China is already a significant regional power and is likely to entertain wider aspirations, given its history as a major power and its view of the Chinese state as the global center. The choices China makes are already beginning to affect the geopolitical distribution of power in Asia, while its economic momentum is bound to give it both greater physical power and increasing ambitions. The rise of a "Greater China" will not leave the Taiwan issue dormant, and that will inevitably impact on the American position in the Far East. The dismantling of the Soviet Union has also created on the western edge of China a series of states, regarding which the Chinese leaders cannot be indifferent. Thus, Russia will also be much affected by China's more active emergence on the world scene.

The eastern periphery of Eurasia poses a paradox. Japan is clearly a major power in world affairs, and the American-Japanese alliance has often—and correctly—been defined as America's most important bilateral relationship. As one of the very top economic powers in the world, Japan clearly possesses the potential for the exercise of first-class political power. Yet it does not act on this, eschewing any aspirations for regional domination and preferring instead to operate under American protection. Like Great Britain in the case of Europe, Japan prefers not to become engaged in the politics of the Asian mainland, though at least a partial reason for this is the continued hostility of many fellow Asians to any Japanese quest for a regionally preeminent political role.

This self-restrained Japanese political profile in turn permits the United States to play a central security role in the Far East. Japan is thus not a geostrategic player, though its obvious potential for quickly becoming one—especially if either China or America were suddenly to alter its current policies—imposes on the United States a special obligation to carefully nurture the American-Japanese relationship. It is not Japanese foreign policy that America must watch, but it is Japan's self-restraint that America must very subtly cultivate. Any significant reduction in American-Japanese political ties would impact directly on the region's stability.

The case for not listing Indonesia as a dynamic geostrategic player is easier to make. In Southeast Asia, Indonesia is the most important country, but even in the region itself, its capacity for projecting significant influence is limited by the relatively underdeveloped state of the Indonesian economy, its continued internal political uncertainties, its dispersed archipelago, and its susceptibility to ethnic conflicts that are exacerbated by the central role exercised in its internal financial affairs by the Chinese minority. At some point, Indonesia could become an important obstacle to Chinese southward aspirations. That eventuality has already been recognized by Australia, which once feared Indonesian expansionism but lately has begun to favor closer Australian-Indonesian security cooperation. But a period of political consolidation and continued economic success is needed before Indonesia can be viewed as the regionally dominant actor.

In contrast, India is in the process of establishing itself as a regional power and views itself as potentially a major global player as well. It also sees itself as a rival to China. That may be a matter of overestimating its own long-term capabilities, but India is unquestionably the most powerful South Asian state, a regional hegemon of sorts. It is also a semisecret nuclear power, and it became one not only in order to intimidate Pakistan but especially to balance China's possession of a nuclear arsenal. India has a geostrategic vision of its regional role, both vis-à-vis its neighbors and in the Indian Ocean. However, its ambitions at this stage only peripherally intrude on America's Eurasian interests, and thus, as a geostrategic player, India is not—at least, not to the same degree as either Russia or China—a source of geopolitical concern.

Ukraine, a new and important space on the Eurasian chessboard, is a geopolitical pivot because its very existence as an independent country helps to transform Russia. Without Ukraine, Russia ceases to be a Eurasian empire. Russia without Ukraine can still strive for imperial status, but it would then become a predominantly Asian imperial state, more likely to be drawn into debilitating conflicts with aroused Central Asians, who would then be resentful of the loss of their recent independence and would be supported by their fellow Islamic states to the south. China would also be likely to oppose any restoration of Russian domination over Central Asia, given its increasing interest in the newly independent states there. However, if Moscow regains control over Ukraine, with its 52 million people and major resources as well as its access to the Black Sea, Russia automatically again regains the wherewithal to become a powerful imperial state, spanning Europe and Asia. Ukraine's loss of independence would have immediate consequences for Central Europe, transforming Poland into the geopolitical pivot on the eastern frontier of a united Europe.

Despite its limited size and small population, Azerbaijan, with its vast energy resources, is also geopolitically critical. It is the cork in the bottle containing the riches of the Caspian Sea basin and Central Asia. The independence of the Central Asian states can be rendered nearly meaningless if Azerbaijan becomes fully subordinated to Moscow's control. Azerbaijan's own and very significant oil resources can also be subjected to Russian control, once Azerbaijan's independence has been nullified. An independent Azerbaijan, linked to Western markets by pipelines that do not pass through Russian-controlled territory, also becomes a major avenue of access from the advanced and energy-consuming economies to the energy rich Central Asian republics. Almost as much as in the case of Ukraine, the future of Azerbaijan and Central Asia is also crucial in defining what Russia might or might not become.

Turkey and Iran are engaged in establishing some degree of influence in the Caspian Sea–Central Asia region, exploiting the retraction of Russian power. For that reason, they might be considered as geostrategic players. However, both states confront serious domestic problems, and their capacity for effecting major regional shifts in the distribution of power is limited. They are also rivals and thus tend to negate each other's influence. For example, in Azerbaijan, where Turkey has gained an influential role, the Iranian posture (arising out of concern over possible Azeri national stirrings within Iran itself) has been more helpful to the Russians.

Both Turkey and Iran, however, are primarily important geopolitical pivots. Turkey stabilizes the Black Sea region, controls access from it to the Mediterranean Sea, balances Russia in the Caucasus, still offers an antidote to Muslim fundamentalism, and serves as the southern anchor for NATO. A destabilized Turkey would be likely to unleash more violence in the southern Balkans, while facilitating the reimposition of Russian control over the newly independent states of the Caucasus. Iran, despite the ambiguity of its attitude toward Azerbaijan, similarly provides stabilizing support for the new political diversity of Central Asia. It dominates the eastern shoreline of the Persian Gulf, while its independence, irrespective of current Iranian hostility toward the United States, acts as a barrier to any long-term Russian threat to American interests in the Persian Gulf region.

Finally, South Korea is a Far Eastern geopolitical pivot. Its close links to the United States enable America to shield Japan and thereby to keep Japan from becoming an independent and major military power, without an overbearing American presence within

Japan itself. Any significant change in South Korea's status, either through unification and/or through a shift into an expanding Chinese sphere of influence, would necessarily alter dramatically America's role in the Far East, thus altering Japan's as well. In addition, South Korea's growing economic power also makes it a more important "space" in its own right, control over which becomes increasingly valuable.

The above list of geostrategic players and geopolitical pivots is neither permanent nor fixed. At times, some states might have to be added or subtracted. Certainly, in some respects, the case could be made that Taiwan, or Thailand, or Pakistan, or perhaps Kazakstan or Uzbekistan should also be included in the latter category. However, at this stage, the case for none of the above seems compelling. Changes in the status of any of them would represent major events and involve some shifts in the distribution of power, but it is doubtful that the catalytic consequences would be far-reaching. The only exception might involve the issue of Taiwan, if one chooses to view it apart from China. Even then, that issue would only arise if China were to use major force to conquer the island, in successful defiance of the United States, thereby threatening more generally America's political credibility in the Far East. The probability of such a course of events seems low, but that consideration still has to be kept in mind when framing U.S. policy toward China.

CRITICAL CHOICES AND POTENTIAL CHALLENGES

The identification of the central players and key pivots helps to define America's grand policy dilemmas and to anticipate the potential major challenges on the Eurasian supercontinent. These can be summarized, before more comprehensive discussion in subsequent chapters, as involving five broad issues:

- What kind of Europe should America prefer and hence promote?

- What kind of Russia is in America's interest, and what and how much can America do about it?

- What are the prospects for the emergence in Central Eurasia of a new "Balkans," and what should America do to minimize the resulting risks?

- What role should China be encouraged to assume in the Far East, and what are the implications of the foregoing not only for the United States but also for Japan?

- What new Eurasian coalitions are possible, which might be most dangerous to U.S. interests, and what needs to be done to preclude them?

The United States has always professed its fidelity to the cause of a united Europe. Ever since the days of the Kennedy administration, the standard invocation has been that of "equal partnership." Official Washington has consistently proclaimed its desire to see Europe emerge as a single entity, powerful enough to share with America both the responsibilities and the burdens of global leadership.

That has been the established rhetoric on the subject. But in practice, the United States has been less clear and less consistent. Does Washington truly desire a Europe that is a genuinely equal partner in world affairs, or does it prefer an unequal alliance? For example, is the United States prepared to share leadership with Europe in the Middle East, a region not only much closer geographically to Europe than to America but also one in which several European states have long-standing interests? The issue of Israel instantly comes to mind. U.S.-European differences over Iran and Iraq have also been treated by the United States not as an issue between equals but as a matter of insubordination.

Ambiguity regarding the degree of American support for European unity also extends to the issue of how European unity is to be defined, especially concerning which country, if any, should lead a united Europe. Washington has not discouraged London's divisive posture regarding Europe's integration, though Washington has also shown a clear preference for German—rather than French—leadership in Europe. That is understandable, given the traditional thrust of French policy, but the preference has also had the effect of encouraging the occasional appearance of a tactical Franco-British entente in order to thwart Germany, as well as periodic French flirtation with Moscow in order to offset the American-German coalition.

The emergence of a truly united Europe—especially if that should occur with constructive American support—will require significant changes in the structure and processes of the NATO alliance, the principal link between America and Europe. NATO provides not only the main mechanism for the exercise of U.S. influence regarding European matters but the basis for the politically critical American military presence in Western Europe. However, European unity will require that structure to adjust to the new reality of an alliance based on two more or less equal partners, instead of an alliance that, to use traditional terminology, involves essentially a hegemon and its vassals. That issue has so far been largely skirted, despite the modest steps taken in 1996 to enhance within NATO the role of the Western European Union (WEU), the military coalition of the Western European states. A real choice in favor of a united Europe will thus compel a far-reaching reordering of NATO, inevitably reducing the American primacy within the alliance.

In brief, a long-range American geostrategy for Europe will have to address explicitly the issues of European unity and real partnership with Europe. An America that truly desires a united and hence also a more independent Europe will have to throw its weight behind those European forces that are genuinely committed to Europe's political and economic integration. Such a strategy will also mean junking the last vestiges of the once-hallowed U.S.-U.K. special relationship.

A policy for a united Europe will also have to address—though jointly with the Europeans—the highly sensitive issue of Europe's geographic scope. How far eastward should the European Union extend? And should the eastern limits of the EU be synonymous with the eastern front line of NATO? The former is more a matter for a European decision, but a European decision on that issue will have direct implications for a NATO decision. The latter, however, engages the United States, and the U.S. voice in NATO is still decisive. Given the growing consensus regarding the desirability of admitting the nations of Central Europe into both the EU and NATO, the practical meaning of this question focuses attention on the future status of the Baltic republics and perhaps also that of Ukraine.

There is thus an important overlap between the European dilemma discussed above and the second one pertaining to Russia. It is easy to respond to the question regarding Russia's future by professing a preference for a democratic Russia, closely linked to Europe. Presumably, a democratic Russia would be more sympathetic to the values shared by America and Europe and hence also more likely to become a junior partner in shaping a more stable and cooperative Eurasia. But Russia's ambitions may go beyond the attainment of recognition and respect as a democracy. Within the Russian foreign policy establishment (composed largely of former Soviet officials), there still thrives a deeply ingrained desire for a special Eurasian role, one that would consequently entail the subordination to Moscow of the newly independent post-Soviet states.

In that context, even friendly western policy is seen by some influential members of the Russian policy-making community as designed to deny Russia its rightful claim to a global status. As two Russian geopoliticians put it:

> [T]he United States and the NATO countries—while sparing Russia's self-esteem to the extent possible, but nevertheless firmly and consistently—are destroying the geopolitical foundations which could, at least in theory, allow Russia to hope to acquire the status as the number two power in world politics that belonged to the Soviet Union.

Moreover, America is seen as pursuing a policy in which

> the new organization of the European space that is being engineered by the West is, in essence, built on the idea of supporting, in this part of the world, new, relatively small and weak national states through their more or less close rapprochement with NATO, the EC, and so forth.[4]

---

[4]A. Bogaturov and V. Kremenyuk (both senior scholars in the Institute of the United States and Canada), in "Current Relations and Prospects for Interaction Between Russia and the United States," *Nezavisimaya Gazeta*, June 28, 1996.

The above quotations define well—even though with some animus—the dilemma that the United States faces. To what extent should Russia be helped economically—which inevitably strengthens Russia politically and militarily—and to what extent should the newly independent states be simultaneously assisted in the defense and consolidation of their independence? Can Russia be both powerful and a democracy at the same time? If it becomes powerful again, will it not seek to regain its lost imperial domain, and can it then be both an empire and a democracy?

U.S. policy toward the vital geopolitical pivots of Ukraine and Azerbaijan cannot skirt that issue, and America thus faces a difficult dilemma regarding tactical balance and strategic purpose. Internal Russian recovery is essential to Russia's democratization and eventual Europeanization. But any recovery of its imperial potential would be inimical to both of these objectives. Moreover, it is over this issue that differences could develop between America and some European states, especially as the EU and NATO expand. Should Russia be considered a candidate for eventual membership in either structure? And what then about Ukraine? The costs of the exclusion of Russia could be high—creating a self-fulfilling prophecy in the Russian mindset—but the results of dilution of either the EU or NATO could also be quite destabilizing.

Another major uncertainty looms in the large and geopolitically fluid space of Central Eurasia, maximized by the potential vulnerability of the Turkish-Iranian pivots. In the area demarcated on the following map from Crimea in the Black Sea directly eastward along the new southern frontiers of Russia, all the way to the Chinese province of Xinjiang, then down to the Indian Ocean and thence westward to the Red Sea, then northward to the eastern Mediterranean Sea and back to Crimea, live about 400 million people, located in some twenty-five states, almost all of them ethnically as well as religiously heterogeneous and practically none of them politically stable. Some of these states may be in the process of acquiring nuclear weapons.

This huge region, torn by volatile hatreds and surrounded by competing powerful neighbors, is likely to be a major battlefield, both for wars among nation-states and, more likely, for protracted ethnic and religious violence. Whether India acts as a restraint or whether it takes advantage of some opportunity to impose its will

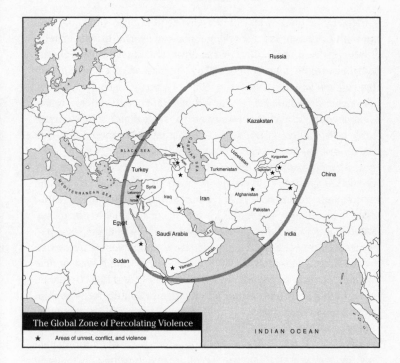

The Global Zone of Percolating Violence
★   Areas of unrest, conflict, and violence

on Pakistan will greatly affect the regional scope of the likely conflicts. The internal strains within Turkey and Iran are likely not
only to get worse but to greatly reduce the stabilizing role these
states are capable of playing within this volcanic region. Such developments will in turn make it more difficult to assimilate the new
Central Asian states into the international community, while also
adversely affecting the American-dominated security of the Persian Gulf region. In any case, both America and the international
community may be faced here with a challenge that will dwarf the
recent crisis in the former Yugoslavia.

A possible challenge to American primacy from Islamic fundamentalism could be part of the problem in this unstable region.
By exploiting religious hostility to the American way of life and
taking advantage of the Arab-Israeli conflict, Islamic fundamentalism could undermine several pro-Western Middle Eastern governments and eventually jeopardize American regional interests,

especially in the Persian Gulf. However, without political cohesion and in the absence of a single genuinely powerful Islamic state, a challenge from Islamic fundamentalism would lack a geopolitical core and would thus be more likely to express itself through diffuse violence.

A geostrategic issue of crucial importance is posed by China's emergence as a major power. The most appealing outcome would be to co-opt a democratizing and free-marketing China into a larger Asian regional framework of cooperation. But suppose China does not democratize but continues to grow in economic and military power? A "Greater China" may be emerging, whatever the desires and calculations of its neighbors, and any effort to prevent that from happening could entail an intensifying conflict with China. Such a conflict could strain American-Japanese relations—for it is far from certain that Japan would want to follow America's lead in containing China—and could therefore have potentially revolutionary consequences for Tokyo's definition of Japan's regional role, perhaps even resulting in the termination of the American presence in the Far East.

However, accommodation with China will also exact its own price. To accept China as a regional power is not a matter of simply endorsing a mere slogan. There will have to be substance to any such regional preeminence. To put it very directly, how large a Chinese sphere of influence, and where, should America be prepared to accept as part of a policy of successfully co-opting China into world affairs? What areas now outside of China's political radius might have to be conceded to the realm of the reemerging Celestial Empire?

In that context, the retention of the American presence in South Korea becomes especially important. Without it, it is difficult to envisage the American-Japanese defense arrangement continuing in its present form, for Japan would have to become militarily more self-sufficient. But any movement toward Korean reunification is likely to disturb the basis for the continued U.S. military presence in South Korea. A reunified Korea may choose not to perpetuate American military protection; that, indeed, could be the price exacted by China for throwing its decisive weight behind the reunification of the peninsula. In brief, U.S. management of its relationship with China will inevitably have direct consequences for the stability of the American-Japanese-Korean triangular security relationship.

Finally, some possible contingencies involving future political alignments should also be briefly noted, subject to fuller discussion in pertinent chapters. In the past, international affairs were largely dominated by contests among individual states for regional domination. Henceforth, the United States may have to determine how to cope with regional coalitions that seek to push America out of Eurasia, thereby threatening America's status as a global power. However, whether any such coalitions do or do not arise to challenge American primacy will in fact depend to a very large degree on how effectively the United States responds to the major dilemmas identified here.

Potentially, the most dangerous scenario would be a grand coalition of China, Russia, and perhaps Iran, an "antihegemonic" coalition united not by ideology but by complementary grievances. It would be reminiscent in scale and scope of the challenge once posed by the Sino-Soviet bloc, though this time China would likely be the leader and Russia the follower. Averting this contingency, however remote it may be, will require a display of U.S. geostrategic skill on the western, eastern, and southern perimeters of Eurasia simultaneously.

A geographically more limited but potentially even more consequential challenge could involve a Sino-Japanese axis, in the wake of a collapse of the American position in the Far East and a revolutionary change in Japan's world outlook. It would combine the power of two extraordinarily productive peoples, and it could exploit some form of "Asianism" as a unifying anti-American doctrine. However, it does not appear likely that in the foreseeable future China and Japan will form an alliance, given their recent historical experience; and a farsighted American policy in the Far East should certainly be able to prevent this eventuality from occurring.

Also quite remote, but not to be entirely excluded, is the possibility of a grand European realignment, involving either a German-Russian collusion or a Franco-Russian entente. There are obvious historical precedents for both, and either could emerge if European unification were to grind to a halt and if relations between Europe and America were to deteriorate gravely. Indeed, in the latter eventuality, one could imagine a European-Russian accommodation to exclude America from the continent. At this stage, all of these variants seem improbable. They would require not only a massive mishandling by America of its European policy but also a dramatic reorientation on the part of the key European states.

Whatever the future, it is reasonable to conclude that American primacy on the Eurasian continent will be buffeted by turbulence and perhaps at least by sporadic violence. America's primacy is potentially vulnerable to new challenges, either from regional contenders or novel constellations. The currently dominant American global system, within which "the threat of war is off the table," is likely to be stable only in those parts of the world in which American primacy, guided by a long-term geostrategy, rests on compatible and congenial sociopolitical systems, linked together by American-dominated multilateral frameworks.

CHAPTER 3

The Democratic Bridgehead

EUROPE IS AMERICA'S NATURAL ALLY. It shares the same values; partakes, in the main, of the same religious heritage; practices the same democratic politics; and is the original homeland of a large majority of Americans. By pioneering in the integration of nation-states into a shared supranational economic and eventually political union, Europe is also pointing the way toward larger forms of postnational organization, beyond the narrow visions and the destructive passions of the age of nationalism. It is already the most multilaterally organized region of the world (see chart on page 58). Success in its political unification would create a single entity of about 400 million people, living under a democratic roof and enjoying a standard of living comparable to that of the United States. Such a Europe would inevitably be a global power.

Europe also serves as the springboard for the progressive expansion of democracy deeper into Eurasia. Europe's expansion eastward would consolidate the democratic victory of the 1990s. It would match on the political and economic plane the essential civilizational scope of Europe—what has been called the Petrine Europe—as defined by Europe's ancient and common religious

European Organizations

OSCE

NATO

EU

Ireland
Austria
Sweden
Finland

Denmark

Greece

WEU

Belgium
Germany
France
Italy
Luxembourg
Netherlands
Portugal
Spain
United Kingdom

USA
Canada
Turkey
Iceland
Norway

Poland
Czech Republic
Slovakia
Hungary
Bulgaria
Romania
Estonia
Latvia
Lithuania
Albania
Slovenia
Croatia
Bosnia-Herzegovina
Yugoslavia

Malta
Holy See
San Marino

Switzerland
Liechtenstein
Cyprus
Monaco

Russia
Belarus
Ukraine
Moldova
Kazakhstan
Kyrgyzstan
Uzbekistan
Turkmenistan
Tajikistan
Armenia
Azerbaijan
Georgia

heritage, derived from Western-rite Christianity. Such a Europe once existed, long before the age of nationalism and even longer before the recent division of Europe into its American- and Soviet-dominated halves. Such a larger Europe would be able to exercise a magnetic attraction on the states located even farther east, building a network of ties with Ukraine, Belarus, and Russia, drawing them into increasingly binding cooperation while proselytizing common democratic principles. Eventually, such a Europe could become one of the vital pillars of an American-sponsored larger Eurasian structure of security and cooperation.

But first of all, Europe is America's essential geopolitical bridgehead on the Eurasian continent. America's geostrategic stake in Europe is enormous. Unlike America's links with Japan, the Atlantic alliance entrenches American political influence and military power directly on the Eurasian mainland. At this stage of American-European relations, with the allied European nations still highly dependent on U.S. security protection, any expansion in the scope of Europe becomes automatically an expansion in the scope of direct U.S. influence as well. Conversely, without close transatlantic ties, America's primacy in Eurasia promptly fades away. U.S. control over the Atlantic Ocean and the ability to project influence and power deeper into Eurasia would be severely circumscribed.

The problem, however, is that a truly European "Europe" as such does not exist. It is a vision, a concept, and a goal, but it is not yet reality. Western Europe is already a common market, but it is still far from being a single political entity. A political Europe has yet to emerge. The crisis in Bosnia offered painful proof of Europe's continued absence, if proof were still needed. The brutal fact is that Western Europe, and increasingly also Central Europe, remains largely an American protectorate, with its allied states reminiscent of ancient vassals and tributaries. This is not a healthy condition, either for America or for the European nations.

Matters are made worse by a more pervasive decline in Europe's internal vitality. Both the legitimacy of the existing socio-economic system and even the surfacing sense of European identity appear to be vulnerable. In a number of European states, one can detect a crisis of confidence and a loss of creative momentum, as well as an inward perspective that is both isolationist and escapist from the larger dilemmas of the world. It is not clear whether most Europeans even want Europe to be a major power and whether they are prepared to do what is needed for it to become one. Even residual European anti-Americanism, currently quite weak, is curiously cynical: the Europeans deplore American "hegemony" but take comfort in being sheltered by it.

The political momentum for Europe's unification was once driven by three main impulses: the memories of the destructive two world wars, the desire for economic recovery, and the insecurity generated by the Soviet threat. By the mid-nineties, however, these impulses had faded. Economic recovery by and large has been achieved; if anything, the problem Europe increasingly faces is that of an excessively burdensome welfare system that is sapping its economic vitality, while the passionate resistance to any reform by special interests is diverting European political attention inward. The Soviet threat has disappeared, while the desire of some Europeans to gain independence from American tutelage has not translated into a compelling impulse for continental unification.

The European cause has been increasingly sustained by the bureaucratic momentum generated by the large institutional machinery created by the European Community and its successor, the European Union. The idea of unity still enjoys significant popular support, but it tends to be lukewarm, lacking in passion and a sense of mission. In general, the Western Europe of today conveys the impression of a troubled, unfocused, comfortable yet socially uneasy set of societies, not partaking of any larger vision. European unification is increasingly a process and not a cause.

Still, the political elites of two leading European nations— France and Germany—remain largely committed to the goal of shaping and defining a Europe that would truly be Europe. They are thus Europe's principal architects. Working together, they could construct a Europe worthy of its past and of its potential. But each is committed to a somewhat different vision and design, and neither is strong enough to prevail by itself.

This condition creates for the United States a special opportunity for decisive intervention. It necessitates American engagement on behalf of Europe's unity, for otherwise unification could grind to a halt and then gradually even be undone. But any effective American involvement in Europe's construction has to be guided by clarity in American thinking regarding what kind of Europe America prefers and is ready to promote—an equal partner or a junior ally—and regarding the eventual scope of both the European Union and NATO. It also requires careful management of Europe's two principal architects.

GRANDEUR AND REDEMPTION

France seeks reincarnation as Europe; Germany hopes for redemption through Europe. These varying motivations go a long way toward explaining and defining the substance of the alternative French and German designs for Europe.

For France, Europe is the means for regaining France's past greatness. Even before World War II, serious French thinkers on international affairs already worried about the progressive decline of Europe's centrality in world affairs. During the several decades of the Cold War, that worry turned into resentment over the "Anglo-Saxon" domination of the West, not to speak of contempt for the related "Americanization" of Western culture. The creation of a genuine Europe—in Charles De Gaulle's words, "from the Atlantic to the Urals"—was to remedy that deplorable state of affairs. And such a Europe, since it would be led by Paris, would simultaneously regain for France the grandeur that the French still feel remains their nation's special destiny.

For Germany, a commitment to Europe is the basis for national redemption, while an intimate connection to America is central to its security. Accordingly, a Europe more assertively independent of America is not a viable option. For Germany, redemption + security = Europe + America. That formula defines Germany's posture and policy, making Germany simultaneously Europe's truly good citizen and America's strongest European supporter.

Germany sees in its fervent commitment to Europe a historical cleansing, a restoration of its moral and political credentials. By redeeming itself through Europe, Germany is restoring its own greatness while gaining a mission that would not automatically mobilize European resentments and fears against Germany. If Germans seek the German national interest, that runs the risk of alienating other Europeans; if Germans promote Europe's common interest, that garners European support and respect.

On the central issues of the Cold War, France was a loyal, dedicated, and determined ally. It stood shoulder to shoulder with America when the chips were down. Whether during the two Berlin blockades or during the Cuban missile crisis, there was no doubt about French steadfastness. But France's support for NATO was tempered by a simultaneous French desire to assert a separate French political identity and to preserve for France its essential freedom of action, especially on matters that pertained to France's global status or to the future of Europe.

There is an element of delusional obsession in the French political elite's preoccupation with the notion that France is still a global power. When Prime Minister Alain Juppé, echoing his predecessors, declared to the National Assembly in May 1995 that "France can and must assert its vocation as a world power," the gathering broke out into spontaneous applause. The French insistence on the development of its own nuclear deterrent was motivated largely by the view that France would thereby enhance its own freedom of action and at the same time gain the capacity to influence American life-and-death decisions regarding the security of the Western alliance as a whole. It was not vis-à-vis the Soviet Union that France sought to upgrade its status, for the French nuclear deterrent had, at the very best, only a marginal impact on Soviet war-making capabilities. Paris felt instead that its own nuclear weapons would give France a role in the Cold War's top-level and most dangerous decision-making processes.

In French thinking, the possession of nuclear weapons fortified France's claim to being a global power, of having a voice that had to be respected worldwide. It tangibly reinforced France's position as one of the five veto-wielding UN Security Council members, all five also nuclear powers. In the French perspective, the British nuclear deterrent was simply an extension of the American, especially given the British commitment to the special relationship and the British abstention from the effort to construct an independent Europe. (That the French nuclear program significantly benefited from covert U.S. assistance was, to the French, of no consequence for France's strategic calculus.) The French nuclear deterrent also consolidated, in the French mindset, France's commanding position as the leading continental power, the only truly European state so endowed.

France's global ambitions were also expressed through its determined efforts to sustain a special security role in most of the Francophone African countries. Despite the loss, after prolonged combat, of Vietnam and Algeria and the abandonment of a wider empire, that security mission, as well as continued French control over scattered Pacific islands (which have provided the venue for controversial French atomic tests), has reinforced the conviction of the French elite that France, indeed, still has a global role to play, despite the reality of being essentially a middle-rank postimperial European power.

All of the foregoing has sustained as well as motivated France's claim to the mantle of European leadership. With Britain self-marginalized and essentially an appendage to U.S. power and with Germany divided for much of the Cold War and still handicapped by its twentieth-century history, France could seize the idea of Europe, identify itself with it, and usurp it as identical with France's conception of itself. The country that first invented the idea of the sovereign nation-state and made nationalism into a civic religion thus found it quite natural to see itself—with the same emotional commitment that was once invested in "la patrie"—as the embodiment of an independent but united Europe. The grandeur of a French-led Europe would then be France's as well.

This special vocation, generated by a deeply felt sense of historical destiny and fortified by a unique cultural pride, has major policy implications. The key geopolitical space that France had to keep within its orbit of influence—or, at least, prevent from being dominated by a more powerful state than itself—can be drawn on the map in the form of a semicircle. It includes the Iberian Peninsula, the northern shore of the western Mediterranean, and Germany up to East-Central Europe (see map on page 64). That is not only the minimal radius of French security; it is also the essential zone of French political interest. Only with the support of the southern states assured, and with Germany's backing guaranteed, can the goal of constructing a unified and independent Europe, led by France, be effectively pursued. And obviously, within that geopolitical orbit, the increasingly powerful Germany is bound to be the most difficult to manage.

In the French vision, the central goal of a united and independent Europe can be achieved by combining the unification of Europe

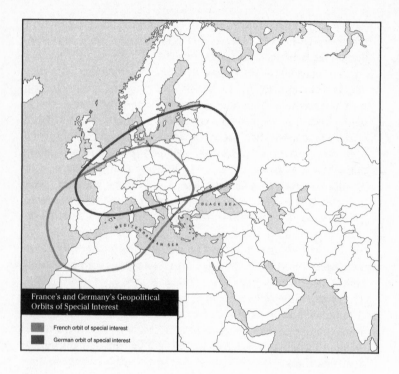

France's and Germany's Geopolitical
Orbits of Special Interest

French orbit of special interest
German orbit of special interest

under French leadership with the simultaneous but gradual diminution of the American primacy on the continent. But if France is to
shape Europe's future, it must both engage and shackle Germany,
while also seeking step-by-step to strip Washington of its political
leadership in European affairs. The resulting key policy dilemmas
for France are essentially twofold: how to preserve the American
security commitment to Europe—which France recognizes is still
essential—while steadily reducing the American presence; and how
to sustain Franco-German partnership as the combined political-
economic engine of European unification while precluding German
leadership in Europe.

If France were truly a global power, the resolution of these dilemmas in the pursuit of France's central goal might not be difficult.
None of the other European states, save Germany, are endowed with
the same ambition or driven by the same sense of mission. Even
Germany could perhaps be seduced into acceptance of French lead-

ership in a united but independent (of America) Europe, but only if it felt that France was in fact a global power and could thus provide Europe with the security that Germany cannot but America does.

Germany, however, knows the real limits of French power. France is much weaker than Germany economically, while its military establishment (as the Gulf War of 1991 showed) is not very competent. It is good enough to squash internal coups in satellite African states, but it can neither protect Europe nor project significant power far from Europe. France is no more and no less than a middle-rank European power. Accordingly, in order to construct Europe, Germany has been willing to propitiate French pride, but in order to keep Europe truly secure, it has not been willing to follow French leadership blindly. It has continued to insist on a central role in European security for America.

That reality, painful for French self-esteem, emerged more clearly after Germany's reunification. Until then, the Franco-German reconciliation did have the appearance of French political leadership riding comfortably on German economic dynamism. That perception actually suited both parties. It mitigated the traditional European fears of Germany, and it had the effect of fortifying and gratifying French illusions by generating the impression that the construction of Europe was led by France, backed by an economically dynamic West Germany.

Franco-German reconciliation, even with its misconceptions, was nonetheless a positive development for Europe, and its importance cannot be overstated. It has provided the crucial foundation for all of the progress so far achieved in Europe's difficult process of unification. Thus, it was also fully compatible with American interests and in keeping with the long-standing American commitment to the promotion of transnational cooperation in Europe. A breakdown of Franco-German cooperation would be a fatal setback for Europe and a disaster for America's position in Europe.

Tacit American support made it possible for France and Germany to push the process of Europe's unification forward. Germany's reunification, moreover, increased the incentive for the French to lock Germany into a binding European framework. Thus, on December 6, 1990, the French president and the German chancellor committed themselves to the goal of a federal Europe, and ten days later, the Rome intergovernmental conference on political union issued—British reservations notwithstanding—a clear mandate to the twelve foreign ministers of the European Community to prepare a Draft Treaty on Political Union.

However, Germany's reunification also dramatically changed the real parameters of European politics. It was simultaneously a geopolitical defeat for Russia and for France. United Germany not only ceased to be a political junior partner of France, but it automatically became the undisputed prime power in Western Europe and even a partial global power, especially through its major financial contributions to the support of the key international institutions.[1] The new reality bred some mutual disenchantment in the Franco-German relationship, for Germany was now able and willing to articulate and openly promote its own vision of a future Europe, still as France's partner but no longer as its protégé.

For France, the resulting diminished political leverage dictated several policy consequences. France somehow had to regain greater influence within NATO—from which it had largely abstained as a protest against U.S. domination—while also compensating for its relative weakness through greater diplomatic maneuver. Returning to NATO might enable France to influence America more; occasional flirtation with Moscow or London might generate pressure from the outside on America as well as on Germany.

Consequently, as part of its policy of maneuver rather than contestation, France returned to NATO's command structure. By 1994, France was again a de facto active participant in NATO's political and military decision making; by late 1995, the French foreign and defense ministers were again regular attendees at alliance sessions. But at a price: once fully inside, they reaffirmed their determination to reform the alliance's structure in order to make for greater balance between its American leadership and its European participation. They wanted a higher profile and a bigger role for a collective European component. As the French foreign minister, Hervé de Charette, stated in a speech on April 8, 1996, "For France,

---

[1]For example, as a percentage of overall budget, Germany accounts for EU: 28.5 percent; NATO: 22.8 percent; UN 8.93 percent, in addition to being the largest shareholder in the World Bank and the EBRD (European Bank for Reconstruction and Development).

the basic goal [of the rapprochement] is to assert a European identity within the alliance that is operationally credible and politically visible."

At the same time, Paris was quite prepared to exploit tactically its traditional links with Russia to constrain America's European policy and to resuscitate whenever expedient the old Franco-British entente to offset Germany's growing European primacy. The French foreign minister came close to saying so explicitly in August 1996, when he declared that "if France wants to play an international role, it stands to benefit from the existence of a strong Russia, from helping it to reaffirm itself as a major power," prompting the Russian foreign minister to reciprocate by stating that "of all the world leaders, the French are the closest to having constructive attitudes in their relations with Russia."[2]

France's initially lukewarm support for NATO's eastward expansion—indeed, a barely suppressed skepticism regarding its desirability—was thus partially a tactic designed to gain leverage in dealing with the United States. Precisely because America and Germany were the chief proponents of NATO expansion, it suited France to play cool, to go along reticently, to voice concern regarding the potential impact of that initiative on Russia, and to act as Europe's most sensitive interlocutor with Moscow. To some Central Europeans, it appeared that the French even conveyed the impression that they were not averse to a Russian sphere of influence in Eastern Europe. The Russian card thus not only balanced America and conveyed a none-too-subtle message to Germany, but it also increased the pressure on the United States to consider favorably French proposals for NATO reform.

Ultimately, NATO expansion will require unanimity among the alliance's sixteen members. Paris knew that its acquiescence was not only vital for that unanimity but that France's actual support was needed to avoid obstruction from other alliance members. Thus, it made no secret of the French intention to make support for NATO expansion a hostage to America's eventually satisfying the French determination to alter both the balance of power within the alliance and its fundamental organization.

France was at first similarly tepid in its support for the east-

[2]As quoted by *Le Nouvel Observateur*, August 12, 1996.

ward expansion of the European Union. Here the lead was taken largely by Germany, with American support but without the same degree of U.S. engagement as in the case of NATO expansion. Even though in NATO France tended to argue that the EU's expansion would provide a more suitable umbrella for the former Communist states, as soon as Germany started pressing for the more rapid enlargement of the EU to include Central Europe, France began to raise technical concerns and also to demand that the EU pay equal attention to Europe's exposed Mediterranean southern flank. (These differences emerged as early as the November 1994 Franco-German summit.) French emphasis on the latter issue also had the effect of gaining for France the support of NATO's southern members, thereby maximizing France's overall bargaining power. But the cost was a widening gap in the respective geopolitical visions of Europe held by France and Germany, a gap only partially narrowed by France's belated endorsement in the second half of 1996 of Poland's accession to both NATO and the EU.

That gap was inevitable, given the changing historical context. Ever since the end of World War II, democratic Germany had recognized that Franco-German reconciliation was required to build a European community within the western half of divided Europe. That reconciliation was also central to Germany's historical rehabilitation. Hence, the acceptance of French leadership was a fair price to pay. At the same time, the continued Soviet threat to a vulnerable West Germany made loyalty to America the essential precondition for survival—and even the French recognized that. But after the Soviet collapse, to build a larger and more united Europe, subordination to France was neither necessary nor propitious. An equal Franco-German partnership, with the reunified Germany in fact now being the stronger partner, was more than a fair deal for Paris; hence, the French would simply have to accept Germany's preference for a primary security link with its transatlantic ally and protector.

With the end of the Cold War, that link assumed new importance for Germany. In the past, it had sheltered Germany from an external but very proximate threat and was the necessary precondition for the eventual reunification of the country. With the Soviet Union gone and Germany reunified, the link to America now provided the umbrella under which Germany could more openly assume a leadership role in Central Europe without simultaneously threatening its neighbors. The American connection provided more than the certificate of good behavior: it reassured Germany's neighbors that a close relationship with Germany also meant a closer relationship with America. All of that made it easier for Germany to define more openly its own geopolitical priorities.

Germany—safely anchored in Europe and rendered harmless but secure by the visible American military presence—could now promote the assimilation of the newly freed Central Europe into the European structures. It would not be the old Mitteleuropa of German imperialism but a more benign community of economic renewal stimulated by German investments and trade, with Germany also acting as the sponsor of the eventually formal inclusion of the new Mitteleuropa in both the European Union and NATO. With the Franco-German alliance providing the vital platform for the assertion of a more decisive regional role, Germany no longer needed to be shy in asserting itself within an orbit of its special interest.

On the map of Europe, the zone of German special interest could be sketched in the shape of an oblong, in the West including of course France and in the East spanning the newly emancipated post-Communist states of Central Europe, including the Baltic republics, embracing Ukraine and Belarus, and reaching even into Russia (see map on page 64). In many respects, that zone corresponds to the historical radius of constructive German cultural influence, carved out in the prenationalist era by German urban and agricultural colonists in East-Central Europe and in the Baltic republics, all of whom were wiped out in the course of World War II. More important, the areas of special concern to the French (discussed earlier) and the Germans, when viewed together as in the map below, in effect define the western and eastern limits of Europe, while the overlap between them underlines the decisive geopolitical importance of the Franco-German connection as the vital core of Europe.

The critical breakthrough for the more openly assertive German role in Central Europe was provided by the German-Polish reconciliation that occurred during the mid-nineties. Despite some initial reluctance, the reunited Germany (with American prodding) did formally recognize as permanent the Oder-Neisse border with Poland, and that step in turn removed the single most important

Polish reservation regarding a closer relationship with Germany. Following some further mutual gestures of goodwill and forgiveness, the relationship underwent a dramatic change. Not only did German-Polish trade literally explode (in 1995 Poland superseded Russia as Germany's largest trading partner in the East), but Germany became Poland's principal sponsor for membership in the EU and (together with the United States) in NATO. It is no exaggeration to say that by the middle of the decade, Polish-German reconciliation was assuming a geopolitical importance in Central Europe matching the earlier impact on Western Europe of the Franco-German reconciliation.

Through Poland, German influence could radiate northward—into the Baltic states—and eastward—into Ukraine and Belarus. Moreover, the scope of the German-Polish reconciliation was somewhat widened by Poland's occasional inclusion in important Franco-German discussions regarding Europe's future. The so-called Weimar Triangle (named after the German city in which the first high-level trilateral Franco-German-Polish consultations, which subsequently became periodic, had taken place) created a potentially significant geopolitical axis on the European continent, embracing some 180 million people from three nations with a highly defined sense of national identity. On the one hand, this further enhanced Germany's dominant role in Central Europe, but on the other hand, that role was somewhat balanced by the Franco-Polish participation in the three-way dialogue.

Central European acceptance of German leadership—and such was even more the case with the smaller Central European states—was eased by the very evident German commitment to the eastward expansion of Europe's key institutions. In so committing itself, Germany undertook a historical mission much at variance with some rather deeply rooted Western European outlooks. In that latter perspective, events occurring east of Germany and Austria were perceived as somehow beyond the limits of concern to the real Europe. That attitude—articulated in the early eighteenth century by Lord Bolingbroke,[3] who argued that political violence in

---

[3] Cf. his *History of Europe, from the Pyrenean Peace to the Death of Louis XIV.*

the East was of no consequence to the Western Europeans—resurfaced during the Munich crisis of 1938; and it made a tragic reappearance in the British and French attitudes during the conflict of the mid-1990s in Bosnia. It still lurks beneath the surface in the ongoing debates regarding the future of Europe.

In contrast, the only real debate in Germany was whether NATO or the EU should be expanded first—the defense minister favored the former, the foreign minister advocated the latter—with the net result that Germany became the undisputed apostle of a larger and more united Europe. The German chancellor spoke of the year 2000 as the goal for the EU's first eastward enlargement, and the German defense minister was among the first to suggest that the fiftieth anniversary of NATO's founding was an appropriately symbolic date for the alliance's eastern expansion. Germany's conception of Europe's future thus differed from its principal European allies: the British proclaimed their preference for a larger Europe because they saw in enlargement the means for diluting Europe's unity; the French feared that enlargement would enhance Germany's role and hence favored more narrowly based integration. Germany stood for both and thus gained a standing in Central Europe all its own.

AMERICA'S CENTRAL OBJECTIVE

The central issue for America is how to construct a Europe that is based on the Franco-German connection, a Europe that is viable, that remains linked to the United States, and that widens the scope of the cooperative democratic international system on which the effective exercise of American global primacy so much depends. Hence, it is not a matter of making a choice between France and Germany. Without either France or Germany, there will be no Europe.

Three broad conclusions emerge from the foregoing discussion:

1. American engagement in the cause of European unification is needed to compensate for the internal crisis of morale and purpose that has been sapping European vitality, to overcome the

widespread European suspicion that ultimately America does not favor genuine European unity, and to infuse into the European undertaking the needed dose of democratic fervor. *That requires a clear-cut American commitment to the eventual acceptance of Europe as America's global partner.*

2. In the short run, tactical opposition to French policy and support for German leadership is justified; in the longer run, European unity will have to involve a more distinctive European political and military identity if a genuine Europe is actually to become reality. *That requires some progressive accommodation to the French view regarding the distribution of power within transatlantic institutions.*

3. Neither France nor Germany is sufficiently strong to construct Europe on its own or to resolve with Russia the ambiguities inherent in the definition of Europe's geographic scope. *That requires energetic, focused, and determined American involvement, particularly with the Germans, in defining Europe's scope and hence also in coping with such sensitive—especially to Russia—issues as the eventual status within the European system of the Baltic republics and Ukraine.*

Just one glance at the map of the vast Eurasian landmass underlines the geopolitical significance to America of the European bridgehead—as well as its geographic modesty. The preservation of that bridgehead and its expansion as the springboard for democracy are directly relevant to America's security. The existing gap between America's global concern for stability and for the related dissemination of democracy and Europe's seeming indifference to these issues (despite France's self-proclaimed status as a global power) needs to be closed, and it can only be narrowed if Europe increasingly assumes a more confederated character. Europe cannot become a single nation-state, because of the tenacity of its diverse national traditions, but it can become an entity that through common political institutions cumulatively reflects shared democratic values, identifies its own interests with their universalization, and exercises a magnetic attraction on its co-inhabitants of the Eurasian space.

Left to themselves, the Europeans run the risk of becoming absorbed by their internal social concerns. Europe's economic recovery has obscured the longer-run costs of its seeming success. These costs are damaging economically as well as politically. The crisis of political legitimacy and economic vitality that Western Europe increasingly confronts—but is unable to overcome—is deeply rooted in the pervasive expansion of the state-sponsored social structure that favors paternalism, protectionism, and parochialism. The result is a cultural condition that combines escapist hedonism with spiritual emptiness—a condition that can be exploited by nationalist extremists or dogmatic ideologues.

This condition, if it becomes rampant, could prove deadly to democracy and the idea of Europe. The two, in fact, are linked, for the new problems of Europe—be they immigration or economic-technological competitiveness with America or Asia, not to speak of the need for a politically stable reform of existing socioeconomic structures—can only be dealt with effectively in an increasingly continental context. A Europe that is larger than the sum of its parts—that is, a Europe that sees a global role for itself in the promotion of democracy and in the wider proselytization of basic human values—is more likely to be a Europe that is firmly uncongenial to political extremism, narrow nationalism, or social hedonism.

One need neither evoke the old fears of a separate German-Russian accommodation nor exaggerate the consequences of French tactical flirtation with Moscow to entertain concern for the geopolitical stability of Europe—and for America's place in it—resulting from a failure of Europe's still ongoing efforts to unite. Any such failure would in fact probably entail some renewed and rather traditional European maneuvers. It would certainly generate opportunities for either Russian or German geopolitical self-assertion, though if Europe's modern history contains any lesson, neither would be likely to gain an enduring success in that regard. However, at the very least, Germany would probably become more assertive and explicit in the definition of its *national* interests.

Currently, Germany's interests are congruent with, and even sublimated within, those of the EU and of NATO. Even the spokesmen for the leftist Alliance 90/Greens have advocated the expansion of both NATO and the EU. But if the unification and enlargement of Europe should stall, there is some reason to assume that a more nationalist definition of Germany's concept of the European "order" would then surface, to the potential detriment of European stability. Wolfgang Schauble, the leader of the Christian Democrats in the Bundestag and a possible successor to Chancellor Kohl, expressed that mindset when he stated that Germany is no longer "the western bulwark against the East; we have become the center of Europe," pointedly adding that in "the long periods during the Middle Ages . . . Germany was involved *in creating order in Europe.*"[4] In this vision, Mitteleuropa—instead of being a European region in which Germany economically preponderates—would become an area of overt German political primacy as well as the basis for a more unilateral German policy vis-à-vis the East and the West.

Europe would then cease to be the Eurasian bridgehead for American power and the potential springboard for the democratic global system's expansion into Eurasia. This is why unambiguous and tangible American support for Europe's unification must be sustained. Although both during Europe's economic recovery and within the transatlantic security alliance America has frequently proclaimed its support for European unification and supported transnational cooperation in Europe, it has also acted as if it preferred to deal on troubling economic and political issues with individual European states and not with the European Union as such. Occasional American insistence on a voice within the European decision-making process has tended to reinforce European suspicions that America favors cooperation among the Europeans when they follow the American lead but not when they formulate Europe's policies. This is the wrong message to convey.

American commitment to Europe's unity—reiterated forcefully in the joint American-European Madrid Declaration of December 1995—will continue to ring hollow until America is ready not only to declare unambiguously that it is prepared to accept the consequences of Europe becoming truly Europe but to act accordingly. For Europe, the ultimate consequence would entail a true partnership with America rather than the status of a favored but still junior ally. And a true partnership does mean sharing in decisions as well as responsibilities. American support for that cause would

Politiken Sondag, August 2, 1996, italics added.

help to invigorate the transatlantic dialogue and would stimulate among the Europeans a more serious concentration on the role that a truly significant Europe might play in the world.

It is conceivable that at some point a truly united and powerful European Union could become a global political rival to the United States. It could certainly become a difficult economic-technological competitor, while its geopolitical interests in the Middle East and elsewhere could significantly diverge from those of America. But, in fact, such a powerful and politically single-minded Europe is not likely in the foreseeable future. Unlike the conditions prevailing in America at the time of the formation of the United States, there are deep historical roots to the resiliency of the European nation-states and the passion for a transnational Europe has clearly waned.

The real alternatives for the next decade or two are either an expanding and unifying Europe, pursuing—though hesitantly and spasmodically—the goal of continental unity; a stalemated Europe, not moving much beyond its current state of integration and geographic scope, with Central Europe remaining a geopolitical no-man's-land; or, as a likely sequel to the stalemate, a progressively fragmenting Europe, resuming its old power rivalries. In a stalemated Europe, it is almost inevitable that Germany's self-identification with Europe will wane, prompting a more nationalist definition of the German state interest. For America, the first option is clearly the best, but it is an option that requires energizing American support if it is to come to pass.

At this stage of Europe's hesitant construction, America need not get directly involved in intricate debates regarding such issues as whether the EU should make its foreign policy decisions by majority vote (a position favored especially by the Germans); whether the European Parliament should assume decisive legislative powers and the European Commission in Brussels should become in effect the European executive; whether the timetable for implementing the agreement on European economic and monetary union should be relaxed; or, finally, whether Europe should be a broad confederation or a multilayered entity, with a federated inner core and a somewhat looser outer rim. These are matters for the Europeans to thrash out among themselves—and it is more than likely that progress on all of these issues will be uneven, punctuated by pauses, and eventually pushed forward only by complex compromises.

Nonetheless, it is reasonable to assume that the Economic and Monetary Union will come into being by the year 2000, perhaps initially among six to ten of the EU's current fifteen members. This will accelerate Europe's economic integration beyond the monetary dimension, further encouraging its political integration. Thus, by fits and starts and with an inner more integrated core as well as a looser outer layer, a single Europe will increasingly become an important political player on the Eurasian chessboard.

In any case, America should not convey the impression that it prefers a vaguer, even if broader, European association, but it should reiterate, through words and deeds, its willingness to deal eventually with the EU as America's global *political and security* partner and not just as a regional common market made up of states allied with the United States through NATO. To make that commitment more credible and thus go beyond the rhetoric of partnership, joint planning with the EU regarding new bilateral transatlantic decision-making mechanisms could be proposed and initiated.

The same principle applies to NATO as such. Its preservation is vital to the transatlantic connection. On this issue, there is overwhelming American-European consensus. Without NATO, Europe not only would become vulnerable but almost immediately would become politically fragmented as well. NATO ensures European security and provides a stable framework for the pursuit of European unity. That is what makes NATO historically so vital to Europe.

However, as Europe gradually and hesitantly unifies, the internal structure and processes of NATO will have to adjust. On this issue, the French have a point. One cannot someday have a truly united Europe and yet have an alliance that remains integrated on the basis of one superpower plus fifteen dependent powers. Once Europe begins to assume a genuine political identity of its own, with the EU increasingly taking on some of the functions of a supranational government, NATO will have to be altered on the basis of a 1 + 1 (US + EU) formula.

This will not happen overnight and all at once. Progress in that direction, to repeat, will be hesitant. But such progress will have to be reflected in the existing alliance arrangements, lest the absence of such adjustment itself should become an obstacle to further progress. A significant step in that direction was the 1996 decision of the alliance to make room for the Combined Joint Task Forces, thereby envisaging the possibility of some purely European military initiatives based on the alliance's logistics as well as on command, control, communications, and intelligence. Greater U.S. willingness to accommodate French demands for an increased role for the Western European Union within NATO, especially in regard to command and decision making, would also betoken more genuine American support for European unity and should help to narrow somewhat the gap between America and France regarding Europe's eventual self-definition.

In the longer run, it is possible that the WEU will embrace some EU member states that, for varying geopolitical or historical reasons, may choose not to seek NATO membership. That could involve Finland or Sweden, or perhaps even Austria, all of which have already acquired observer status with the WEU.[5] Other states may also seek a WEU connection as a preliminary to eventual NATO membership. The WEU might also choose at some point to emulate NATO's Partnership for Peace program with regard to would-be members of the EU. All of that would help to spin a wider web of security cooperation in Europe, beyond the formal scope of the transatlantic alliance.

In the meantime, until a larger and more united Europe emerges—and that, even under the best of conditions, will not be soon—the United States will have to work closely with both France and Germany in order to help such a more united and larger Europe emerge. Thus, regarding France, the central policy dilemma for America will continue to be how to inveigle France into closer Atlantic political and military integration without compromising the American-German connection, and regarding Germany, how to

[5]It is noteworthy that influential voices both in Finland and in Sweden have began to discuss the possibility of association with NATO. In May 1996, the commander of the Finnish Defense Forces was reported by the Swedish media to have raised the possibility of some NATO deployments on Nordic soil, and in August 1996, the Swedish Parliament's Defense Committee, in an action symptomatic of a gradual drift toward closer security cooperation with NATO, recommended that Sweden join the Western European Armaments Group (WEAG) to which only NATO members belong.

exploit U.S. reliance on German leadership in an Atlanticist Europe without prompting concern in France and Britain as well as in other European countries.

More demonstrable American flexibility on the future shape of the alliance would be helpful in eventually mobilizing greater French support for the alliance's eastward expansion. In the long run, a NATO zone of integrated military security on both sides of Germany would more firmly anchor Germany within a multilateral framework, and that should be a matter of consequence for France. Moreover, the expansion of the alliance would increase the probability that the Weimar Triangle (of Germany, France, and Poland) could become a subtle means for somewhat balancing German leadership in Europe. Although Poland relies on German support for gaining entrance into the alliance (and resents current French hesitations regarding such expansion), once it is inside the alliance a shared Franco-Polish geopolitical perspective is more likely to emerge.

In any case, Washington should not lose sight of the fact that France is only a short-term adversary on matters pertaining to the identity of Europe or to the inner workings of NATO. More important, it should bear in mind the fact that France is an essential partner in the important task of permanently locking a democratic Germany into Europe. That is the historic role of the Franco-German relationship, and the expansion of both the EU and NATO eastward should enhance the importance of that relationship as Europe's inner core. Finally, France is not strong enough either to obstruct America on the geostrategic fundamentals of America's European policy or to become by itself a leader of Europe as such. Hence, its peculiarities and even its tantrums can be tolerated.

It is also germane to note that France does play a constructive role in North Africa and in the Francophone African countries. It is the essential partner for Morocco and Tunisia, while also exercising a stabilizing role in Algeria. There is a good domestic reason for such French involvement: some 5 million Muslims now reside in France. France thus has a vital stake in the stability and orderly development of North Africa. But that interest is of wider benefit to Europe's security. Without the French sense of mission, Europe's southern flank would be much more unstable and threatening. All of southern Europe is becoming increasingly concerned with the social-political threat posed by instability along the Mediterranean's southern littoral. France's intense concern for what transpires across the Mediterranean is thus quite pertinent to NATO's security concerns, and that consideration should be taken into account when America occasionally has to cope with France's exaggerated claims of special leadership status.

Germany is another matter. Germany's dominant role cannot be denied, but caution must be exercised regarding any public endorsements of the German leadership role in Europe. That leadership may be expedient to some European states—like those in Central Europe that appreciate the German initiative on behalf of Europe's eastward expansion—and it may be tolerable to the Western Europeans as long as it is subsumed under America's primacy, but in the long run, Europe's construction cannot be based on it. Too many memories still linger; too many fears are likely to surface. A Europe constructed and led by Berlin is simply not feasible. That is why Germany needs France, why Europe needs the Franco-German connection, and why America cannot choose between Germany and France.

The essential point regarding NATO expansion is that it is a process integrally connected with Europe's own expansion. If the European Union is to become a geographically larger community—with a more-integrated Franco-German leading core and less-integrated outer layers—and if such a Europe is to base its security on a continued alliance with America, then it follows that its geopolitically most exposed sector, Central Europe, cannot be demonstratively excluded from partaking in the sense of security that the rest of Europe enjoys through the transatlantic alliance. On this, America and Germany agree. For them, the impulse for enlargement is political, historical, and constructive. It is not driven by animosity toward Russia, nor by fear of Russia, nor by the desire to isolate Russia.

Hence, America must work particularly closely with Germany in promoting the eastward expansion of Europe. American-German cooperation and joint leadership regarding this issue are essential. Expansion will happen if the United States and Germany jointly encourage the other NATO allies to endorse the step and either negotiate effectively some accommodation with Russia, if it is willing to compromise (see chapter 4), or act assertively, in the correct conviction that the task of constructing Europe cannot be subordinated to Moscow's objections. Combined American-German pressure will be especially needed to obtain the required unanimous agreement of all NATO members, but no NATO member will be able to deny it if America and Germany jointly press for it.

Ultimately at stake in this effort is America's long-range role in Europe. A new Europe is still taking shape, and if that new Europe is to remain geopolitically a part of the "Euro-Atlantic" space, the expansion of NATO is essential. Indeed, a comprehensive U.S. policy for Eurasia as a whole will not be possible if the effort to widen NATO, having been launched by the United States, stalls and falters. That failure would discredit American leadership; it would shatter the concept of an expanding Europe; it would demoralize the Central Europeans; and it could reignite currently dormant or dying Russian geopolitical aspirations in Central Europe. For the West, it would be a self-inflicted wound that would mortally damage the prospects for a truly European pillar in any eventual Eurasian security architecture; and for America, it would thus be not only a regional defeat but a global defeat as well.

The bottom line guiding the progressive expansion of Europe has to be the proposition that no power outside of the existing transatlantic system has the right to veto the participation of any qualified European state in the European system—and hence also in its transatlantic security system—and that no qualified European state should be excluded a priori from eventual membership in either the EU or NATO. Especially the highly vulnerable and increasingly qualified Baltic states are entitled to know that eventually they also can become full-fledged members in both organizations— and that in the meantime, their sovereignty cannot be threatened without engaging the interests of an expanding Europe and its U.S. partner.

In essence, the West—especially America and its Western European allies—must provide an answer to the question eloquently posed by Václav Havel in Aachen on May 15, 1996:

> I know that neither the European Union nor the North Atlantic Alliance can open its doors overnight to all those who aspire to join them. What both most assuredly can do—and what they should do before it is too late—is to give the whole of Eu-

rope, seen as a sphere of common values, the clear assurance that they are not closed clubs. *They should formulate a clear and detailed policy of gradual enlargement that not only contains a timetable but also explains the logic of that timetable.* [italics added]

EUROPE'S HISTORIC TIMETABLE

Although at this stage the ultimate eastern limits of Europe can neither be defined firmly nor finally fixed, in the broadest sense Europe is a common civilization, derived from the shared Christian tradition. Europe's narrower Western definition has been associated with Rome and its historical legacy. But Europe's Christian tradition has involved also Byzantium and its Russian Orthodox emanation. Thus, culturally, Europe is more than the Petrine Europe, and the Petrine Europe in turn is much more than Western Europe—even though in recent years the latter has usurped the identity of "Europe." Even a mere glance at the map on page 82 confirms that the existing Europe is simply not a complete Europe. Worse than that, it is a Europe in which a zone of insecurity between Europe and Russia can have a suction effect on both, inevitably causing tensions and rivalry.

A Charlemagne Europe (limited to Western Europe) by necessity made sense during the Cold War, but such a Europe is now an anomaly. This is so because in addition to being a civilization, the emerging united Europe is also a way of life, a standard of living, and a polity of shared democratic procedures, not burdened by ethnic and territorial conflicts. That Europe in its formally organized scope is currently much less than its actual potential. Several of the more advanced and politically stable Central European states, all part of the Western Petrine tradition, notably the Czech Republic, Poland, Hungary, and perhaps also Slovenia, are clearly qualified and eager for membership in "Europe" and its transatlantic security connection.

In the current circumstances, the expansion of NATO to include Poland, the Czech Republic, and Hungary—probably by 1999—appears to be likely. After this initial but significant step, it is likely that any subsequent expansion of the alliance will either be coinci-

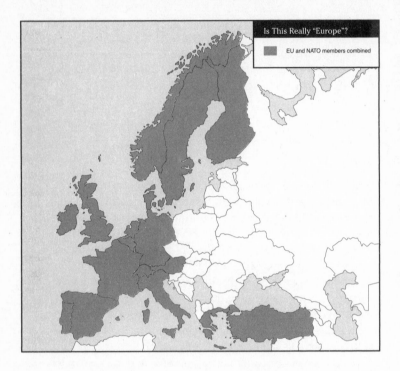

Is This Really "Europe"?

EU and NATO members combined

dental with or will follow the expansion of the EU. The latter involves a much more complicated process, both in the number of qualifying stages and in the meeting of membership requirements (see chart on page 83). Thus, even the first admissions into the EU from Central Europe are not likely before the year 2002 or perhaps somewhat later. Nonetheless, after the first three new NATO members have also joined the EU, both the EU and NATO will have to address the question of extending membership to the Baltic republics, Slovenia, Romania, Bulgaria, and Slovakia, and perhaps also, eventually, to Ukraine.

It is noteworthy that the prospect of eventual membership is already exercising a constructive influence on the affairs and conduct of would-be members. Knowledge that neither the EU nor NATO wishes to be burdened by additional conflicts pertaining either to minority rights or to territorial claims among their members (Turkey versus Greece is more than enough) has already

EU Membership: *Application to Accession*

A European country submits an application for membership to the Council of the European Union (the Council).

↓

The Council asks the Commission to deliver an opinion about the application.

↓

The Commission delivers an opinion about the application to the Council.

↓

The Council decides unanimously to open negotiations for accession.

↓

The Commission proposes, and the Council adopts unanimously, positions to be taken by the Union vis-à-vis the Applicants in accession negotiations.

↓

The Union, represented by the Council President, conducts negotiations with the Applicant.

↓

Agreement reached between Union and Applicant on a Draft Treaty of Accession.

↓

Accession Treaty submitted to the Council and the European Parliament.

↓

European Parliament delivers its assent to the Accession Treaty by an absolute majority.

↓

The Council approves the Accession Treaty unanimously.

↓

Member States and Applicants formally sign the Accession Treaty.

↓

Member States and Applicants ratify the Accession Treaty.

↓

After ratification, the Accession Agreement goes into effect.

Prepared by C.S.I.S. US-EU-Poland Action Commission

given Slovakia, Hungary, and Romania the needed incentive to reach accommodations that meet the standards set by the Council of Europe. Much the same is true for the more general principle that only democracies can qualify for membership. The desire not to be left out is having an important reinforcing impact on the new democracies.

In any case, it ought to be axiomatic that Europe's political unity and security are indivisible. As a practical matter, in fact it is difficult to conceive of a truly united Europe without a common security arrangement with America. It follows, therefore, that states that are in a position to begin and are invited to undertake accession talks with the EU should automatically also be viewed henceforth as subject in effect to NATO's presumptive protection.

Accordingly, the process of widening Europe and enlarging the transatlantic security system is likely to move forward by deliberate stages. Assuming sustained American and Western European commitment, a speculative but cautiously realistic timetable for these stages might be the following:

1. By 1999, the first new Central European members will have been admitted into NATO, though their entry into the EU will probably not happen before 2002 or 2003.

2. In the meantime, the EU will initiate accession talks with the Baltic republics, and NATO will likewise begin to move forward on the issue of their membership as well as Romania's, with their accession likely to be completed by 2005. At some point in this stage, the other Balkan states may likewise become eligible.

3. Accession by the Baltic states might prompt Sweden and Finland also to consider NATO membership.

4. Somewhere between 2005 and 2010, Ukraine, especially if in the meantime the country has made significant progress in its domestic reforms and has succeeded in becoming more evidently identified as a Central European country, should become ready for serious negotiations with both the EU and NATO.

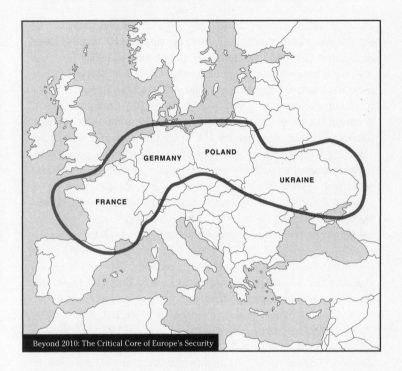

Beyond 2010: The Critical Core of Europe's Security

In the meantime, it is likely that Franco-German-Polish collaboration within the EU and NATO will have deepened considerably, especially in the area of defense. That collaboration could become the Western core of any wider European security arrangements that might eventually embrace both Russia and Ukraine. Given the special geopolitical interest of Germany and Poland in Ukraine's independence, it is also quite possible that Ukraine will gradually be drawn into the special Franco-German-Polish relationship. By the year 2010, Franco-German-Polish-Ukrainian political collaboration, engaging some 230 million people, could evolve into a partnership enhancing Europe's geostrategic depth (see map above).

Whether the above scenario emerges in a benign fashion or in the context of intensifying tensions with Russia is of great importance. Russia should be continuously reassured that the doors to Europe are open, as are the doors to its eventual participation in an expanded transatlantic system of security and, perhaps at some future point, in a new trans-Eurasian system of security. To give credence to these assurances, various cooperative links between Russia and Europe—in all fields—should be very deliberately promoted. (Russia's relationship to Europe, and the role of Ukraine in that regard, are discussed more fully in the next chapter.)

If Europe succeeds both in unifying and in expanding and if Russia in the meantime undertakes successful democratic consolidation and social modernization, at some point Russia can also become eligible for a more organic relationship with Europe. That, in turn, would make possible the eventual merger of the transatlantic security system with a transcontinental Eurasian one. However, as a practical reality, the question of Russia's formal membership will not arise for quite some time to come—and that, if anything, is yet another reason for not pointlessly shutting the doors to it.

To conclude: with the Europe of Yalta gone, it is essential that there be no reversion to the Europe of Versailles. The end of the division of Europe should not precipitate a step back to a Europe of quarrelsome nation-states but should be the point of departure for shaping a larger and increasingly integrated Europe, reinforced by a widened NATO and rendered even more secure by a constructive security relationship with Russia. Hence, America's central geostrategic goal in Europe can be summed up quite simply: it is to consolidate through a more genuine transatlantic partnership the U.S. bridgehead on the Eurasian continent so that an enlarging Europe can become a more viable springboard for projecting into Eurasia the international democratic and cooperative order.

CHAPTER 4

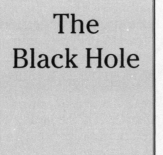

The
Black Hole

THE DISINTEGRATION LATE IN 1991 of the world's territorially
largest state created a "black hole" in the very center of
Eurasia. It was as if the geopoliticians' "heartland" had been
suddenly yanked from the global map.

For America, this new and perplexing geopolitical situation
poses a crucial challenge. Understandably, the immediate task has
to be to reduce the probability of political anarchy or a reversion
to a hostile dictatorship in a crumbling state still possessing a
powerful nuclear arsenal. But the long-range task remains: how to
encourage Russia's democratic transformation and economic recovery while avoiding the reemergence of a Eurasian empire that
could obstruct the American geostrategic goal of shaping a larger
Euro-Atlantic system to which Russia can then be stably and safely
related.

RUSSIA'S NEW GEOPOLITICAL SETTING

The collapse of the Soviet Union was the final stage in the progressive fragmentation of the vast Sino-Soviet Communist bloc that for
a brief period of time matched, and in some areas even surpassed,

the scope of Genghis Khan's realm. But the more modern transcontinental Eurasian bloc lasted very briefly, with the defection by Tito's Yugoslavia and the insubordination of Mao's China signaling early on the Communist camp's vulnerability to nationalist aspirations that proved to be stronger than ideological bonds. The Sino-Soviet bloc lasted roughly ten years; the Soviet Union about seventy.

However, even more geopolitically significant was the undoing of the centuries-old Moscow-ruled Great Russian Empire. The disintegration of that empire was precipitated by the general socioeconomic and political failure of the Soviet system—though much of its malaise was obscured almost until the very end by its systemic secrecy and self-isolation. Hence, the world was stunned by the seeming rapidity of the Soviet Union's self-destruction. In the course of two short weeks in December 1991, the Soviet Union was first defiantly declared as dissolved by the heads of its Russian, Ukrainian, and Belorussian republics, then formally replaced by a vaguer entity—called the Commonwealth of Independent States (CIS)—embracing all of the Soviet republics but the Baltic ones; then the Soviet president reluctantly resigned and the Soviet flag was lowered for the last time from the tower of the Kremlin; and, finally, the Russian Federation—now a predominantly Russian national state of 150 million people—emerged as the de facto successor to the former Soviet Union, while the other republics—accounting for another 150 million people—asserted in varying degrees their independent sovereignty.

The collapse of the Soviet Union produced monumental geopolitical confusion. In the course of a mere fortnight, the Russian people—who, generally speaking, were even less forewarned than the outside world of the Soviet Union's approaching disintegration—suddenly discovered that they were no longer the masters of a transcontinental empire but that the frontiers of Russia had been rolled back to where they had been in the Caucasus in the early 1800s, in Central Asia in the mid-1800s, and—much more dramatically and painfully—in the West in approximately 1600, soon after the reign of Ivan the Terrible. The loss of the Caucasus revived strategic fears of resurgent Turkish influence; the loss of Central Asia generated a sense of deprivation regarding the enormous energy and mineral resources of the region as well as anxiety over a potential Islamic challenge; and Ukraine's independence challenged the very essence of Russia's claim to being the divinely endowed standard-bearer of a common pan-Slavic identity.

The space occupied for centuries by the Tsarist Empire and for three-quarters of a century by the Russian-dominated Soviet Union was now to be filled by a dozen states, with most (except for Russia) hardly prepared for genuine sovereignty and ranging in size from the relatively large Ukraine with its 52 million people to Armenia with its 3.5 million. Their viability seemed uncertain, while Moscow's willingness to accommodate permanently to the new reality was similarly unpredictable. The historic shock suffered by the Russians was magnified by the fact that some 20 million Russian-speaking people were now inhabitants of foreign states dominated politically by increasingly nationalistic elites determined to assert their own identities after decades of more or less coercive Russification.

The collapse of the Russian Empire created a power void in the very heart of Eurasia. Not only was there weakness and confusion in the newly independent states, but in Russia itself, the upheaval produced a massive systemic crisis, especially as the political upheaval was accompanied by the simultaneous attempt to undo the old Soviet socioeconomic model. The national trauma was made worse by Russia's military involvement in Tajikistan, driven by fears of a Muslim takeover of that newly independent state, and was especially heightened by the tragic, brutal, and both economically and politically very costly intervention in Chechnya. Most painful of all, Russia's international status was significantly degraded, with one of the world's two superpowers now viewed by many as little more than a Third World regional power, though still possessing a significant but increasingly antiquated nuclear arsenal.

The geopolitical void was magnified by the scale of Russia's social crisis. Three-quarters of a century of Communist rule had inflicted unprecedented biological damage on the Russian people. A very high proportion of its most gifted and enterprising individuals were killed or perished in the Gulag, in numbers to be counted in the millions. In addition, during this century the country also suffered the ravages of World War I, the killings of a protracted civil war, and the atrocities and deprivations of World War II. The ruling Communist regime imposed a stifling doctrinal orthodoxy, while isolating the country from the rest of the world. Its economic policies were totally indifferent to ecological concerns, with the result that both the environment and the health of the people suffered greatly. According to official Russian statistics, by the mid-1990s only about 40 percent of newborns came into the world healthy, while roughly one-fifth of Russian first graders suffered from some form of mental retardation. Male longevity had declined to 57.3 years, and more Russians were dying than were being born. Russia's social condition was, in fact, typical of a middle-rank Third World country.

One cannot overstate the horrors and tribulations that have befallen the Russian people in the course of this century. Hardly a single Russian family has had the opportunity to lead a normal civilized existence. Consider the social implications of the following sequence of events:

- the Russo-Japanese War of 1905, ending in Russia's humiliating defeat;

- the first "proletarian" revolution of 1905, igniting large-scale urban violence;

- World War I of 1914–1917, with its millions of casualties and massive economic dislocation;

- the civil war of 1918–1921, again consuming several million lives and devastating the land;

- the Russo-Polish War of 1919–1920, ending in a Russian defeat;

- the launching of the Gulag in the early 1920s, including the decimation of the prerevolutionary elite and its large-scale exodus from Russia;

- the industrialization and collectivization drives of the early and mid-1930s, which generated massive famines and millions of deaths in Ukraine and Kazakstan;

- the Great Purges and Terror of the mid- and late 1930s, with millions incarcerated in labor camps and upward of 1 million shot and several million dying from maltreatment;

- World War II of 1941–1945, with its multiple millions of military and civilian casualties and vast economic devastation;

- the reimposition of Stalinist terror in the late 1940s, again involving large-scale arrests and frequent executions;

- the forty-year-long arms race with the United States, lasting from the late 1940s to the late 1980s, with its socially impoverishing effects;

- the economically exhausting efforts to project Soviet power into the Caribbean, Middle East, and Africa during the 1970s and 1980s;

- the debilitating war in Afghanistan from 1979 to 1989;

- the sudden breakup of the Soviet Union, followed by civil disorders, a painful economic crisis, and the bloody and humiliating war against Chechnya.

Not only was the crisis in Russia's internal condition and the loss of international status distressingly unsettling, especially for the Russian political elite, but Russia's geopolitical situation was also adversely affected. In the West, as a consequence of the Soviet Union's disintegration, Russia's frontiers had been altered most painfully, and its sphere of geopolitical influence had dramatically shrunk (see map on page 94). The Baltic states had been Russian-controlled since the 1700s, and the loss of the ports of Riga and Tallinn made Russia's access to the Baltic Sea more limited and subject to winter freezes. Although Moscow managed to retain a politically dominant position in the formally newly independent but highly Russified Belarus, it was far from certain that the nationalist contagion would not eventually also gain the upper hand there as well. And beyond the frontiers of the former Soviet Union, the collapse of the Warsaw Pact meant that the former satellite states of Central Europe, foremost among them Poland, were rapidly gravitating toward NATO and the European Union.

Most troubling of all was the loss of Ukraine. The appearance of an independent Ukrainian state not only challenged all Russians to rethink the nature of their own political and ethnic identity, but it represented a vital geopolitical setback for the Russian state. The repudiation of more than three hundred years of Russian imperial history meant the loss of a potentially rich industrial and agricultural economy and of 52 million people ethnically and religiously sufficiently close to the Russians to make Russia into a truly large and confident imperial state. Ukraine's independence also deprived Russia of its dominant position on the Black Sea, where Odessa had served as Russia's vital gateway to trade with the Mediterranean and the world beyond.

The loss of Ukraine was geopolitically pivotal, for it drastically limited Russia's geostrategic options. Even without the Baltic states and Poland, a Russia that retained control over Ukraine could still seek to be the leader of an assertive Eurasian empire, in which Moscow could dominate the non-Slavs in the South and Southeast of the former Soviet Union. But without Ukraine and its 52 million fellow Slavs, any attempt by Moscow to rebuild the Eurasian empire was likely to leave Russia entangled alone in protracted conflicts with the nationally and religiously aroused non-Slavs, the war with Chechnya perhaps simply being the first example. Moreover, given Russia's declining birthrate and the explosive birthrate among the Central Asians, any new Eurasian entity based purely on Russian power, without Ukraine, would inevitably become less European and more Asiatic with each passing year.

The loss of Ukraine was not only geopolitically pivotal but also geopolitically catalytic. It was Ukrainian actions—the Ukrainian declaration of independence in December 1991, its insistence in the critical negotiations in Bela Vezha that the Soviet Union should be replaced by a looser Commonwealth of Independent States, and especially the sudden coup-like imposition of Ukrainian command over the Soviet army units stationed on Ukrainian soil—that prevented the CIS from becoming merely a new name for a more confederal USSR. Ukraine's political self-determination stunned Moscow and set an example that the other Soviet republics, though initially more timidly, then followed.

Russia's loss of its dominant position on the Baltic Sea was replicated on the Black Sea not only because of Ukraine's independence but also because the newly independent Caucasian states—Georgia, Armenia, and Azerbaijan—enhanced the opportunities for Turkey to reestablish its once-lost influence in the region. Prior to 1991, the Black Sea was the point of departure for the projection of Russian naval power into the Mediterranean. By the mid-1990s, Russia was left with a small coastal strip on the Black Sea and with an unresolved debate with Ukraine over basing rights in Crimea for the remnants of the Soviet Black Sea Fleet, while observing, with evident irritation, joint NATO-Ukrainian naval and shore-landing maneuvers and a growing Turkish role in the Black Sea region. Russia also suspected Turkey of having provided effective aid to the Chechen resistance.

Farther to the southeast, the geopolitical upheaval produced a similarly significant change in the status of the Caspian Sea basin and of Central Asia more generally. Before the Soviet Union's collapse, the Caspian Sea was in effect a Russian lake, with a small southern sector falling within Iran's perimeter. With the emergence of the independent and strongly nationalist Azerbaijan—reinforced by the influx of eager Western oil investors—and the similarly independent Kazakstan and Turkmenistan, Russia became only one of five claimants to the riches of the Caspian Sea basin. It could no longer confidently assume that it could dispose of these resources on its own.

The emergence of the independent Central Asian states meant that in some places Russia's southeastern frontier had been pushed back northward more than one thousand miles. The new states now controlled vast mineral and energy deposits that were bound to attract foreign interests. It was almost inevitable that not only the elites but, before too long, also the peoples of these states would become more nationalistic and perhaps increasingly Islamic in outlook. In Kazakstan, a vast country endowed with enormous natural resources but with its nearly 20 million people split almost

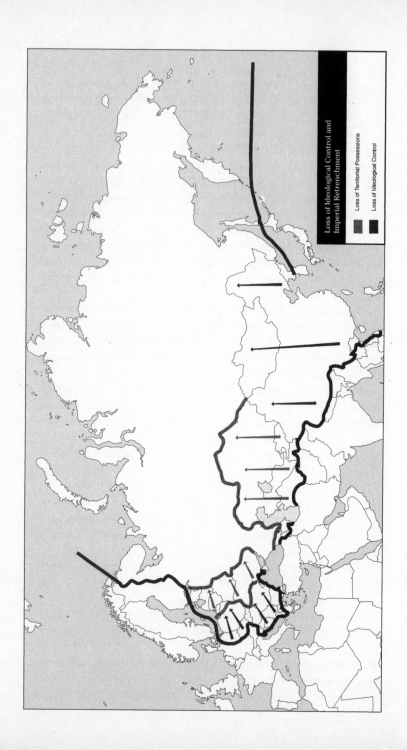

Loss of Ideological Control and Imperial Retrenchment

Loss of Territorial Possessions

Loss of Ideological Control

evenly between Kazaks and Slavs, linguistic and national frictions are likely to intensify. Uzbekistan—with its much more ethnically homogeneous population of approximately 25 million and its leaders emphasizing the country's historic glories—has become increasingly assertive in affirming the region's new postcolonial status. Turkmenistan, geographically shielded by Kazakstan from any direct contact with Russia, has actively developed new links with Iran in order to diminish its prior dependence on the Russian communications system for access to the global markets.

Supported from the outside by Turkey, Iran, Pakistan, and Saudi Arabia, the Central Asian states have not been inclined to trade their new political sovereignty even for the sake of beneficial economic integration with Russia, as many Russians continued to hope they would. At the very least, some tension and hostility in their relationship with Russia is unavoidable, while the painful precedents of Chechnya and Tajikistan suggest that something worse cannot be altogether excluded. For the Russians, the specter of a potential conflict with the Islamic states along Russia's entire southern flank (which, adding in Turkey, Iran, and Pakistan, account for more than 300 million people) has to be a source of serious concern.

Finally, at the time its empire dissolved, Russia was also facing an ominous new geopolitical situation in the Far East, even though no territorial or political changes had taken place. For several centuries, China had been weaker and more backward than Russia, at least in the political-military domains. No Russian concerned with the country's future and perplexed by the dramatic changes of this decade can ignore the fact that China is on its way to being a more advanced, more dynamic, and more successful state than Russia. China's economic power, wedded to the dynamic energy of its 1.2 billion people, is fundamentally reversing the historical equation between the two countries, with the empty spaces of Siberia almost beckoning for Chinese colonization.

This staggering new reality was bound to affect the Russian sense of security in its Far Eastern region as well as Russian interests in Central Asia. Before long, this development might even overshadow the geopolitical importance of Russia's loss of Ukraine. Its strategic implications were well expressed by Vladimir Lukin, Russia's first post-Communist ambassador to the United States and later the chairman of the Duma's Foreign Affairs Committee:

> In the past, Russia saw itself as being ahead of Asia, though lagging behind Europe. But since then, Asia has developed much faster. . . . we find ourselves to be not so much between "modern Europe" and "backward Asia" but rather occupying some strange middle space between two "Europes."[1]

In brief, Russia, until recently the forger of a great territorial empire and the leader of an ideological bloc of satellite states extending into the very heart of Europe and at one point to the South China Sea, had become a troubled national state, without easy geographic access to the outside world and potentially vulnerable to debilitating conflicts with its neighbors on its western, southern, and eastern flanks. Only the uninhabitable and inaccessible northern spaces, almost permanently frozen, seemed geopolitically secure.

GEOSTRATEGIC PHANTASMAGORIA

A period of historic and strategic confusion in postimperial Russia was hence unavoidable. The shocking collapse of the Soviet Union and especially the stunning and generally unexpected disintegration of the Great Russian Empire have given rise in Russia to enormous soul-searching, to a wide-ranging debate over what ought to be Russia's current historical self-definition, to intense public and private arguments over questions that in most major nations are not even raised: What is Russia? Where is Russia? What does it mean to be a Russian?

These questions are not merely theoretical: any reply contains significant geopolitical content. Is Russia a national state, based on purely Russian ethnicity, or is Russia by definition something more (as Britain is more than England) and hence destined to be an imperial state? What are—historically, strategically, and ethnically—the proper frontiers of Russia? Should the independent Ukraine be

[1]In "Our Security Predicament," *Foreign Policy* 88 (Fall 1992):60.

viewed as a temporary aberration when assessed in such historic, strategic, and ethnic terms? (Many Russians are inclined to feel that way.) To be a Russian, does one have to be ethnically a Russian ("Russkyi"), or can one be a Russian politically but not ethnically (that is, be a "Rossyanin"—the equivalent to "British" but not to "English")? For example, Yeltsin and some Russians have argued (with tragic consequences) that the Chechens could—indeed, should—be considered Russians.

A year before the Soviet Union's demise, a Russian nationalist, one of the few who saw the end approaching, cried out in a desperate affirmation:

> If the terrible disaster, which is unthinkable to the Russian people, does occur and the state is torn apart, and the people, robbed and deceived by their 1,000-year history, suddenly end up alone, and their recent "brothers" have taken their belongings and disappeared into their "national lifeboats" and sail away from the listing ship—well, we have nowhere to go. . . .
>
> Russian statehood, which embodies the "Russian idea" politically, economically, and spiritually, will be built anew. It will gather up all the best from its long 1,000-year kingdom and the 70 years of Soviet history that have flown by in a moment.[2]

But how? The difficulty of defining an answer that would be acceptable to the Russian people and yet realistic has been compounded by the historic crisis of the Russian state itself. Throughout almost its entire history, that state was simultaneously an instrument of territorial expansion and economic development. It was also a state that deliberately did not conceive itself to be a purely national instrument, in the West European tradition, but defined itself as the executor of a special supranational mission, with the "Russian idea" variously defined in religious, geopolitical, or ideological terms. Now, suddenly, that mission was repudiated as the state shrank territorially to a largely ethnic dimension.

Moreover, the post-Soviet crisis of the Russian state (of its "essence," so to speak) was compounded by the fact that Russia

[2]Aleksandr Prokhanov. "Tragedy of Centralism," *Literaturnaya Rossiya*, January 1990, pp. 4–5.

was not only faced with the challenge of having been suddenly deprived of its imperial missionary vocation but, in order to close the yawning gap between Russia's social backwardness and the more advanced parts of Eurasia, was now being pressed by domestic modernizers (and their Western consultants) to withdraw from its traditional economic role as the mentor, owner, and disposer of social wealth. This called for nothing short of a politically revolutionary limitation of the international and domestic role of the Russian state. This was profoundly disruptive to the most established patterns of Russian domestic life and contributed to a divisive sense of geopolitical disorientation within the Russian political elite.

In that perplexing setting, as one might have expected, "Whither Russia and what is Russia?" prompted a variety of responses. Russia's extensive Eurasian location has long predisposed that elite to think in geopolitical terms. The first foreign minister of the postimperial and post-Communist Russia, Andrei Kozyrev, reaffirmed that mode of thought in one of his early attempts to define how the new Russia should conduct itself on the international scene. Barely a month after the dissolution of the Soviet Union, he noted: "In abandoning messianism we set course for pragmatism. . . . we rapidly came to understand that geopolitics . . . is replacing ideology."[3]

Generally speaking, three broad and partially overlapping geostrategic options, each ultimately related to Russia's preoccupation with its status vis-à-vis America and each also containing some internal variants, can be said to have emerged in reaction to the Soviet Union's collapse. These several schools of thought can be classified as follows:

1. priority for "the mature strategic partnership" with America, which for some of its adherents was actually a code term for a global condominium;

2. emphasis on the "near abroad" as Russia's central concern, with some advocating a form of Moscow-dominated economic integration but with others also expecting an even-

[3]Interview in *Rossiyskaya Gazeta*, January 12, 1992.

tual restoration of some measure of imperial control, thereby creating a power more capable of balancing America and Europe; and

3. a counteralliance, involving some sort of a Eurasian anti-U.S. coalition designed to reduce the American preponderance in Eurasia.

Although the first of the foregoing was initially dominant among President Yeltsin's new ruling team, the second option surfaced into political prominence shortly thereafter, in part as a critique of Yeltsin's geopolitical priorities; the third made itself heard somewhat later, around the mid-1990s, in reaction to the spreading sense that Russia's post-Soviet geostrategy was both unclear and failing. As it happens, all three proved to be historically maladroit and derived from rather phantasmagoric views of Russia's current power, international potential, and foreign interests.

In the immediate wake of the Soviet Union's collapse, Yeltsin's initial posture represented the cresting of the old but never entirely successful "westernizer" conception in Russian political thought: that Russia belonged in the West, should be part of the West, and should as much as possible imitate the West in its own domestic development. That view was espoused by Yeltsin himself and by his foreign minister, with Yeltsin being quite explicit in denouncing the Russian imperial legacy. Speaking in Kiev on November 19, 1990, in words that the Ukrainians or Chechens could subsequently turn against him, Yeltsin eloquently declared:

> Russia does not aspire to become the center of some sort of new empire . . . Russia understands better than others the perniciousness of that role, inasmuch as it was Russia that performed that role for a long time. What did it gain from this? Did Russians become freer as a result? Wealthier? Happier? . . . history has taught us that a people that rules over others cannot be fortunate.

The deliberately friendly posture adopted by the West, especially by the United States, toward the new Russian leadership was a source of encouragement to the post-Soviet "westernizers" in the

Russian foreign policy establishment. It both reinforced its pro-American inclinations and seduced its membership personally. The new leaders were flattered to be on a first-name basis with the top policy makers of the world's only superpower, and they found it easy to deceive themselves into thinking that they, too, were the leaders of a superpower. When the Americans launched the slogan of "the mature strategic partnership" between Washington and Moscow, to the Russians it seemed as if a new democratic American-Russian condominium—replacing the former contest—had thus been sanctified.

That condominium would be global in scope. Russia thereby would not only be the legal successor to the former Soviet Union but the de facto partner in a global accommodation, based on genuine equality. As the new Russian leaders never tired of asserting, that meant not only that the rest of the world should recognize Russia as America's equal but that no global problem could be tackled or resolved without Russia's participation and/or permission. Although it was not openly stated, implicit in this illusion was also the notion that Central Europe would somehow remain, or might even choose to remain, a region of special political proximity to Russia. The dissolution of the Warsaw Pact and Comecon would not be followed by the gravitation of their former members either toward NATO or even only toward the EU.

Western aid, in the meantime, would enable the Russian government to undertake domestic reforms, withdrawing the state from economic life and permitting the consolidation of democratic institutions. Russia's economic recovery, its special status as America's coequal partner, and its sheer attractiveness would then encourage the recently independent states of the new CIS—grateful that the new Russia was not threatening them and increasingly aware of the benefits of some form of union with Russia—to engage in ever-closer economic and then political integration with Russia, thereby also enhancing Russia's scope and power.

The problem with this approach was that it was devoid of either international or domestic realism. While the concept of "mature strategic partnership" was flattering, it was also deceptive. America was neither inclined to share global power with Russia nor could it, even if it had wanted to do so. The new Russia was simply too weak, too devastated by three-quarters of a century of

Communist rule, and too socially backward to be a real global partner. In Washington's view, Germany, Japan, and China were at least as important and influential. Moreover, on some of the central geostrategic issues of national interest to America—in Europe, the Middle East, and the Far East—it was far from the case that American and Russian aspirations were the same. Once differences inevitably started to surface, the disproportion in political power, financial clout, technological innovation, and cultural appeal made the "mature strategic partnership" seem hollow—and it struck an increasing number of Russians as deliberately designed to deceive Russia.

Perhaps that disappointment might have been averted if earlier on—during the American-Russian honeymoon—America had embraced the concept of NATO expansion and had at the same time offered Russia "a deal it could not refuse," namely, a special cooperative relationship between Russia and NATO. Had America clearly and decisively embraced the idea of widening the alliance, with the stipulation that Russia should somehow be included in the process, perhaps Moscow's subsequent sense of disappointment with "the mature partnership" as well as the progressive weakening of the political position of the westernizers in the Kremlin might have been averted.

The moment to have done so was during the second half of 1993, right after Yeltsin's public endorsement in August of Poland's interest in joining the transatlantic alliance as being consistent with "the interests of Russia." Instead, the Clinton administration, then still pursuing its "Russia first" policy, agonized for two more years, while the Kremlin changed its tune and became increasingly hostile to the emerging but indecisive signals of the American intention to widen NATO. By the time Washington decided, in 1996, to make NATO enlargement a central goal in America's policy of shaping a larger and more secure Euro-Atlantic community, the Russians had locked themselves into rigid opposition. Hence, the year 1993 might be viewed as the year of a missed historic opportunity.

Admittedly, not all of the Russian concerns regarding NATO expansion lacked legitimacy or were motivated by malevolent motives. Some opponents, to be sure, especially among the Russian military, partook of a Cold War mentality, viewing NATO expansion not as an integral part of Europe's own growth but rather as the advance toward Russia of an American-led and still hostile alliance. Some of the Russian foreign policy elite—most of whom were actually former Soviet officials—persisted in the long-standing geostrategic view that America had no place in Eurasia and that NATO expansion was largely driven by the American desire to increase its sphere of influence. Some of their opposition also derived from the hope that an unattached Central Europe would some day again revert to Moscow's sphere of geopolitical influence, once Russia had regained its health.

But many Russian democrats also feared that the expansion of NATO would mean that Russia would be left outside of Europe, ostracized politically, and considered unworthy of membership in the institutional framework of European civilization. Cultural insecurity compounded the political fears, making NATO expansion seem like the culmination of the long-standing Western policy designed to isolate Russia, leaving it alone in the world and vulnerable to its various enemies. Moreover, the Russian democrats simply could not grasp the depth either of the Central Europeans' resentment over half a century of Moscow's domination or of their desire to be part of a larger Euro-Atlantic system.

On balance, it is probable that neither the disappointment nor the weakening of the Russian westernizers could have been avoided. For one thing, the new Russian elite, quite divided within itself and with neither its president nor its foreign minister capable of providing consistent geostrategic leadership, was not able to define clearly what the new Russia wanted in Europe, nor could it realistically assess the actual limitations of Russia's weakened condition. Moscow's politically embattled democrats could not bring themselves to state boldly that a democratic Russia does not oppose the enlargement of the transatlantic democratic community and that it wishes to be associated with it. The delusion of a shared global status with America made it difficult for the Moscow political elite to abandon the idea of a privileged geopolitical position for Russia, not only in the area of the former Soviet Union itself but even in regard to the former Central European satellite states.

These developments played into the hands of the nationalists, who by 1994 were beginning to recover their voices, and the militarists, who by then had become Yeltsin's critically important domestic supporters. Their increasingly shrill and occasionally threatening reactions to the aspirations of the Central Europeans merely intensified the determination of the former satellite states—mindful of their only recently achieved liberation from Russian rule—to gain the safe haven of NATO.

The gulf between Washington and Moscow was widened further by the Kremlin's unwillingness to disavow all of Stalin's conquests. Western public opinion, especially in Scandinavia but also in the United States, was especially troubled by the ambiguity of the Russian attitude toward the Baltic republics. While recognizing their independence and not pressing for their membership in the CIS, even the democratic Russian leaders periodically resorted to threats in order to obtain preferential treatment for the large communities of Russian colonists who had deliberately been settled in these countries during the Stalinist years. The atmosphere was further clouded by the pointed unwillingness of the Kremlin to denounce the secret Nazi-Soviet agreement of 1939 that had paved the way for the forcible incorporation of these republics into the Soviet Union. Even five years after the Soviet Union's collapse, spokesmen for the Kremlin insisted (in the official statement of September 10, 1996) that in 1940 the Baltic states had voluntarily "joined" the Soviet Union.

The post-Soviet Russian elite had apparently also expected that the West would aid in, or at least not impede, the restoration of a central Russian role in the post-Soviet space. They thus resented the West's willingness to help the newly independent post-Soviet states consolidate their separate political existence. Even while warning that a "confrontation with the United States . . . is an option that should be avoided," senior Russian analysts of American foreign policy argued (not altogether incorrectly) that the United States was seeking "the reorganization of interstate relations in the whole of Eurasia . . . whereby there was not one sole leading power on the continent but many medium, relatively stable, and moderately strong ones . . . but necessarily inferior to the United States in their individual or even collective capabilities."[4]

[4]A. Bogaturov and V. Kremenyuk (both senior scholars in the Institute of the United States and Canada), in "The Americans Themselves Will Never Stop," *Nezavisimaya Gazeta*, June 28, 1996.

In this regard, Ukraine was critical. The growing American inclination, especially by 1994, to assign a high priority to American-Ukrainian relations and to help Ukraine sustain its new national freedom was viewed by many in Moscow—even by its "westernizers"—as a policy directed at the vital Russian interest in eventually bringing Ukraine back into the common fold. That Ukraine will eventually somehow be "reintegrated" remains an article of faith among many members of the Russian political elite.[5] As a result, Russia's geopolitical and historical questioning of Ukraine's separate status collided head-on with the American view that an imperial Russia could not be a democratic Russia.

Additionally, there were purely domestic reasons that a "mature strategic partnership" between two "democracies" proved to be illusory. Russia was just too backward and too devastated by Communist rule to be a viable democratic partner of the United States. That central reality could not be obscured by high-sounding rhetoric about partnership. Post-Soviet Russia, moreover, had made only a partial break with the past. Almost all of its "democratic" leaders—even if genuinely disillusioned with the Soviet past—were not only the products of the Soviet system but former senior members of its ruling elite. They were not former dissidents, as in Poland or the Czech Republic. The key institutions of Soviet power—though weakened, demoralized, and corrupted—were still there. Symbolic of that reality and of the lingering hold of the Communist past was the historic centerpiece of Moscow: the continued presence of the Lenin mausoleum. It was as if post-Nazi Germany were governed by former middle-level Nazi "Gauleiters" spouting democratic slogans, with a Hitler mausoleum still standing in the center of Berlin.

[5]For example, even Yeltsin's top adviser, Dmitryi Ryurikov, was quoted by *Interfax* (November 20, 1996) as considering Ukraine to be "a temporary phenomenon," while Moscow's *Obshchaya Gazeta* (December 10, 1996) reported that "in the foreseeable future events in eastern Ukraine may confront Russia with a very difficult problem. Mass manifestations of discontent . . . will be accompanied by appeals to Russia, or even demands, to take over the region. Quite a few people in Moscow would be ready to support such plans." Western concerns regarding Russian intentions were certainly not eased by Russian demands for Crimea and Sevastopol, nor by such provocative acts as the deliberate inclusion in late 1996 of Sevastopol in Russian public television's nightly weather forecasts for Russian cities.

The political weakness of the new democratic elite was compounded by the very scale of the Russian economic crisis. The need for massive reforms—for the withdrawal of the Russian state from the economy—generated excessive expectations of Western, especially American, aid. Although that aid, especially from Germany and America, gradually did assume large proportions, even under the best of circumstances it still could not prompt a quick economic recovery. The resulting social dissatisfaction provided additional underpinning for a mounting chorus of disappointed critics who alleged that the partnership with the United States was a sham, beneficial to America but damaging to Russia.

In brief, neither the objective nor the subjective preconditions for an effective global partnership existed in the immediate years following the Soviet Union's collapse. The democratic "westernizers" simply wanted too much and could deliver too little. They desired an equal partnership—or, rather, a condominium—with America, a relatively free hand within the CIS, and a geopolitical no-man's-land in Central Europe. Yet their ambivalence about Soviet history, their lack of realism regarding global power, the depth of the economic crisis, and the absence of widespread social support meant that they could not deliver the stable and truly democratic Russia that the concept of equal partnership implied. Russia first had to go through a prolonged process of political reform, an equally long process of democratic stabilization, and an even longer process of socioeconomic modernization and then manage a deeper shift from an imperial to a national mindset regarding the new geopolitical realities not only in Central Europe but especially within the former Russian Empire before a real partnership with America could become a viable geopolitical option.

Under these circumstances, it is not surprising that the "near abroad" priority became both the major critique of the pro-West option as well as an early foreign policy alternative. It was based on the argument that the "partnership" concept slighted what ought to be most important to Russia: namely, its relations with the former Soviet republics. The "near abroad" came to be the shorthand formulation for advocacy of a policy that would place primary emphasis on the need to reconstruct some sort of a viable framework, with Moscow as the decision-making center, in the geopolitical space once occupied by the Soviet Union. On this premise, there was widespread agreement that a policy of concentration on the West, especially on America, was yielding little and costing too much. It simply made it easier for the West to exploit the opportunities created by the Soviet Union's collapse.

However, the "near abroad" school of thought was a broad umbrella under which several varying geopolitical conceptions could cluster. It embraced not only the economic functionalists and determinists (including some "westernizers") who believed that the CIS could evolve into a Moscow-led version of the EU but also others who saw in economic integration merely one of several tools of imperial restoration that could operate either under the CIS umbrella or through special arrangements (formulated in 1996) between Russia and Belarus or among Russia, Belarus, Kazakstan, and Kyrgyzstan; it also included Slavophile romantics who advocated a Slavic Union of Russia, Ukraine, and Belarus, and, finally, proponents of the somewhat mystical notion of Eurasianism as the substantive definition of Russia's enduring historical mission.

In its narrowest form, the "near abroad" priority involved the perfectly reasonable proposition that Russia must first concentrate on relations with the newly independent states, especially as all of them remained tied to Russia by the realities of the deliberately fostered Soviet policy of promoting economic interdependence among them. That made both economic and geopolitical sense. The "common economic space," of which the new Russian leaders spoke often, was a reality that could not be ignored by the leaders of the newly independent states. Cooperation, and even some integration, was an economic necessity. Thus, it was not only normal but desirable to promote joint CIS institutions in order to reverse the economic disruptions and fragmentation produced by the political breakup of the Soviet Union.

For some Russians, the promotion of economic integration was thus a functionally effective and politically responsible reaction to what had transpired. The analogy with the EU was often cited as pertinent to the post-Soviet situation. A restoration of the empire was explicitly rejected by the more moderate advocates of economic integration. For example, an influential report entitled "A Strategy for Russia," which was issued as early as August 1992 by the Council for Foreign and Defense Policy, a group of prominent personalities and government officials, very pointedly advocated "post-imperial enlightened integration" as the proper program for the post-Soviet "common economic space."

However, emphasis on the "near abroad" was not merely a politically benign doctrine of regional economic cooperation. Its geopolitical content had imperial overtones. Even the relatively moderate 1992 report spoke of a recovered Russia that would eventually establish a strategic partnership with the West, in which Russia would have the role of "regulating the situation in Eastern Europe, Central Asia and the Far East." Other advocates of this priority were more unabashed, speaking explicitly of Russia's "exclusive role" in the post-Soviet space and accusing the West of engaging in an anti-Russian policy by providing aid to Ukraine and the other newly independent states.

A typical but by no means extreme example was the argument made by Y. Ambartsumov, the chairman in 1993 of the parliamentary Foreign Affairs Committee and a former advocate of the "partnership" priority, who openly asserted that the former Soviet space was an exclusive Russian sphere of geopolitical influence. In January 1994, he was echoed by the heretofore energetic advocate of the pro-Western priority, Foreign Minister Andrei Kozyrev, who stated that Russia "must preserve its military presence in regions that have been in its sphere of interest for centuries." In fact, *Izvestiia* reported on April 8, 1994, that Russia had succeeded in retaining no fewer than twenty-eight military bases on the soil of the newly independent states—and a line drawn on a map linking the Russian military deployments in Kaliningrad, Moldova, Crimea, Armenia, Tajikistan, and the Kuril Islands would roughly approximate the outer limits of the former Soviet Union, as in the map on page 108.

In September 1995, President Yeltsin issued an official document on Russian policy toward the CIS that codified Russian goals as follows:

> The main objective of Russia's policy toward the CIS is to create an economically and politically integrated association of states capable of claiming its proper place in the world community . . . to consolidate Russia as the leading force in the formation of a new system of interstate political and economic relations on the territory of the post-Union space.

Russian Military Bases in the Former Soviet Space

● Bases on fringe of old Soviet frontiers

One should note the emphasis placed on the political dimension of the effort, on the reference to a single entity claiming "*its*" place in the world system, and on Russia's dominant role within that new entity. In keeping with this emphasis, Moscow insisted that political and military ties between Russia and the newly constituted CIS also be reinforced: that a common military command be created; that the armed forces of the CIS states be linked by a formal treaty; that the "external" borders of the CIS be subject to centralized (meaning Moscow's) control; that Russian forces play the decisive role in any peacekeeping actions within the CIS; and that a common foreign policy be shaped within the CIS, whose main institutions have come to be located in Moscow (and not in Minsk, as originally agreed in 1991), with the Russian president presiding at the CIS summit meetings.

And that was not all. The September 1995 document also declared that

Russian television and radio broadcasting in the near abroad should be guaranteed, the dissemination of Russian press in the region should be supported, and Russia should train national cadres for CIS states.

Special attention should be given to restoring Russia's position as the main educational center on the territory of the post-Soviet space, bearing in mind the need to educate the young generation in CIS states in a spirit of friendly relations with Russia.

Reflecting this mood, in early 1996 the Russian Duma went so far as to declare the dissolution of the Soviet Union to be invalid. Moreover, during spring of the same year, Russia signed two agreements providing for closer economic and political integration between Russia and the more accommodating members of the CIS. One agreement, signed with great pomp and circumstance, in effect provided for a union between Russia and Belarus within a new "Community of Sovereign Republics" (the Russian abbreviation "SSR" was pointedly reminiscent of the Soviet Union's "SSSR"), and the other—signed by Russia, Kazakstan, Belarus, and Kyrgyzstan—postulated the creation in the long term of a "Community of Integrated States." Both initiatives indicated impatience over the slow progress of integration within the CIS and Russia's determination to persist in promoting it.

The "near abroad" emphasis on enhancing the central mechanisms of the CIS thus combined some elements of reliance on objective economic determinism with a strong dose of subjective imperial determination. But neither provided a more philosophical and also a geopolitical answer to the still gnawing question "What is Russia, what is its true mission and rightful scope?"

It was this void that the increasingly appealing doctrine of Eurasianism—with its focus also on the "near abroad"—attempted to fill. The point of departure for this orientation—defined in rather cultural and even mystical terminology—was the premise that geopolitically and culturally, Russia is neither quite European nor quite Asian and that, therefore, it has a distinctive Eurasian identity of its own. That identity is the legacy of Russia's unique spatial control over the enormous landmass between Central Europe and the shores of the Pacific Ocean, the legacy of the imperial statehood that Moscow forged through four centuries of eastward expansion. That expansion assimilated into Russia a large non-Russian and non-European population, creating thereby also a singular Eurasian political and cultural personality.

Eurasianism as a doctrine was not a post-Soviet emanation. It first surfaced in the nineteenth century but became more pervasive in the twentieth, as an articulate alternative to Soviet communism and as a reaction to the alleged decadence of the West. Russian émigrés were especially active in propagating the doctrine as an alternative to Sovietism, realizing that the national awakening of the non-Russians within the Soviet Union required an overarching supranational doctrine, lest the eventual fall of communism lead also to the disintegration of the old Great Russian Empire.

As early as the mid-1920s, this case was articulated persuasively by Prince N. S. Trubetzkoy, a leading exponent of Eurasianism, who wrote that

> [c]ommunism was in fact a disguised version of Europeanism in destroying the spiritual foundations and national uniqueness of Russian life, in propagating there the materialist frame of reference that actually governs both Europe and America . . .
>
> Our task is to create a completely new culture, our own culture, which will not resemble European civilization . . . when Russia ceases to be a distorted reflection of European civilization . . . when she becomes once again herself: Russia-Eurasia, the conscious heir to and bearer of the great legacy of Genghis Khan.[6]

That view found an eager audience in the confused post-Soviet setting. On the one hand, communism was condemned as a betrayal of Russian orthodoxy and of the special, mystical "Russian idea"; and on the other, westernism was repudiated because the West, especially America, was seen as corrupt, anti-Russian culturally, and inclined to deny to Russia its historically and geographically rooted claim to exclusive control over the Eurasian landmass.

Eurasianism was given an academic gloss in the much-quoted writings of Lev Gumilev, a historian, geographer, and ethnogra-

[6]N. S. Trubetzkoy. "The Legacy of Genghis Khan," *Cross Currents* 9 (1990):68.

pher, whose books *Medieval Russia and the Great Steppe, The Rhythms of Eurasia,* and *The Geography of Ethnos in Historical Time* make a powerful case for the proposition that Eurasia is the natural geographic setting for the Russian people's distinctive "ethnos," the consequence of a historic symbiosis between them and the non-Russian inhabitants of the open steppes, creating thereby a unique Eurasian cultural and spiritual identity. Gumilev warned that adaptation to the West would mean nothing less for the Russian people than the loss of their own "ethnos and soul."

These views were echoed, though more primitively, by a variety of Russian nationalist politicians. Yeltsin's former vice president, Aleksandr Rutskoi, for example, asserted that "it is apparent from looking at our country's geopolitical situation that Russia represents the only bridge between Asia and Europe. Whoever becomes the master of this space will become the master of the world."[7] Yeltsin's 1996 Communist challenger, Gennadii Zyuganov, despite his Marxist-Leninist vocation, embraced Eurasianism's mystical emphasis on the special spiritual and missionary role of the Russian people in the vast spaces of Eurasia, arguing that Russia was thereby endowed both with a unique cultural vocation and with a specially advantageous geographic basis for the exercise of global leadership.

A more sober and pragmatic version of Eurasianism was also advanced by the leader of Kazakstan, Nursultan Nazarbayev. Faced at home with an almost even demographic split between native Kazaks and Russian settlers and seeking a formula that would somewhat dilute Moscow's pressures for political integration, Nazarbayev propagated the concept of the "Eurasian Union" as an alternative to the faceless and ineffective CIS. Although his version lacked the mystical content of the more traditional Eurasianist thinking and certainly did not posit a special missionary role for the Russians as leaders of Eurasia, it was derived from the notion that Eurasia—defined geographically in terms analogous to that of the Soviet Union—constituted an organic whole, which must also have a political dimension.

To a degree, the attempt to assign to the "near abroad" the highest priority in Russian geopolitical thinking was justified in the

[7]Interview with *L'Espresso* (Rome), July 15, 1994.

sense that some measure of order and accommodation between postimperial Russia and the newly independent states was an absolute necessity, in terms of security and economics. However, what gave much of the discussion a surrealistic touch was the lingering notion that in some fashion, whether it came about either voluntarily (because of economics) or as a consequence of Russia's eventual recovery of its lost power—not to speak of Russia's special Eurasian or Slavic mission—the political "integration" of the former empire was both desirable and feasible.

In this regard, the frequently invoked comparison with the EU neglects a crucial distinction: the EU, even allowing for Germany's special influence, is not dominated by a single power that alone overshadows all the other members combined, in relative GNP, population, or territory. Nor is the EU the successor to a national empire, with the liberated members deeply suspicious that "integration" is a code word for renewed subordination. Even so, one can easily imagine what the reaction of the European states would have been if Germany had declared formally that its goal was to consolidate and expand its leading role in the EU along the lines of Russia's pronouncement of September 1995 cited earlier.

The analogy with the EU suffers from yet another deficiency. The open and relatively developed Western European economies were ready for democratic integration, and the majority of Western Europeans perceived tangible economic and political benefits in such integration. The poorer West European countries were also able to benefit from substantial subsidies. In contrast, the newly independent states viewed Russia as politically unstable, as still entertaining domineering ambitions, and, economically, as an obstacle to their participation in the global economy and to their access to much-needed foreign investment.

Opposition to Moscow's notions of "integration" was particularly strong in Ukraine. Its leaders quickly recognized that such "integration," especially in light of Russian reservations regarding the legitimacy of Ukrainian independence, would eventually lead to the loss of national sovereignty. Moreover, the heavy-handed Russian treatment of the new Ukrainian state—its unwillingness to grant recognition of Ukraine's borders, its questioning of Ukraine's right to Crimea, its insistence on exclusive extraterritorial control over the port of Sevastopol—gave the aroused Ukrainian nationalism a distinctively anti-Russian edge. The self-definition of Ukrainian nationhood, during the critical formative stage in the history of the new state, was thus diverted from its traditional anti-Polish or anti-Romanian orientation and became focused instead on opposition to any Russian proposals for a more integrated CIS, for a special Slavic community (with Russia and Belarus), or for a Eurasian Union, deciphering them as Russian imperial tactics.

Ukraine's determination to preserve its independence was encouraged by external support. Although initially the West, especially the United States, had been tardy in recognizing the geopolitical importance of a separate Ukrainian state, by the mid-1990s both America and Germany had become strong backers of Kiev's separate identity. In July 1996, the U.S. secretary of defense declared, "I cannot overestimate the importance of Ukraine as an independent country to the security and stability of all of Europe," while in September, the German chancellor—notwithstanding his strong support for President Yeltsin—went even further in declaring that "Ukraine's firm place in Europe can no longer be challenged by anyone . . . No one will be able any more to dispute Ukraine's independence and territorial integrity." American policy makers also came to describe the American-Ukrainian relationship as "a strategic partnership," deliberately invoking the same phrase used to describe the American-Russian relationship.

Without Ukraine, as already noted, an imperial restoration based either on the CIS or on Eurasianism was not a viable option. An empire without Ukraine would eventually mean a Russia that would become more "Asianized" and more remote from Europe. Moreover, Eurasianism was also not especially appealing to the newly independent Central Asians, few of whom were eager for a new union with Moscow. Uzbekistan became particularly assertive in supporting Ukraine's objections to any elevation of the CIS into a supranational entity and in opposing the Russian initiatives designed to enhance the CIS.

Other CIS states, also wary of Moscow's intentions, tended to cluster around Ukraine and Uzbekistan in opposing or evading Moscow's pressures for closer political and military integration. Moreover, a sense of national consciousness was deepening in almost all of the new states, a consciousness increasingly focused on repudiating past submission to Moscow as colonialism and on eradicating its various legacies. Thus, even the ethnically vulnerable Kazakstan joined the other Central Asian states in abandoning the Cyrillic alphabet and replacing it with the Latin script as adapted earlier by Turkey. In effect, by the mid-1990s a bloc, quietly led by Ukraine and comprising Uzbekistan, Turkmenistan, Azerbaijan, and sometimes also Kazakstan, Georgia, and Moldova, had informally emerged to obstruct Russian efforts to use the CIS as the tool for political integration.

Ukrainian insistence on only limited and largely economic integration had the further effect of depriving the notion of a "Slavic Union" of any practical meaning. Propagated by some Slavophiles and given prominence by Aleksandr Solzhenitsyn's support, this idea automatically became geopolitically meaningless once it was repudiated by Ukraine. It left Belarus alone with Russia; and it also implied a possible partition of Kazakstan, with its Russian-populated northern regions potentially part of such a union. Such an option was understandably not reassuring to the new rulers of Kazakstan and merely intensified the anti-Russian thrust of their nationalism. In Belarus, a Slavic Union without Ukraine meant nothing less than incorporation into Russia, thereby also igniting more volatile feelings of nationalist resentment.

These external obstacles to a "near abroad" policy were powerfully reinforced by an important internal restraint: the mood of the Russian people. Despite the rhetoric and the political agitation among the political elite regarding Russia's special mission in the space of the former empire, the Russian people—partially out of sheer fatigue but also out of pure common sense—showed little enthusiasm for any ambitious program of imperial restoration. They favored open borders, open trade, freedom of movement, and special status for the Russian language, but political integration, especially if it was to involve economic costs or require bloodshed, evoked little enthusiasm. The disintegration of the "union" was regretted, its restoration favored; but public reaction to the war in Chechnya indicated that any policy that went beyond the application of economic leverage and/or political pressure would lack popular support.

In brief, the ultimate geopolitical inadequacy of the "near abroad" priority was that Russia was not strong enough politically to impose its will and not attractive enough economically to be able to seduce the new states. Russian pressure merely made them seek more external ties, first and foremost with the West but in some cases also with China and the key Islamic countries to the south. When Russia threatened to form its own military bloc in response to NATO's expansion, it begged the question "With whom?" And it begged the even more painful answer: at the most, maybe with Belarus and Tajikistan.

The new states, if anything, were increasingly inclined to distrust even perfectly legitimate and needed forms of economic integration with Russia, fearing their potential political consequences. At the same time, the notions of Russia's alleged Eurasian mission and of the Slavic mystique served only to isolate Russia further from Europe and, more generally, from the West, thereby perpetuating the post-Soviet crisis and delaying the needed modernization and westernization of Russian society along the lines of what Kemal Ataturk did in Turkey in the wake of the Ottoman Empire's collapse. The "near abroad" option thus offered Russia not a geopolitical solution but a geopolitical illusion.

If not a condominium with America and if not the "near abroad," then what other geostrategic option was open to Russia? The failure of the Western orientation to produce the desired global co-equality with America for a "democratic Russia," which was more a slogan than reality, caused a letdown among the democrats, whereas the reluctant recognition that "reintegration" of the old empire was at best a remote possibility tempted some Russian geopoliticians to toy with the idea of some sort of counteralliance aimed at America's hegemonic position in Eurasia.

In early 1996, President Yeltsin replaced his Western-oriented foreign minister, Kozyrev, with the more experienced but also orthodox former Communist international specialist Evgenniy Primakov, whose long-standing interest has been Iran and China. Some Russian commentators speculated that Primakov's orientation might precipitate an effort to forge a new "antihegemonic" coalition, formed around the three powers with the greatest geopolitical stake in reducing America's primacy in Eurasia. Some of Primakov's initial travel and comments reinforced that impression. Moreover, the existing Sino-Iranian connection in weapons trade as well as the Russian inclination to cooperate in Iran's efforts to increase its access to nuclear energy seemed to provide a perfect fit for closer political dialogue and eventual alliance. The result could, at least theoretically, bring together the world's leading Slavic power, the world's most militant Islamic power, and the world's most populated and powerful Asian power, thereby creating a potent coalition.

The necessary point of departure for any such counteralliance option involved a renewal of the bilateral Sino-Russian connection, capitalizing on the resentment among the political elites of both states over the emergence of America as the only global superpower. In early 1996, Yeltsin traveled to Beijing and signed a declaration that explicitly denounced global "hegemonic" tendencies, thereby implying that the two states would align themselves against the United States. In December, the Chinese prime minister, Li Peng, returned the visit, and both sides not only reiterated their opposition to an international system "dominated by one power" but also endorsed the reinforcement of existing alliances. Russian commentators welcomed this development, viewing it as a positive shift in the global correlation of power and as an appropriate response to America's sponsorship of NATO's expansion. Some even sounded gleeful that the Sino-Russian alliance would give America its deserved comeuppance.

However, a coalition allying Russia with both China and Iran can develop only if the United States is shortsighted enough to antagonize China and Iran simultaneously. To be sure, that eventuality cannot be excluded, and American conduct in 1995–1996 almost seemed consistent with the notion that the United States was seeking an antagonistic relationship with both Teheran and Beijing. However, neither Iran nor China was prepared to cast its lot strategically with a Russia that was both unstable and weak. Both realized that any such coalition, once it went beyond some occasional tactical orchestration, would risk their respective access to the more advanced world, with its exclusive capacity for investment and with its needed cutting-edge technology. Russia had too little to offer to make it a truly worthy partner in an antihegemonic coalition.

In fact, lacking any shared ideology and united merely by an "antihegemonic" emotion, any such coalition would be essentially an alliance of a part of the Third World against the most advanced portions of the First World. None of its members would gain much, and China especially would risk losing its enormous investment inflows. For Russia, too, "the phantom of a Russia-China alliance . . . would sharply increase the chances that Russia would once again become restricted from Western technology and capital," as a critical Russian geopolitician noted.[8] The alignment would eventually condemn all of its participants, whether two or three in number, to prolonged isolation and shared backwardness.

Moreover, China would be the senior partner in any serious Russian effort to jell such an "antihegemonic" coalition. Being more populous, more industrious, more innovative, more dynamic, and harboring some potential territorial designs on Russia, China would inevitably consign Russia to the status of a junior partner, while at the same time lacking the means (and probably any real desire) to help Russia overcome its backwardness. Russia would thus become a buffer between an expanding Europe and an expansionist China.

Finally, some Russian foreign affairs experts continued to entertain the hope that a stalemate in European integration, including perhaps internal Western disagreements over the future shape of NATO, might eventually create at least tactical opportunities for a Russo-German or a Russo-French flirtation, in either case to the detriment of Europe's transatlantic connection with America. This perspective was hardly new, for throughout the Cold War, Moscow periodically tried to play either the German or the French card. Nonetheless, it was not unreasonable for some of Moscow's geopoliticians to calculate that a stalemate in European affairs could create tactical openings that might be exploited to America's disadvantage.

But that is about all that could thereby be attained: purely tactical options. Neither France nor Germany is likely to forsake the American connection. An occasional flirtation, especially with the French, focused on some narrow issue, cannot be excluded—but a geopolitical reversal of alliances would have to be preceded by a massive upheaval in European affairs, a breakdown in European unification and in transatlantic ties. And even then, it is unlikely

[8]Aleksei Bogaturov. "Current Relations and Prospects for Interaction Between Russia and the United States," *Nezavisimaya Gazeta*, June 28, 1996.

that the European states would be inclined to pursue a truly comprehensive geopolitical alignment with a disoriented Russia.

Thus, none of the counteralliance options, in the final analysis, offer a viable alternative. The solution to Russia's new geopolitical dilemmas will not be found in counteralliance, nor will it come about through the illusion of a coequal strategic partnership with America or in the effort to create some new politically and economically "integrated" structure in the space of the former Soviet Union. All evade the only choice that is in fact open to Russia.

THE DILEMMA OF THE ONE ALTERNATIVE

Russia's only real geostrategic option—the option that could give Russia a realistic international role and also maximize the opportunity of transforming and socially modernizing itself—is Europe. And not just any Europe, but the transatlantic Europe of the enlarging EU and NATO. Such a Europe is taking shape, as we have seen in chapter 3, and it is also likely to remain linked closely to America. That is the Europe to which Russia will have to relate, if it is to avoid dangerous geopolitical isolation.

For America, Russia is much too weak to be a partner but still too strong to be simply its patient. It is more likely to become a problem, unless America fosters a setting that helps to convince the Russians that the best choice for their country is an increasingly organic connection with a transatlantic Europe. Although a long-term Russo-Chinese and Russo-Iranian strategic alliance is not likely, it is obviously important for America to avoid policies that could distract Russia from making the needed geopolitical choice. To the extent possible, American relations with China and Iran should, therefore, be formulated with their impact on Russian geopolitical calculations also kept in mind. Perpetuating illusions regarding grand geostrategic options can only delay the historic choice that Russia must make in order to bring to an end its deep malaise.

Only a Russia that is willing to accept the new realities of Europe, both economic and geopolitical, will be able to benefit internally from the enlarging scope of transcontinental European cooperation in commerce, communications, investment, and education. Russia's participation in the Council of Europe is thus a step very much in the right direction. It is a foretaste of further institutional links between the new Russia and the growing Europe. It also implies that if Russia pursues this path, it will have no choice other than eventually to emulate the course chosen by post-Ottoman Turkey, when it decided to shed its imperial ambitions and embarked very deliberately on the road of modernization, Europeanization, and democratization.

No other option can offer Russia the benefits that a modern, rich, and democratic Europe linked to America can. Europe and America are not a threat to a Russia that is a nonexpansive national and democratic state. They have no territorial designs on Russia, which China someday might have, nor do they share an insecure and potentially violent frontier, which is certainly the case with Russia's ethnically and territorially unclear border with the Muslim nations to the south. On the contrary, for Europe as well as for America, a national and democratic Russia is a geopolitically desirable entity, a source of stability in the volatile Eurasian complex.

Russia consequently faces the dilemma that the choice in favor of Europe and America, in order for it to yield tangible benefits, requires, first of all, a clear-cut abjuration of the imperial past and, second, no tergiversation regarding the enlarging Europe's political and security links with America. The first requirement means accommodation to the geopolitical pluralism that has come to prevail in the space of the former Soviet Union. Such accommodation does not exclude economic cooperation, rather on the model of the old European Free Trade Area, but it cannot include limits on the political sovereignty of the new states—for the simple reason that they do not wish it. Most important in that respect is the need for clear and unambiguous acceptance by Russia of Ukraine's separate existence, of its borders, and of its distinctive national identity.

The second requirement may be even more difficult to swallow. A truly cooperative relationship with the transatlantic community cannot be based on the notion that those democratic states of Europe that wish to be part of it can be excluded because of a Russian say-so. The expansion of that community need not be rushed, and it certainly should not be promoted on an anti-Russian theme. But neither can it, nor should it, be halted by a political fiat that itself reflects an antiquated notion of European security relations. An

expanding and democratic Europe has to be an open-ended historical process, not subject to politically arbitrary geographic limits.

For many Russians, the dilemma of the one alternative may at
first, and for some time to come, be too difficult to resolve. It will
require an enormous act of political will and perhaps also an outstanding leader, capable of making the choice and articulating the
vision of a democratic, national, truly modern and European Russia. That may not happen for some time. Overcoming the post-
Communist and postimperial crises will require not only more
time than is the case with the post-Communist transformation of
Central Europe but also the emergence of a farsighted and stable
political leadership. No Russian Ataturk is now in sight. Nonetheless, Russians will eventually have to come to recognize that Russia's national redefinition is not an act of capitulation but one of
liberation.[9] They will have to accept that what Yeltsin said in Kiev
in 1990 about a nonimperial future for Russia was absolutely on
the mark. And a genuinely nonimperial Russia will still be a great
power, spanning Eurasia, the world's largest territorial unit by far.

In any case, a redefinition of "What is Russia and where is Russia" will probably occur only by stages, and it will require a wise
and firm Western posture. America and Europe will have to help.
They should offer Russia not only a special treaty or charter with
NATO, but they should also begin the process of exploring with
Russia the shaping of an eventual transcontinental system of security and cooperation that goes considerably beyond the loose
structure of the Organization for Security and Cooperation in Europe (OSCE). And if Russia consolidates its internal democratic institutions and makes tangible progress in free-market-based
economic development, its ever-closer association with NATO and
the EU should not be ruled out.

At the same time, it is equally important for the West, especially for America, to pursue policies that perpetuate the dilemma
of the one alternative for Russia. The political and economic stabilization of the new post-Soviet states is a major factor in necessi-
tating Russia's historical self-redefinition. Hence, support for the

[9]In early 1996, General Aleksandr Lebed published a remarkable article
("The Fading of Empire or the Rebirth of Russia," *Segodnya*, April 26, 1996)
that went a long way toward making that case.

new post-Soviet states—for geopolitical pluralism in the space of the former Soviet empire—has to be an integral part of a policy designed to induce Russia to exercise unambiguously its European option. Among these states, three are geopolitically especially important: Azerbaijan, Uzbekistan, and Ukraine.

An independent Azerbaijan can serve as a corridor for Western access to the energy-rich Caspian Sea basin and Central Asia. Conversely, a subdued Azerbaijan would mean that Central Asia can be sealed off from the outside world and thus rendered politically vulnerable to Russian pressures for reintegration. Uzbekistan, nationally the most vital and the most populous of the Central Asian states, represents a major obstacle to any renewed Russian control over the region. Its independence is critical to the survival of the other Central Asian states, and it is the least vulnerable to Russian pressures.

Most important, however, is Ukraine. As the EU and NATO expand, Ukraine will eventually be in the position to choose whether it wishes to be part of either organization. It is likely that, in order to reinforce its separate status, Ukraine will wish to join both, once they border upon it and once its own internal transformation begins to qualify it for membership. Although that will take time, it is not too early for the West—while further enhancing its economic and security ties with Kiev—to begin pointing to the decade 2005–2015 as a reasonable time frame for the initiation of Ukraine's progressive inclusion, thereby reducing the risk that the Ukrainians may fear that Europe's expansion will halt on the Polish-Ukrainian border.

Russia, despite its protestations, is likely to acquiesce in the expansion of NATO in 1999 to include several Central European countries, because the cultural and social gap between Russia and Central Europe has widened so much since the fall of communism. By contrast, Russia will find it incomparably harder to acquiesce in Ukraine's accession to NATO, for to do so would be to acknowledge that Ukraine's destiny is no longer organically linked to Russia's. Yet if Ukraine is to survive as an independent state, it will have to become part of Central Europe rather than Eurasia, and if it is to be part of Central Europe, then it will have to partake fully of Central Europe's links to NATO and the European Union. Russia's acceptance of these links would then define Russia's own decision to be also truly a part of Europe. Russia's refusal would be tanta-mount to the rejection of Europe in favor of a solitary "Eurasian" identity and existence.

The key point to bear in mind is that Russia cannot be in Europe without Ukraine also being in Europe, whereas Ukraine can be in Europe without Russia being in Europe. Assuming that Russia decides to cast its lot with Europe, it follows that ultimately it is in Russia's own interest that Ukraine be included in the expanding European structures. Indeed, Ukraine's relationship to Europe could be the turning point for Russia itself. But that also means that the defining moment for Russia's relationship to Europe is still some time off—"defining" in the sense that Ukraine's choice in favor of Europe will bring to a head Russia's decision regarding the next phase of its history: either to be a part of Europe as well or to become a Eurasian outcast, neither truly of Europe nor Asia and mired in its "near abroad" conflicts.

It is to be hoped that a cooperative relationship between an enlarging Europe and Russia can move from formal bilateral links to more organic and binding economic, political, and security ties. In that manner, in the course of the first two decades of the next century, Russia could increasingly become an integral part of a Europe that embraces not only Ukraine but reaches to the Urals and even beyond. An association or even some form of membership for Russia in the European and transatlantic structures would in turn open the doors to the inclusion of the three Caucasian countries—Georgia, Armenia, and Azerbaijan—that so desperately aspire to a European connection.

One cannot predict how fast that process can move, but one thing is certain: it will move faster if a geopolitical context is shaped that propels Russia in that direction, while foreclosing other temptations. And the faster Russia moves toward Europe, the sooner the black hole of Eurasia will be filled by a society that is increasingly modern and democratic. Indeed, for Russia the dilemma of the one alternative is no longer a matter of making a geopolitical choice but of facing up to the imperatives of survival.

CHAPTER 5

The Eurasian Balkans

IN EUROPE, THE WORD "BALKANS" conjures up images of ethnic conflicts and great-power regional rivalries. Eurasia, too, has its "Balkans," but the Eurasian Balkans are much larger, more populated, even more religiously and ethnically heterogeneous. They are located within that large geographic oblong that demarcates the central zone of global instability identified in chapter 2 and that embraces portions of southeastern Europe, Central Asia and parts of South Asia, the Persian Gulf area, and the Middle East.

The Eurasian Balkans form the inner core of that large oblong (see map on page 124), and they differ from its outer zone in one particularly significant way: they are a power vacuum. Although most of the states located in the Persian Gulf and the Middle East are also unstable, American power is that region's ultimate arbiter. The unstable region in the outer zone is thus an area of single power hegemony and is tempered by that hegemony. In contrast, the Eurasian Balkans are truly reminiscent of the older, more familiar Balkans of southeastern Europe: not only are its political entities unstable but they tempt and invite the intrusion of more powerful neighbors, each of whom is determined to oppose the re-

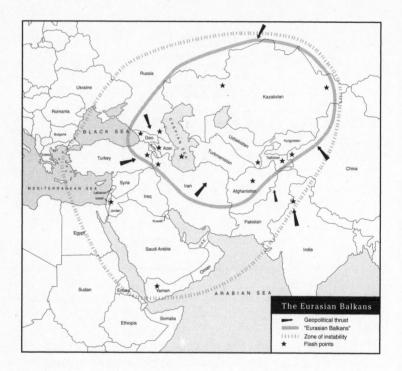

The Eurasian Balkans

➤ Geopolitical thrust
▨ "Eurasian Balkans"
⌇⌇⌇ Zone of instability
★ Flash points

gion's domination by another. It is this familiar combination of a power vacuum and power suction that justifies the appellation "Eurasian Balkans."

The traditional Balkans represented a potential geopolitical prize in the struggle for European supremacy. The Eurasian Balkans, astride the inevitably emerging transportation network meant to link more directly Eurasia's richest and most industrious western and eastern extremities, are also geopolitically significant. Moreover, they are of importance from the standpoint of security and historical ambitions to at least three of their most immediate and more powerful neighbors, namely, Russia, Turkey, and Iran, with China also signaling an increasing political interest in the region. But the Eurasian Balkans are infinitely more important as a potential economic prize: an enormous concentration of natural gas and oil reserves is located in the region, in addition to important minerals, including gold.

The world's energy consumption is bound to vastly increase over the next two or three decades. Estimates by the U.S. Department of Energy anticipate that world demand will rise by more than 50 percent between 1993 and 2015, with the most significant increase in consumption occurring in the Far East. The momentum of Asia's economic development is already generating massive pressures for the exploration and exploitation of new sources of energy, and the Central Asian region and the Caspian Sea basin are known to contain reserves of natural gas and oil that dwarf those of Kuwait, the Gulf of Mexico, or the North Sea.

Access to that resource and sharing in its potential wealth represent objectives that stir national ambitions, motivate corporate interests, rekindle historical claims, revive imperial aspirations, and fuel international rivalries. The situation is made all the more volatile by the fact that the region is not only a power vacuum but is also internally unstable. Every one of its countries suffers from serious internal difficulties, all of them have frontiers that are either the object of claims by neighbors or are zones of ethnic resentment, few are nationally homogeneous, and some are already embroiled in territorial, ethnic, or religious violence.

THE ETHNIC CAULDRON

The Eurasian Balkans include nine countries that one way or another fit the foregoing description, with two others as potential candidates. The nine are Kazakstan, Kyrgyzstan, Tajikistan, Uzbekistan, Turkmenistan, Azerbaijan, Armenia, and Georgia—all of them formerly part of the defunct Soviet Union—as well as Afghanistan. The potential additions to the list are Turkey and Iran, both of them much more politically and economically viable, both active contestants for regional influence within the Eurasian Balkans, and thus both significant geostrategic players in the region. At the same time, both are potentially vulnerable to internal ethnic conflicts. If either or both of them were to be destabilized, the internal problems of the region would become unmanageable, while efforts to restrain regional domination by Russia could even become futile.

The three states of the Caucasus—Armenia, Georgia, and Azer-

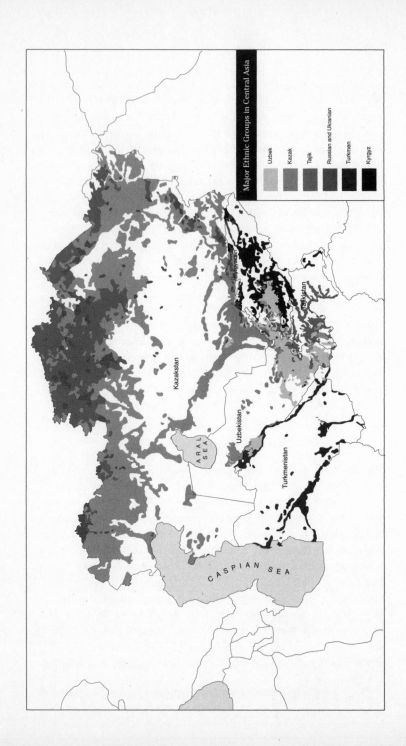

Major Ethnic Groups in Central Asia

Uzbek
Kazak
Tajik
Russian and Ukranian
Turkmen
Kyrgyz

Kazakstan

Kyrgyzstan

Tajikistan

Uzbekistan

Turkmenistan

ARAL SEA

CASPIAN SEA

	Afghanistan	Armenia	Azerbaijan	Georgia	Kazakhstan	Kyrgyzstan	Tajikistan	Turkmenistan	Uzbekistan
Population (Million, '95)	21.3	3.6	7.8	5.7	17.4	4.8	6.2	4.1	23.1
Life Expectancy	45.4	72.4	71.1	73.1	68.3	68.1	69.0	65.4	68.8
Ethnic Divisions ('95 est.)	Pashtun (38%) Tajik (25%) Hazara (19%) Uzbek (6%)	Armenian (93%) Azeri (3%) Russian (2%) Other (2%)	Azeri (90%) Dagestani (3.2%) Russian (2.5%) Armenian (2.3%) Other (2%)	Georgian (70.1%) Armenian (8.1%) Russian (6.3%) Azeri (5.7%) Ossetian (3%) Abkhaz (1.8%) Other (5%)	Kazak (41.9%) Russian (37%) Ukrainian (5.2%) German (4.7%) Uzbek (2.1%) Tatar (2%) Other (7%)	Kyrgyz (52.4%) Russian (21.5%) Uzbek (12.9%) Ukrainian (2.5%) German (2.4%) Other (8.3%)	Tajik (64.9%) Uzbek (25%) Russian (3.5%) Other (6.6%)	Turkmen (73.3%) Russian (9.8%) Uzbek (9%) Kazak (2%) Other (5.9%)	Uzbek (71.4%) Russian (8.3%) Tajik (4.7%) Kazak (4.1%) Tatar (2.4%) Karakalpak (2.1%) Other (7%)
GDP ($ billion)*	NA	8.1	13.8	6.0	55.2	8.4	8.5	13.1	54.5
Major Exports:	Wheat Livestock Fruits Carpets Wool Gems	Gold Aluminum Transport eq. Elec. eq.	Oil, Gas Chemicals Oilfield eq. Textiles Cotton	Citrus fruits Tea Wine Machinery Ferrous m. Non-ferrous m.	Oil Ferrous m. Non-ferrous m. Chemicals Grain Wool Meat Coal	Wool Chemicals Cotton Ferrous m. Non-ferrous m. Shoes Machinery Tobacco	Cotton Aluminum Fruits Vegetable oil Textiles	Natural gas Cotton** Petroleum prod.** Electricity Textiles Carpets	Cotton Gold Natural gas Mineral fertilizers Ferrous metals Textiles Food products

*Purchasing power parity: '94, as extrapolated from World Bank est. for 1992. **Turkmenistan is the world's tenth largest cotton producer, it has the world's fifth largest reserves of natural gas and significant oil reserves.

baijan—can be said to be based on truly historic nations. As a result, their nationalisms tend to be both pervasive and intense, and external conflicts have tended to be the key challenge to their well-being. The five new Central Asian states, by contrast, can be said to be rather more in the nation-building phase, with tribal and ethnic identities still strong, making internal dissension the major difficulty. In either type of state, these vulnerabilities have tempted exploitation by their more powerful and imperially minded neighbors.

The Eurasian Balkans are an ethnic mosaic (see preceding table and map). The frontiers of its states were drawn arbitrarily by Soviet cartographers in the 1920s and 1930s, when the respective Soviet republics were formally established. (Afghanistan, never having been part of the Soviet Union, is the exception.) Their borders were carved out largely on the ethnic principle, but they also reflected the Kremlin's interest in keeping the southern region of the Russian Empire internally divided and thus more subservient.

Accordingly, Moscow rejected proposals by Central Asian nationalists to meld the various Central Asian peoples (most of whom were not yet nationalistically motivated) into a single political unit—to be called "Turkestan"—preferring instead to create five separate "republics," each with a distinctive new name and jigsaw borders. Presumably out of a similar calculation, the Kremlin abandoned plans for a single Caucasian federation. Therefore, it is not surprising that, upon the collapse of the Soviet Union, neither the three states of the Caucasus nor the five states of Central Asia were fully prepared for their newly independent status nor for the needed regional cooperation.

In the Caucasus, Armenia's less than 4 million people and Azerbaijan's more than 8 million promptly became embroiled in open warfare over the status of Nagorno-Karabakh, a largely Armenian-populated enclave within Azerbaijan. The conflict generated large-scale ethnic cleansings, with hundreds of thousands of refugees and expellees fleeing in both directions. Given the fact that Armenia is Christian and Azerbaijan Muslim, the war has some overtones of a religious conflict. The economically devastating war made it much more difficult for either country to establish itself as stably independent. Armenia was driven to rely more on Russia, which had provided significant military help, while Azerbaijan's new independence and internal stability were compromised by the loss of Nagorno-Karabakh.

Azerbaijan's vulnerability has wider regional implications because the country's location makes it a geopolitical pivot. It can be described as the vitally important "cork" controlling access to the "bottle" that contains the riches of the Caspian Sea basin and Central Asia. An independent, Turkic-speaking Azerbaijan, with pipelines running from it to the ethnically related and politically supportive Turkey, would prevent Russia from exercising a monopoly on access to the region and would thus also deprive Russia of decisive political leverage over the policies of the new Central Asian states. Yet Azerbaijan is very vulnerable to pressures from powerful Russia to the north and from Iran to the south. There are twice as many Azeris—some estimate as many as 20 million—living in northwestern Iran as in Azerbaijan proper. That reality makes Iran fearful of potential separatism among its Azeris and hence quite ambivalent regarding Azerbaijan's sovereign status, despite the two nations' shared Muslim faith. As a result, Azerbaijan has become the object of combined Russian and Iranian pressures to restrict its dealings with the West.

Unlike either Armenia or Azerbaijan, both of which are ethnically quite homogeneous, about 30 percent of Georgia's 6 million people are minorities. Moreover, these small communities, rather tribal in organization and identity, have intensely resented Georgian domination. Upon the dissolution of the Soviet Union, the Ossetians and the Abkhazians therefore took advantage of internal Georgian political strife to attempt secession, which Russia quietly backed in order to compel Georgia to accede to Russian pressures to remain within the CIS (from which Georgia initially wanted to secede altogether) and to accept Russian military bases on Georgian soil in order to seal the area off from Turkey.

In Central Asia, internal factors have been more significant in promoting instability. Culturally and linguistically, four of the five newly independent Central Asian states are part of the Turkic world. Tajikistan is linguistically and culturally Persian, while Afghanistan (outside of the former Soviet Union) is a Pathan, Tajik, Pashtun, and Persian ethnic mosaic. All six countries are Muslim. Most of them, over the years, were under the passing influence of the Persian, Turkish, and Russian empires, but that experience has not served to foster a spirit of a shared regional interest among them. On the contrary, their diverse ethnic composition makes them vulnerable to internal and external conflicts, which cumulatively tempt intrusion by more powerful neighbors.

Of the five newly independent Central Asian states, Kazakstan and Uzbekistan are the most important. Regionally, Kazakstan is the shield and Uzbekistan is the soul for the region's diverse national awakenings. Kazakstan's geographic size and location shelter the others from direct Russian physical pressure, since Kazakstan alone borders on Russia. However, its population of about 18 million is approximately 35 percent Russian (the Russian population throughout the area is steadily declining), with another 20 percent also non-Kazak, a fact that has made it much more difficult for the new Kazak rulers—themselves increasingly nationalistic but representing only about one-half of the country's total population—to pursue the goal of nation building on the basis of ethnicity and language.

The Russians residing in the new state are naturally resentful of the new Kazak leadership, and being the formerly ruling colonial class and thus also better educated and situated, they are fearful of the loss of privilege. Furthermore, they tend to view the new Kazak nationalism with barely concealed cultural disdain. With both the northwestern and northeastern regions of Kazakstan heavily dominated by Russian colonists, Kazakstan would face the danger of territorial secession if Kazak-Russian relations were to deteriorate seriously. At the same time, several hundred thousand Kazaks reside on the Russian side of the state borders and in northeastern Uzbekistan, the state that the Kazaks view as their principal rival for Central Asian leadership.

Uzbekistan is, in fact, the prime candidate for regional leadership in Central Asia. Although smaller in size and less endowed with natural resources than Kazakstan, it has a larger population (nearly 25 million) and, much more important, a considerably more homogeneous population than Kazakstan's. Given higher indigenous birthrates and the gradual exodus of the formerly dominant Russians, soon about 75 percent of its people will be Uzbek, with only an insignificant Russian minority remaining largely in Tashkent, the capital.

Moreover, the country's political elite deliberately identifies the new state as the direct descendant of the vast medieval empire of Tamerlane (1336–1404), whose capital, Samarkand, became the region's renowned center for the study of religion, astronomy, and the arts. This lineage imbues modern Uzbekistan with a deeper sense of historical continuity and regional mission than its neighbors. Indeed, some Uzbek leaders see Uzbekistan as the national core of a single Central Asian entity, presumably with Tashkent as its capital. More than in any of the other Central Asian states, Uzbekistan's political elite and increasingly also its people, already partake of the subjective makings of a modern nation-state and are determined—domestic difficulties notwithstanding—never to revert to colonial status.

That condition makes Uzbekistan both the leader in fostering a sense of post-ethnic modern nationalism and an object of some uneasiness among its neighbors. Even as the Uzbek leaders set the pace in nation building and in the advocacy of greater regional self-sufficiency, the country's relatively greater national homogeneity and more intense national consciousness inspire fear among the rulers of Turkmenistan, Kyrgyzstan, Tajikistan, and even Kazakstan that Uzbek regional leadership could evolve into Uzbek regional domination. That concern inhibits regional cooperation among the newly sovereign states—which is not encouraged by the Russians in any case—and perpetuates regional vulnerability.

However, like the others, Uzbekistan is not entirely free of ethnic tensions. Parts of southern Uzbekistan, particularly around the historically and culturally important centers of Samarkand and Bukhara, have significant Tajik populations, which remain resentful of the frontiers drawn by Moscow. Complicating matters further is the presence of Uzbeks in western Tajikistan and of both Uzbeks and Tajiks in Kyrgyzstan's economically important Fergana Valley (where in recent years bloody ethnic violence has erupted), not to mention the presence of Uzbeks in northern Afghanistan.

Of the other three Central Asian states that have emerged from Russian colonial rule—Kyrgyzstan, Tajikistan, and Turkmenistan—only the third is relatively cohesive ethnically. Approximately 75 percent of its 4.5 million people are Turkmen, with Uzbeks and Russians each accounting for less than 10 percent. Turkmenistan's shielded geographic location makes it relatively remote from Russia, with Uzbekistan and Iran of far greater geopolitical relevance to the country's future. Once pipelines to the area have been developed, Turkmenistan's truly vast natural gas reserves augur a prosperous future for the country's people.

Kyrgyzstan's 5 million people are much more diverse. The Kyrgyz themselves account for about 55 percent of the total and the Uzbeks for about 13 percent, with the Russians lately dropping from over 20 percent to slightly over 15 percent. Prior to independence, the Russians largely composed the technical-engineering intelligentsia, and their exodus has hurt the country's economy. Although rich in minerals and endowed with a natural beauty that has led some to describe the country as the Switzerland of Central Asia (and thus potentially as a new tourist frontier), Kyrgyzstan's geopolitical location, squeezed between China and Kazakstan, makes it highly dependent on the degree to which Kazakstan itself succeeds in maintaining its independence.

Tajikistan is only somewhat more ethnically homogeneous. Of its 6.5 million people, fewer than two-thirds are Tajik and more than 25 percent are Uzbek (who are viewed with some hostility by the Tajiks), while the remaining Russians account for only about 3 percent. However, as elsewhere, even the dominant ethnic community is sharply—even violently—divided along tribal lines, with modern nationalism confined largely to the urban political elite. As a result, independence has produced not only civil strife but a convenient excuse for Russia to continue deploying its army in the country. The ethnic situation is even further complicated by the large presence of Tajiks across the border, in northeastern Afghanistan. In fact, almost as many ethnic Tajiks live in Afghanistan as in Tajikistan, another factor that serves to undermine regional stability.

Afghanistan's current state of disarray is likewise a Soviet legacy, even though the country is not a former Soviet republic. Fragmented by the Soviet occupation and the prolonged guerrilla warfare conducted against it, Afghanistan is a nation-state in name only. Its 22 million people have become sharply divided along ethnic lines, with growing divisions among the country's Pashtuns, Tajiks, and Hazaras. At the same time, the jihad against the Russian occupiers has made religion the dominant dimension of the country's political life, infusing dogmatic fervor into already sharp political differences. Afghanistan thus has to be seen not only as a part of the Central Asian ethnic conundrum but also as politically very much part of the Eurasian Balkans.

Although all of the formerly Soviet Central Asian states, as well as Azerbaijan, are populated predominantly by Muslims, their political elites—still largely the products of the Soviet era—are almost uniformly nonreligious in outlook and the states are formally secular. However, as their populations shift from a primarily traditional clannish or tribal identity to a more modern national awareness, they are likely to become imbued with an intensifying Islamic consciousness. In fact, an Islamic revival—already abetted from the outside not only by Iran but also by Saudi Arabia—is likely to become the mobilizing impulse for the increasingly pervasive new nationalisms, determined to oppose any reintegration under Russian—and hence infidel—control.

Indeed, the process of Islamization is likely to prove contagious also to the Muslims who have remained within Russia proper. They number about 20 million—more than twice the number of disaffected Russians (circa 9.5 million) who continue to live under foreign rule in the independent Central Asian states. The Russian Muslims thus account for about 13 percent of Russia's population, and it is almost inevitable that they will become more assertive in claiming their rights to a distinctive religious and political identity. Even if that claim does not take the form of a quest for outright independence, as it has in Chechnya, it will overlap with the dilemmas that Russia, given its recent imperial involvement and the Russian minorities in the new states, will continue to face in Central Asia.

Gravely increasing the instability of the Eurasian Balkans and making the situation potentially much more explosive is the fact that two of the adjoining major nation-states, each with a historically imperial, cultural, religious, and economic interest in the region—namely, Turkey and Iran—are themselves volatile in their geopolitical orientation and are internally potentially vulnerable. Were these two states to become destabilized, it is quite likely that the entire region would be plunged into massive disorder, with the ongoing ethnic and territorial conflicts spinning out of control and the region's already delicate balance of power severely disrupted. Accordingly, Turkey and Iran are not only important geostrategic players but are also geopolitical pivots, whose own internal condition is of critical importance to the fate of the region. Both are middle-sized powers, with strong regional aspirations and a sense of their historical significance. Yet the future geopolitical orientation and even the national cohesion of both states remains uncertain.

Turkey, a postimperial state still in the process of redefining its identity, is pulled in three directions: the modernists would like to see it become a European state and thus look to the west; the Islamists lean in the direction of the Middle East and a Muslim community and thus look to the south; and the historically minded nationalists see in the Turkic peoples of the Caspian Sea basin and Central Asia a new mission for a regionally dominant Turkey and thus look eastward. Each of these perspectives posits a different strategic axis, and the clash between them introduces for the first time since the Kemalist revolution a measure of uncertainty regarding Turkey's regional role.

Moreover, Turkey itself could become at least a partial victim of the region's ethnic conflicts. Although its population of about 65 million is predominantly Turkish, with about 80 percent Turkic stock (though including a variety of Circassians, Albanians, Bosnians, Bulgarians, and Arabs), as much as 20 percent or perhaps even more are Kurdish. Concentrated in the country's eastern regions, the Turkish Kurds have increasingly been drawn into the struggle for national independence waged by the Iraqi and Iranian Kurds. Any internal tensions within Turkey regarding the country's overall direction would doubtless encourage the Kurds to press even more violently for a separate national status.

Iran's future orientation is even more problematic. The fundamentalist Shiite revolution that triumphed in the late 1970s may be entering its "Thermidorian" phase, and that heightens the uncertainty regarding Iran's geostrategic role. On the one hand, the collapse of the atheistic Soviet Union opened up Iran's newly independent northern neighbors to religious proselytizing but, on the other, Iran's hostility to the United States has inclined Teheran to adopt at least a tactically pro-Moscow orientation, reinforced by Iran's concerns regarding the impact on its own cohesion of Azerbaijan's new independence.

That concern is derived from Iran's vulnerability to ethnic tensions. Of the country's 65 million people (almost identical in number to Turkey's), only somewhat more than one-half are Persians. Roughly one-fourth are Azeri, and the remainder include Kurds, Baluchis, Turkmens, Arabs, and other tribes. Outside of the Kurds and the Azeris, the others at present do not have the capacity to threaten Iran's national integrity, especially given the high degree of national, even imperial, consciousness among the Persians. But that could change quite quickly, particularly in the event of a new political crisis in Iranian politics.

Furthermore, the very fact that several newly independent "stans" now exist in the area and that even the 1 million Chechens have been able to assert their political aspirations is bound to have an infectious effect on the Kurds as well as on all the other ethnic minorities in Iran. If Azerbaijan succeeds in stable political and economic development, the Iranian Azeris will probably become increasingly committed to the idea of a greater Azerbaijan. Thus, political instability and divisions in Teheran could expand into a challenge to the cohesion of the Iranian state, thereby dramatically extending the scope and increasing the stakes of what is involved in the Eurasian Balkans.

THE MULTIPLE CONTEST

The traditional Balkans of Europe involved head-on competition among three imperial rivals: the Ottoman Empire, the Austro-Hungarian Empire, and the Russian Empire. There were also three indirect participants who were concerned that their European interests would be adversely affected by the victory of a particular protagonist: Germany feared Russian power, France opposed Austria-Hungary, and Great Britain preferred to see a weakening Ottoman Empire in control of the Dardanelles than the emergence of any one of the other major contestants in control of the Balkans. In the course of the nineteenth century, these powers managed to contain Balkan conflicts without prejudice to anyone's vital interests, but they failed to do so in 1914, with disastrous consequences for all.

Today's competition within the Eurasian Balkans also directly involves three neighboring powers: Russia, Turkey, and Iran, though China may eventually become a major protagonist as well. Also involved in the competition, but more remotely, are Ukraine,

Pakistan, India, and the distant America. Each of the three principal and most directly engaged contestants is driven not only by the prospect of future geopolitical and economic benefits but also by strong historical impulses. Each was at one time or another either the politically or the culturally dominant power in the region. Each views the others with suspicion. Although head-on warfare among them is unlikely, the cumulative impact of their external rivalry could contribute to regional chaos.

In the case of the Russians, the attitude of hostility to the Turks verges on the obsessive. The Russian media portrays the Turks as bent on control over the region, as instigators of local resistance to Russia (with some justification in the case of Chechnya), and as threatening Russia's overall security to a degree that is altogether out of proportion to Turkey's actual capabilities. The Turks reciprocate in kind and view their role as that of liberators of their brethren from prolonged Russian oppression. The Turks and the Iranians (Persians) have also been historical rivals in the region, and that rivalry has in recent years been revived, with Turkey projecting the image of a modern and secular alternative to the Iranian concept of an Islamic society.

Although each of the three can be said to seek at least a sphere of influence, in the case of Russia, Moscow's ambitions have a much broader sweep because of the relatively fresh memories of imperial control, the presence in the area of several million Russians, and the Kremlin's desire to reinstate Russia as a major global power. Moscow's foreign policy statements have made it plain that it views the entire space of the former Soviet Union as a zone of the Kremlin's special geostrategic interest, from which outside political—and even economic—influence should be excluded.

In contrast, although Turkish aspirations for regional influence retain some vestiges of an imperial, albeit more dated, past (the Ottoman Empire reached its apogee in 1590 with the conquest of the Caucasus and Azerbaijan, though it did not include Central Asia), they tend to be more rooted in an ethnic-linguistic sense of identity with the Turkic peoples of the area (see map on page 137). Given Turkey's much more limited political and military power, a sphere of exclusive political influence is simply unattainable. Rather, Turkey sees itself as potential leader of a loose Turkic-speaking community, taking advantage to that end of its appealing

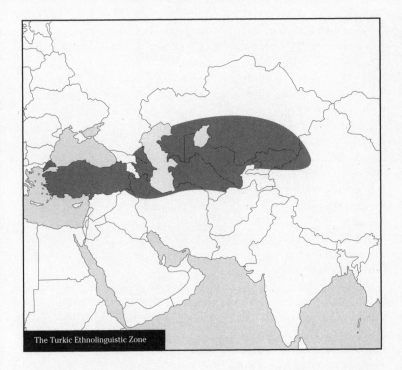

The Turkic Ethnolinguistic Zone

relative modernity, its linguistic affinity, and its economic means to establish itself as the most influential force in the nation-building processes underway in the area.

Iran's aspirations are vaguer still, but in the long run no less threatening to Russia's ambitions. The Persian Empire is a much more distant memory. At its peak, circa 500 B.C., it embraced the current territory of the three Caucasian states, Turkmenistan, Uzbekistan, and Tajikistan, and Afghanistan, as well as Turkey, Iraq, Syria, Lebanon, and Israel. Although Iran's current geopolitical aspirations are narrower than Turkey's, pointing mainly at Azerbaijan and Afghanistan, the entire Muslim population in the area—even within Russia itself—is the object of Iranian religious interest. Indeed, the revival of Islam in Central Asia has become an organic part of the aspirations of Iran's current rulers.

The competitive interests of Russia, Turkey, and Iran are represented on the map on page 138: in the case of the geopolitical

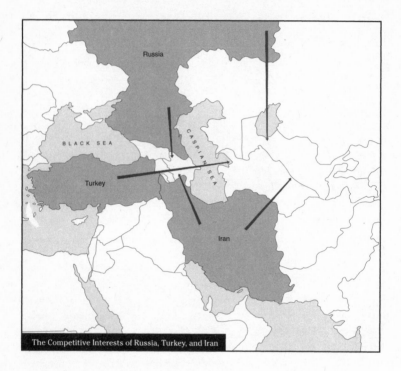

The Competitive Interests of Russia, Turkey, and Iran

thrust of Russia, by two arrows pointing directly south at Azerbai-jan and Kazakstan; in Turkey's case, by a single arrow pointing eastward through Azerbaijan and the Caspian Sea at Central Asia; and in Iran's case, by two arrows aiming northward at Azerbaijan and northeast at Turkmenistan, Afghanistan, and Tajikistan. These arrows not only crisscross; they can collide.

At this stage, China's role is more limited and its goals less evi-dent. It stands to reason that China prefers to face a collection of relatively independent states in the West rather than a Russian Empire. At a minimum, the new states serve as a buffer, but China is also anxious that its own Turkic minorities in Xinjiang Province might see in the newly independent Central Asian states an attrac-tive example for themselves, and for that reason, China has sought assurances from Kazakstan that cross-border minority activism will be suppressed. In the long run, the energy resources of the re-gion are bound to be of special interest to Beijing, and direct access to them, not subject to Moscow's control, has to be China's central goal. Thus, the overall geopolitical interest of China tends to clash with Russia's quest for a dominant role and is complementary to Turkish and Iranian aspirations.

For Ukraine, the central issues are the future character of the CIS and freer access to energy sources, which would lessen Ukraine's dependence on Russia. In that regard, closer relations with Azerbaijan, Turkmenistan, and Uzbekistan have become important to Kiev, with Ukrainian support for the more independent-minded states being an extension of Ukraine's efforts to enhance its own independence from Moscow. Accordingly, Ukraine has supported Georgia's efforts to become the westward route for Azeri oil exports. Ukraine has also collaborated with Turkey in order to weaken Russian influence in the Black Sea and has supported Turkish efforts to direct oil flows from Central Asia to Turkish terminals.

The involvement of Pakistan and India is more remote still, but neither is indifferent to what may be transpiring in these new Eurasian Balkans. For Pakistan, the primary interest is to gain geostrategic depth through political influence in Afghanistan—and to deny to Iran the exercise of such influence in Afghanistan and Tajikistan—and to benefit eventually from any pipeline construction linking Central Asia with the Arabian Sea. India, in reaction to Pakistan and possibly concerned about China's long-range influence in the region, views Iranian influence in Afghanistan and a greater Russian presence in the former Soviet space more favorably.

Although distant, the United States, with its stake in the maintenance of geopolitical pluralism in post-Soviet Eurasia, looms in the background as an increasingly important if indirect player, clearly interested not only in developing the region's resources but also in preventing Russia from exclusively dominating the region's geopolitical space. In so doing, America is not only pursuing its larger Eurasian geostrategic goals but is also representing its own growing economic interest, as well as that of Europe and the Far East, in gaining unlimited access to this hitherto closed area.

Thus, at stake in this conundrum are geopolitical power, access to potentially great wealth, the fulfillment of national and/or religious missions, and security. The particular focus of the contest, however, is on access. Until the collapse of the Soviet Union, access to the region was monopolized by Moscow. All rail transport, gas and oil pipelines, and even air travel were channeled through the center. Russian geopoliticians would prefer it to remain so, since they know that whoever either controls or dominates access to the region is the one most likely to win the geopolitical and economic prize.

It is this consideration that has made the pipeline issue so central to the future of the Caspian Sea basin and Central Asia. If the main pipelines to the region continue to pass through Russian territory to the Russian outlet on the Black Sea at Novorossiysk, the political consequences of this condition will make themselves felt, even without any overt Russian power plays. The region will remain a political dependency, with Moscow in a strong position to determine how the region's new wealth is to be shared. Conversely, if another pipeline crosses the Caspian Sea to Azerbaijan and thence to the Mediterranean through Turkey and if one more goes to the Arabian Sea through Afghanistan, no single power will have monopoly over access.

The troubling fact is that some elements in the Russian political elite act as if they prefer that the area's resources not be developed at all if Russia cannot have complete control over access. Let the wealth remain unexploited if the alternative is that foreign investment will lead to more direct presence by foreign economic, and thus also political, interests. That proprietary attitude is rooted in history, and it will take time and outside pressures before it changes.

The Tsarist expansion into the Caucasus and Central Asia occurred over a period of about three hundred years, but its recent end was shockingly abrupt. As the Ottoman Empire declined in vitality, the Russian Empire pushed southward, along the shores of the Caspian Sea toward Persia. It seized the Astrakhan khanate in 1556 and reached Persia by 1607. It conquered Crimea during 1774–1784, then took over the kingdom of Georgia in 1801 and overwhelmed the tribes astride the Caucasian mountain range (with the Chechens resisting with unique tenacity) during the second half of the 1800s, completing the takeover of Armenia by 1878.

The conquest of Central Asia was less a matter of overcoming a rival empire than of subjugating essentially isolated and quasi-tribal feudal khanates and emirates, capable of offering only sporadic and isolated resistance. Uzbekistan and Kazakstan were taken over through a series of military expeditions during the years 1801–1881, with Turkmenistan crushed and incorporated in campaigns lasting from 1873 to 1886. However, by 1850, the conquest of most of Central Asia was essentially completed, though periodic outbreaks of local resistance occurred even during the Soviet era.

The collapse of the Soviet Union produced a dramatic historical reversal. In the course of merely a few weeks in December 1991, Russia's Asian space suddenly shrank by about 20 percent, and the population Russia controlled in Asia was cut from 75 million to about 30 million. In addition, another 18 million residents in the Caucasus were also detached from Russia. Making these reversals even more painful to the Russian political elite was the awareness that the economic potential of these areas was now being targeted by foreign interests with the financial means to invest in, develop, and exploit resources that until very recently were accessible to Russia alone.

Yet Russia faces a dilemma: it is too weak politically to seal off the region entirely from the outside and too poor financially to develop the area exclusively on its own. Moreover, sensible Russian leaders realize that the demographic explosion underway in the new states means that their failure to sustain economic growth will eventually create an explosive situation along Russia's entire southern frontier. Russia's experience in Afghanistan and Chechnya could be repeated along the entire borderline that stretches from the Black Sea to Mongolia, especially given the national and Islamic resurgence now underway among the previously subjugated peoples.

It follows that Russia must somehow find a way of accommodating to the new postimperial reality, as it seeks to contain the Turkish and Iranian presence, to prevent the gravitation of the new states toward its principal rivals, to discourage the formation of any truly independent Central Asian regional cooperation, and to limit American geopolitical influence in the newly sovereign capitals. The issue thus is no longer that of imperial restoration—which would be too costly and would be fiercely resisted—but instead involves creating a new web of relations that would constrain the new states and preserve Russia's dominant geopolitical and economic position.

The chosen instrument for accomplishing that task has primarily been the CIS, though in some places the use of the Russian military and the skillful employment of Russian diplomacy to "divide and rule" has served the Kremlin's interests just as well. Moscow has used its leverage to seek from the new states the maximum degree of compliance to its vision of an increasingly integrated "commonwealth" and has pressed for a centrally directed system of control over the external borders of the CIS; for closer military integration, within the framework of a common foreign policy; and for the further expansion of the existing (originally Soviet) pipeline network, to the exclusion of any new ones that could skirt Russia. Russian strategic analyses have explicitly stated that Moscow views the area as its own special geopolitical space, even if it is no longer an integral part of its empire.

A clue to Russian geopolitical intentions is provided by the insistence with which the Kremlin has sought to retain a Russian military presence on the territories of the new states. Taking advantage of the Abkhazian secession movement, Moscow obtained basing rights in Georgia, legitimated its military presence on Armenian soil by exploiting Armenia's need for support in the war against Azerbaijan, and applied political and financial pressure to obtain Kazakstan's agreement to Russian bases; in addition, the civil war in Tajikistan made possible the continued presence there of the former Soviet army.

In defining its policy, Moscow has proceeded on the apparent expectation that its postimperial web of relationships with Central Asia will gradually emasculate the substance of the sovereignty of the individually weak new states and that it will place them in a subordinate relationship to the command center of the "integrated" CIS. To accomplish that goal, Russia is discouraging the new states from creating their own separate armies, from fostering the use of their distinctive languages (in which they are gradually replacing the Cyrillic alphabet with the Latin), from cultivating close ties with outsiders, and from developing new pipelines directly to outlets in the Arabian or Mediterranean Seas. If the policy succeeds, Russia could then dominate their foreign relations and determine revenue sharing.

In pursuing that goal, Russian spokesmen often invoke, as we have seen in chapter 4, the example of the European Union. In fact, however, Russia's policy toward the Central Asian states and the Caucasus is much more reminiscent of the Francophone African community—with the French military contingents and budgetary subsidies determining the politics and policies of the French-speaking postcolonial African states.

While the restoration of the maximum feasible degree of Russian political and economic influence in the region is the overall goal and the reinforcement of the CIS is the principal mechanism for achieving it, Moscow's primary geopolitical targets for political subordination appear to be Azerbaijan and Kazakstan. For a Russian political counteroffensive to be successful, Moscow must not only cork access to the region but must also penetrate its geographic shield.

For Russia, Azerbaijan has to be a priority target. Its subordination would help to seal off Central Asia from the West, especially from Turkey, thereby further increasing Russia's leverage vis-à-vis the recalcitrant Uzbekistan and Turkmenistan. To that end, tactical cooperation with Iran regarding such controversial issues as how to divide the drilling concessions to the Caspian seabed serves the important objective of compelling Baku to accommodate itself to Moscow's wishes. A subservient Azerbaijan would also facilitate the consolidation of a dominant Russian position in both Georgia and Armenia.

Kazakstan offers an especially tempting primary target as well, because its ethnic vulnerability makes it impossible for the Kazak government to prevail in an open confrontation with Moscow. Moscow can also exploit the Kazak fear of China's growing dynamism, as well as the likelihood of growing Kazak resentment over the Sinification of the adjoining Xinjiang Province in China. Kazakstan's gradual subordination would have the geopolitical effect of almost automatically drawing Kyrgyzstan and Tajikistan into Moscow's sphere of control, while exposing both Uzbekistan and Turkmenistan to more direct Russian pressure.

The Russian strategy, however, runs counter to the aspirations of almost all of the states located in the Eurasian Balkans. Their new political elites will not voluntarily yield the power and privilege they have gained through independence. As the local Russians gradually vacate their previously privileged positions, the new elites are rapidly developing a vested interest in sovereignty, a

dynamic and socially contagious process. Moreover, the once politically passive populations are also becoming more nationalistic
and, outside of Georgia and Armenia, also more conscious of their
Islamic identity.

Insofar as foreign affairs are concerned, both Georgia and Armenia (despite the latter's dependence on Russian support against
Azerbaijan) would like to become gradually more associated with
Europe. The resource-rich Central Asian states, along with Azerbaijan, would like to maximize the economic presence on their soil
of American, European, Japanese, and lately Korean capital, hop-
ing thereby to greatly accelerate their own economic development
and consolidate their independence. To this end, they also welcome the increasing role of Turkey and Iran, seeing in them a coun-
terweight to Russian power and a bridge to the large Muslim world
to the south.

Azerbaijan—encouraged by both Turkey and America—has
thus not only rejected Russian demands for military bases but it
also defied Russian demands for a single pipeline to a Russian Black
Sea port, opting instead for a dual solution involving a second
pipeline through Georgia to Turkey. (A pipeline southward through
Iran, to be financed by an American company, had to be abandoned
because of the U.S. financial embargo on deals with Iran.) In 1995,
amid much fanfare, a new rail link between Turkmenistan and Iran
was opened, making it feasible for Europe to trade with Central Asia
by rail, skirting Russia altogether. There was a touch of symbolic
drama to this reopening of the ancient Silk Route, with Russia thus
no longer able to separate Europe from Asia.

Uzbekistan has also become increasingly assertive in its opposition to Russia's efforts at "integration." Its foreign minister declared flatly in August 1996 that "Uzbekistan opposes the creation
of CIS supranational institutions which can be used as instruments
of centralized control." Its strongly nationalistic posture had already prompted sharp denunciations in the Russian press concerning Uzbekistan's

> emphatically pro-West orientation in the economy, the harsh
> invective apropos integration treaties within the CIS, the deci-
> sive refusal to join even the Customs Union, and a methodical
> anti-Russian nationality policy (even kindergartens which use

Russian are being closed down). . . . For the United States, which is pursuing in the Asia region a policy of the weakening of Russia, this position is so attractive.[1]

Even Kazakstan, in reaction to Russian pressures, has come to favor a secondary non-Russian route for its own outflows. As Umirserik Kasenov, the adviser to the Kazak president, put it:

> It is a fact that Kazakstan's search for alternative pipelines has been fostered by Russia's own actions, such as the limitation of shipments of Kazakstan's oil to Novorossiysk and of Tyumen oil to the Pavlodar Refinery. Turkmenistan's efforts to promote the construction of a gas line to Iran are partly due to the fact that the CIS countries pay only 60 percent of the world price or do not pay for it at all.[2]

Turkmenistan, for much the same reason, has been actively exploring the construction of a new pipeline through Afghanistan and Pakistan to the Arabian Sea, in addition to the energetic construction of new rail links with Kazakstan and Uzbekistan to the north and with Iran and Afghanistan to the south. Very preliminary and exploratory talks have also been held among the Kazaks, the Chinese, and the Japanese regarding an ambitious pipeline project that would stretch from Central Asia to the China Sea (see map on page 146). With long-term Western oil and gas investment commitments in Azerbaijan reaching some $13 billion and in Kazakstan going well over $20 billion (1996 figures), the economic and political isolation of this area is clearly breaking down in the face of global economic pressures and limited Russian financial options.

Fear of Russia has also had the effect of driving the Central Asian states into greater regional cooperation. The initially dormant Central Asian Economic Union, formed in January 1993, has been gradually activated. Even President Nursultan Nazarbayev of Kazakstan, at first an articulate advocate of a new "Eurasian Union," gradually became a convert to ideas of closer Central

---

[1]*Zavtra* 28 (June 1996).

[2]"What Russia Wants in the Transcaucasus and Central Asia," *Nezavisimaya Gazeta*, January 24, 1995.

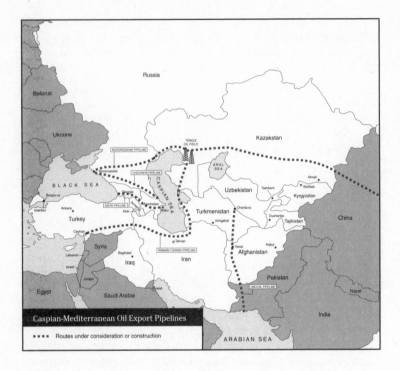

Caspian-Mediterranean Oil Export Pipelines

▪▪▪▪ Routes under consideration or construction

Asian cooperation, increased military collaboration among the region's states, support for Azerbaijan's efforts to channel Caspian Sea and Kazak oil through Turkey, and joint opposition to Russian and Iranian efforts to prevent the sectoral division of the Caspian Sea's continental shelf and mineral resources among the coastal states.

Given the fact that the governments in the area tend to be highly authoritarian, perhaps even more important has been the personal reconciliation among the principal leaders. It was common knowledge that the presidents of Kazakstan, Uzbekistan, and Turkmenistan were not particularly fond of one another (which they made eminently plain to foreign visitors), and that personal antagonism initially made it easier for the Kremlin to play off one against the other. By the mid-1990s, the three had come to realize that closer cooperation among them was essential to the preservation of their new sovereignty, and they began to engage in highly publicized displays of their allegedly close relations, stressing that henceforth they would coordinate their foreign policies.

But more important still has been the emergence within the CIS of an informal coalition, led by Ukraine and Uzbekistan, dedicated to the idea of a "cooperative," but not "integrated," commonwealth. Toward this end, Ukraine has signed agreements on military cooperation with Uzbekistan, Turkmenistan, and Georgia; and in September 1996, the foreign ministers of Ukraine and Uzbekistan even engaged in the highly symbolic act of issuing a declaration, demanding that henceforth CIS summits not be chaired by Russia's president but that the chairmanship be rotated.

The example set by Ukraine and Uzbekistan has had an impact even on the leaders who have been more deferential to Moscow's central concerns. The Kremlin must have been especially disturbed to hear Kazakstan's Nursultan Nazarbayev and Georgia's Eduard Shevardnadze declare in September 1996 that they would leave the CIS "if our independence is threatened." More generally, as a counter to the CIS, the Central Asian states and Azerbaijan stepped up their level of activity in the Organization of Economic Cooperation, a still relatively loose association of the region's Islamic states—including Turkey, Iran, and Pakistan—dedicated to the enhancement of financial, economic, and transportation links among its members. Moscow has been publicly critical of these initiatives, viewing them, quite correctly, as diluting the pertinent states' membership in the CIS.

In a similar vein, there has been steady enhancement of ties with Turkey and, to a lesser extent, Iran. The Turkic-speaking countries have eagerly accepted Turkey's offers of military training for the new national officer corps and the laying down of the Turkish welcome mat for some ten thousand students. The fourth summit meeting of the Turkic-speaking countries, held in Tashkent in October 1996 and prepared with Turkish backing, focused heavily on the enhancement of transportation links, on increased trade, and also on common educational standards as well as closer cultural cooperation with Turkey. Both Turkey and Iran have been particularly active in assisting the new states with their television programming, thereby directly influencing large audiences.

A ceremony in Alma-Ata, the capital of Kazakstan, in December 1996 was particularly symbolic of Turkey's identification with the independence of the region's states. On the occasion of the fifth anniversary of Kazakstan's independence, the Turkish president, Suleyman Demirel, stood at the side of President Nazarbayev at the unveiling of a gold-colored column twenty-eight meters high, crowned with a legendary Kazak/Turkic warrior's figure atop a griffinlike creature. At the event, Kazakstan hailed Turkey for "standing by Kazakstan at every step of its development as an independent state," and the Turks reciprocated by granting Kazakstan a credit line of $300 million, beyond existing private Turkish investment of about $1.2 billion.

While neither Turkey nor Iran has the means to exclude Russia from regional influence, Turkey and (more narrowly) Iran have thus been reinforcing the will and the capacity of the new states to resist reintegration with their northern neighbor and former master. And that certainly helps to keep the region's geopolitical future open.

NEITHER DOMINION NOR EXCLUSION

The geostrategic implications for America are clear: America is too distant to be dominant in this part of Eurasia but too powerful not to be engaged. All the states in the area view American engagement as necessary to their survival. Russia is too weak to regain imperial domination over the region or to exclude others from it, but it is also too close and too strong to be excluded. Turkey and Iran are strong enough to be influential, but their own vulnerabilities could make the area unable to cope with both the challenge from the north and the region's internal conflicts. China is too powerful not to be feared by Russia and the Central Asian states, yet its very presence and economic dynamism facilitates Central Asia's quest for wider global outreach.

It follows that America's primary interest is to help ensure that no single power comes to control this geopolitical space and that the global community has unhindered financial and economic access to it. Geopolitical pluralism will become an enduring reality only when a network of pipeline and transportation routes links the region directly to the major centers of global economic activity via the Mediterranean and Arabian Seas, as well as overland.

Hence, Russian efforts to monopolize access need to be opposed as inimical to regional stability.

However, the exclusion of Russia from the area is neither desirable nor feasible, nor is the fanning of hostility between the area's new states and Russia. In fact, Russia's active economic participation in the region's development is essential to the area's stability—and having Russia as a partner, but not as an exclusive dominator, can also reap significant economic benefits as a result. Greater stability and increased wealth within the region would contribute directly to Russia's well-being and give real meaning to the "commonwealth" promised by the acronym CIS. But that cooperative option will become Russia's policy only when much more ambitious, historically anachronistic designs that are painfully reminiscent of the original Balkans are effectively precluded.

The states deserving America's strongest geopolitical support are Azerbaijan, Uzbekistan, and (outside this region) Ukraine, all three being geopolitically pivotal. Indeed, Kiev's role reinforces the argument that Ukraine is the critical state, insofar as Russia's own future evolution is concerned. At the same time, Kazakstan—given its size, economic potential, and geographically important location—is also deserving of prudent international backing and especially of sustained economic assistance. In time, economic growth in Kazakstan might help to bridge the ethnic split that makes this Central Asian "shield" so vulnerable to Russian pressure.

In this region, America shares a common interest not only with a stable, pro-Western Turkey but also with Iran and China. A gradual improvement in American-Iranian relations would greatly increase global access to the region and, more specifically, reduce the more immediate threat to Azerbaijan's survival. China's growing economic presence in the region and its political stake in the area's independence are also congruent with America's interests. China's backing of Pakistan's efforts in Afghanistan is also a positive factor, for closer Pakistani-Afghan relations would make international access to Turkmenistan more feasible, thereby helping to reinforce both that state and Uzbekistan (in the event that Kazakstan were to falter).

Turkey's evolution and orientation are likely to be especially decisive for the future of the Caucasian states. If Turkey sustains its path to Europe—and if Europe does not close its doors to

Turkey—the states of the Caucasus are also likely to gravitate into the European orbit, a prospect they fervently desire. But if Turkey's Europeanization grinds to a halt, for either internal or external reasons, then Georgia and Armenia will have no choice but to adapt to Russia's inclinations. Their future will then become a function of Russia's own evolving relationship with the expanding Europe, for good or ill.

Iran's role is likely to be even more problematic A return to a pro-Western posture would certainly facilitate the stabilization and consolidation of the region, and it is therefore strategically desirable for America to encourage such a turn in Iran's conduct. But until that happens, Iran is likely to play a negative role, adversely affecting Azerbaijan's prospects, even as it takes positive steps like opening Turkmenistan to the world and, despite Iran's current fundamentalism, reinforcing the Central Asians' sense of their religious heritage.

Ultimately, Central Asia's future is likely to be shaped by an even more complex set of circumstances, with the fate of its states determined by the intricate interplay of Russian, Turkish, Iranian, and Chinese interests, as well as by the degree to which the United States conditions its relations with Russia on Russia's respect for the independence of the new states. The reality of that interplay precludes either empire or monopoly as a meaningful goal for any of the geostrategic players involved. Rather, the basic choice is between a delicate regional balance—which would permit the gradual inclusion of the area in the emerging global economy while the states of the region consolidate themselves and probably also acquire a more pronounced Islamic identity—or ethnic conflict, political fragmentation, and possibly even open hostilities along Russia's southern frontiers. The attainment and consolidation of that regional balance has to be a major goal in any comprehensive U.S. geostrategy for Eurasia.

CHAPTER 6

The Far Eastern Anchor

A<small>N EFFECTIVE</small> A<small>MERICAN POLICY</small> for Eurasia has to have a Far Eastern anchor. That need will not be met if America is excluded or excludes itself from the Asian mainland. A close relationship with maritime Japan is essential for America's global policy, but a cooperative relationship with mainland China is imperative for America's Eurasian geostrategy. The implications of that reality need to be faced, for the ongoing interaction in the Far East between three major powers—America, China, and Japan—creates a potentially dangerous regional conundrum and is almost certain to generate geopolitically tectonic shifts.

For China, America across the Pacific should be a natural ally since America has no designs on the Asian mainland and has historically opposed both Japanese and Russian encroachments on a weaker China. To the Chinese, Japan has been the principal enemy over the last century; Russia, "the hungry land" in Chinese, has long been distrusted; and India, too, now looms as a potential rival. The principle "my neighbor's neighbor is my ally" thus fits the geopolitical and historical relationship between China and America.

However, America is no longer Japan's adversary across the ocean but is now closely allied with Japan. America also has strong ties with Taiwan and with several of the Southeast Asian nations. The Chinese are also sensitive to America's doctrinal reservations regarding the internal character of the current Chinese regime. Thus, America is also seen as the principal obstacle in China's quest not only to become globally preeminent but even just regionally predominant. Is a collision between America and China, therefore, inevitable?

For Japan, America has been the umbrella under which the country could safely recover from a devastating defeat, regain its economic momentum, and on that basis progressively attain a position as one of the world's prime powers. But the very fact of that umbrella imposes a limit on Japan's freedom of action, creating the paradoxical situation of a world-class power being simultaneously a protectorate. For Japan, America continues to be the vital partner in Japan's emergence as an international leader. But America is also the main reason for Japan's continued lack of national self-reliance in the security area. How long can this situation endure?

In other words, in the foreseeable future two centrally important—and very directly interacting—geopolitical issues will define America's role in Eurasia's Far East:

1. What is the practical definition and—from America's point of view—the acceptable scope of China's potential emergence as the dominant regional power and of its growing aspirations for the status of a global power?

2. As Japan seeks to define a global role for itself, how should America manage the regional consequences of the inevitable reduction in the degree of Japan's acquiescence in its status as an American protectorate?

The East Asian geopolitical scene is currently characterized by metastable power relations. Metastability involves a condition of external rigidity but of relatively little flexibility, in that regard more reminiscent of iron than steel. It is vulnerable to a destructive chain reaction generated by a powerful jarring blow. Today's Far East is experiencing extraordinary economic dynamism alongside growing political uncertainty. Asian economic growth may in fact even contribute to that uncertainty, because prosperity obscures the region's political vulnerabilities even as it intensifies national ambitions and expands social expectations.

That Asia is an economic success without parallel in human development goes without saying. Just a few basic statistics dramatically highlight that reality. Less than four decades ago, East Asia (including Japan) accounted for a mere 4 percent or so of the world's total GNP, while North America led with approximately 35–40 percent; by the mid-1990s, the two regions were roughly equal (in the neighborhood of 25 percent). Moreover, Asia's pace of growth has been historically unprecedented. Economists have noted that in the takeoff stage of industrialization, Great Britain took more than fifty years and America just somewhat less than fifty years to double their respective outputs per head, whereas both China and South Korea accomplished the same gain in approximately ten years. Barring some massive regional disruption, within a quarter of a century, Asia is likely to outstrip both North America and Europe in total GNP.

However, in addition to becoming the world's center of economic gravity, Asia is also its potential political volcano. Although surpassing Europe in economic development, Asia is singularly deficient in regional political development. It lacks the cooperative multilateral structures that so dominate the European political landscape and that dilute, absorb, and contain Europe's more traditional territorial, ethnic, and national conflicts. There is nothing comparable in Asia to either the European Union or NATO. None of the three regional associations—ASEAN (Association of Southeast Asian Nations), ARF (Asian Regional Forum, ASEAN's platform for a political-security dialogue), and APEC (Asia-Pacific Economic Cooperation Group)—even remotely approximates the web of multilateral and regional cooperative ties that bind Europe together.

On the contrary, Asia is today the seat of the world's greatest concentration of rising and recently awakened mass nationalisms, fueled by sudden access to mass communications, hyperactivated by expanding social expectations generated by growing economic prosperity as well as by widening disparities in social wealth, and made more susceptible to political mobilization by the explosive increase both in population and urbanization. This condition is rendered even more ominous by the scale of Asia's arms buildup. In 1995, the region became—according to the International Institute of Strategic Studies—the world's biggest importer of arms, outstripping Europe and the Middle East.

In brief, East Asia is seething with dynamic activity, which so far has been channeled in peaceful directions by the region's rapid pace of economic growth. But that safety valve could at some point be overwhelmed by unleashed political passions, once they have been triggered by some flash point, even a relatively trivial one. The potential for such a flash point is present in a large number of contentious issues, each vulnerable to demagogic exploitation and thus potentially explosive:

- China's resentment of Taiwan's separate status is intensifying as China gains in strength and as the increasingly prosperous Taiwan begins to flirt with a formally separate status as a nation-state.

- The Paracel and Spratly Islands in the South China Sea pose the risk of a collision between China and several Southeast Asian states over access to potentially valuable seabed energy sources, with China imperially viewing the South China Sea as its legitimate national patrimony.

- The Senkaku Islands are contested by both Japan and China (with the rivals Taiwan and mainland China ferociously of a single mind on this issue), and the historical rivalry for regional preeminence between Japan and China infuses this issue with symbolic significance as well.

- The division of Korea and the inherent instability of North Korea—made all the more dangerous by North Korea's quest for nuclear capability—pose the risk that a sudden explosion could engulf the peninsula in warfare, which in turn would engage the United States and indirectly involve Japan.

- The issue of the southernmost Kuril Islands, unilaterally seized in 1945 by the Soviet Union, continues to paralyze and poison Russo-Japanese relations.

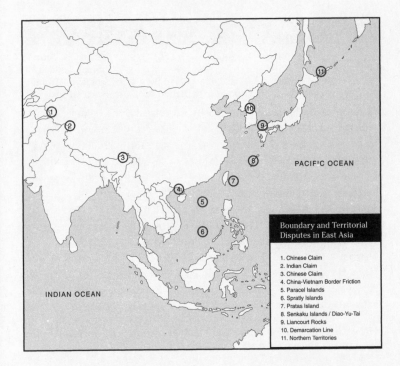

Boundary and Territorial
Disputes in East Asia

1. Chinese Claim
2. Indian Claim
3. Chinese Claim
4. China-Vietnam Border Friction
5. Paracel Islands
6. Spratly Islands
7. Pratas Island
8. Senkaku Islands / Diao-Yu-Tai
9. Liancourt Rocks
10. Demarcation Line
11. Northern Territories

- Other latent territorial-ethnic conflicts involve Russo-Chinese, Chinese-Vietnamese, Japanese-Korean, and Chinese-Indian border issues; ethnic unrest in Xinjiang Province; and Chinese-Indonesian disputes over oceanic boundaries. (See map above.)

The distribution of power in the region is also unbalanced. China, with its nuclear arsenal and its large armed forces, is clearly the dominant military power (see table on page 156). The Chinese navy has already adopted a strategic doctrine of "offshore active defense," seeking to acquire within the next fifteen years an ocean-going capability for "effective control of the seas within the first island chain," meaning the Taiwan Strait and the South China Sea. To be sure, Japan's military capability is also increasing, and in terms of quality, it has no regional peer. At present, however, the Japanese armed forces are not a tool of Japanese foreign policy and are

	Personnel	Tanks		Fighters		Surface Ships		Sub-marines	
Asian Armed Forces									
	Total	Total		Total		Total		Total	
				(Numbers in parentheses are advanced systems)					
China	3,030,000	9,400	(500)	5,224	(124)	57	(40)	53	(7)
Pakistan	577,000	1,890	(40)	336	(160)	11	(8)	6	(6)
India	1,100,000	3,500	(2,700)	700	(374)	21	(14)	18	(12)
Thailand	295,000	633	(313)	74	(18)	14	(6)	0	(0)
Singapore	55,500	350	(0)	143	(6)	0	(0)	0	(0)
North Korea	1,127,000	4,200	(2,225)	730	(136)	3	(0)	23	(0)
South Korea	633,000	1,860	(450)	334	(48)	17	(9)	3	(3)
Japan	237,700	1,200	(929)	324	(231)	62	(40)	17	(17)
Taiwan*	442,000	1,400	(0)	460	(10)	38	(11)	4	(2)
Vietnam	857,000	1,900	(400)	240	(0)	7	(5)	0	(0)
Malaysia**	114,500	26	(26)	50	(0)	2	(0)	0	(0)
Philippines	106,500	41	(0)	7	(0)	1	(0)	0	(0)
Indonesia	270,900	235	(110)	54	(12)	17	(4)	2	(2)

*Taiwan has 150 F-16s, 60 Mirage, and 130 other fighter jets on order and several naval vessels under construction.

**Malaysia is purchasing 8 F-18s and possibly 18 MiG-29s.

Note: Personnel means all active military; tanks are main battle tanks and light tanks; fighters are air-to-air and ground attack aircraft; surface ships are carriers, cruisers, destroyers, and frigates; and submarines are all types. Advanced systems are at least mid-1960s design with advanced technologies, such as laser range finders for tanks.

Source: General Accounting Office report, "Impact of China's Military Modernization in the Pacific Region," June 1995.

largely viewed as an extension of the American military presence in the region.

The emergence of China has already prompted its southeastern neighbors to be increasingly deferential to Chinese concerns. It is noteworthy that during the minicrisis of early 1996 concerning Taiwan (in which China engaged in some threatening military maneuvers and barred air and sea access to a zone near Taiwan, precipitating a demonstrative U.S. naval deployment), the foreign minister of Thailand hastily declared that such a ban was normal, his Indonesian counterpart stated that this was purely a Chinese affair, and the Philippines and Malaysia declared a policy of neutrality on the issue.

The absence of a regional balance of power has in recent years prompted both Australia and Indonesia—heretofore rather wary of each other—to initiate growing military coordination. Both countries made little secret of their anxiety over the longer-range prospects of Chinese regional military domination and over the staying power of the United States as the region's security guarantor. This concern has also caused Singapore to explore closer security cooperation with these nations. In fact, throughout the region, the central but unanswered question among strategists has become this: "For how long can peace in the world's most populated and increasingly most armed region be assured by one hundred thousand American soldiers, and for how much longer in any case are they likely to stay?"

It is in this volatile setting of intensifying nationalisms, increasing populations, growing prosperity, exploding expectations, and overlapping power aspirations that genuinely tectonic shifts are occurring in East Asia's geopolitical landscape:

- China, whatever its specific prospects, is a rising and potentially dominant power.

- America's security role is becoming increasingly dependent on collaboration with Japan.

- Japan is groping for a more defined and autonomous political role.

- Russia's role has greatly diminished, while the formerly Russian-dominated Central Asia has become an object of international rivalry.

- The division of Korea is becoming less tenable, making Korea's future orientation a matter of increasing geostrategic interest to its major neighbors.

These tectonic shifts give added salience to the two central issues posed at the outset of this chapter.

CHINA: NOT GLOBAL BUT REGIONAL

China's history is one of national greatness. The currently intense nationalism of the Chinese people is new only in its social pervasiveness, for it engages the self-identification and the emotions of an unprecedented number of Chinese. It is no longer a phenomenon confined largely to the students who, in the early years of this century, formed the precursors of the Kuomintang and the Chinese Communist Party. Chinese nationalism is now a mass phenomenon, defining the mindset of the world's most populous state.

That mindset has deep historical roots. History has predisposed the Chinese elite to think of China as the natural center of the world. In fact, the Chinese word for China—Chung-kuo, or the "Middle Kingdom"—both conveys the notion of China's centrality in world affairs and reaffirms the importance of national unity. That perspective also implies a hierarchical radiation of influence from the center to the peripheries, and thus China as the center expects deference from others.

Moreover, since time immemorial, China, with its vast population, has been a distinctive and proud civilization all its own. That civilization was highly advanced in all areas: philosophy, culture, the arts, social skills, technical inventiveness, and political power. The Chinese recall that until approximately 1600, China led the world in agricultural productivity, industrial innovation, and standard of living. But unlike the European and the Islamic civilizations, which have spawned some seventy-five-odd states, China has remained for most of its history a single state, which at the time of America's declaration of independence already contained more than 200 million people and was also the world's leading manufacturing power.

From that perspective, China's fall from greatness—the last 150 years of China's humiliation—is an aberration, a desecration of China's special quality, and a personal insult to every individual Chinese. It must be erased, and its perpetrators deserve due punishment. These perpetrators, in varying degrees, have primarily been four: Great Britain, Japan, Russia, and America—Great Britain, because of the Opium War and its consequent shameful debasement of China; Japan, because of the predatory wars spanning the last century, resulting in terrible (and still unrepented) infliction of suffering on the Chinese people; Russia, because of protracted encroachment on Chinese territories in the North as well as Stalin's domineering insensitivity toward Chinese self-esteem; and finally America, because through its Asian presence and support of Japan, it stands in the way of China's external aspirations.

In the Chinese view, two of these four powers have already been punished, so to speak, by history. Great Britain is no longer an empire, and the lowering of the Union Jack in Hong Kong forever closes that particularly painful chapter. Russia remains next door, though much diminished in stature, prestige, and territory. It is America and Japan that pose the most serious problems for China, and it is in the interaction with them that China's regional and global role will be substantively defined.

That definition, however, will depend in the first instance on how China itself evolves, on how much of an economic and military power it actually becomes. On this score, the prognosis for China is generally promising, though not without some major uncertainties and qualifications. Both the pace of China's economic growth and the scale of foreign investment in China—each among the highest in the world—provide the statistical basis for the conventional prognosis that within two decades or so China will become a global power, roughly on a par with the United States and Europe (assuming that the latter both unites and expands further). China might by then have a GDP considerably in excess of Japan's, and it already exceeds Russia's by a significant margin. That economic momentum should permit China to acquire military power on a scale that will be intimidating to all its neighbors, perhaps even to the more geographically distant opponents of China's aspirations. Further strengthened by the incorporation of Hong Kong and Macao, and perhaps also eventually by the political subordination of Taiwan, a Greater China will emerge not only as the dominant state in the Far East but as a world power of the first rank.

However, there are pitfalls in any such prognosis for the "Middle Kingdom's" inevitable resurrection as a central global power, the most obvious of which pertains to the mechanical reliance on statistical projection. That very error was made not long ago by those who prophesied that Japan would supplant the United States as the world's leading economy and that Japan was destined to be the new superstate. That perspective failed to take into account both the factor of Japan's economic vulnerability and the problem of political discontinuity—and the same error is being made by those who proclaim, and also fear, the inevitable emergence of China as a world power.

First of all, it is far from certain that China's explosive growth rates can be maintained over the next two decades. An economic slowdown cannot be excluded, and that by itself would discredit the conventional prognosis. In fact, for these rates to be sustained over a historically long period of time would require an unusually felicitous combination of effective national leadership, political tranquillity, domestic social discipline, high rates of savings, continued very high inflow of foreign investment, and regional stability. A prolonged combination of all of these positive factors is problematic.

Moreover, China's fast pace of growth is likely to produce political side effects that could limit its freedom of action. Chinese consumption of energy is already expanding at a rate that far exceeds domestic production. That excess will widen in any case, but especially so if China's rate of growth continues to be very high. The same is the case with food. Even given the slowdown in China's demographic growth, the Chinese population is still increasing in large absolute numbers, with food imports becoming more essential to internal well-being and political stability. Dependence on imports will not only impose strains on Chinese economic resources because of higher costs, but they will also make China more vulnerable to external pressures.

Militarily, China might partially qualify as a global power, since the very size of its economy and its high growth rates should enable its rulers to divert a significant ratio of the country's GDP to sustain a major expansion and modernization of China's armed forces, including a further buildup of its strategic nuclear arsenal. However, if that effort is excessive (and according to some Western estimates, in the mid-1990s it was already consuming about 20 percent of China's GDP), it could have the same negative effect on China's long-term economic growth that the failed attempt by the Soviet Union to compete in the arms race with the United States had on the Soviet economy. Furthermore, a major Chinese effort in this area would be likely to precipitate a countervailing Japanese arms buildup, thereby negating some of the political benefits of

China's growing military prowess. And one must not ignore the fact that outside of its nuclear forces, China is likely to lack the means, for some time to come, to project its military power beyond its regional perimeter.

Tensions within China could also intensify, as a result of the inevitable unevenness of highly accelerated economic growth, driven heavily by the uninhibited exploitation of marginal advantages. The coastal South and East as well as the principal urban centers—more accessible to foreign investment and overseas trade—have so far been the major beneficiaries of China's impressive economic growth. In contrast, the inland rural areas in general and some of the outlying regions have lagged (with upward of 100 million rural unemployed).

The resulting resentment over regional disparities could begin to interact with anger over social inequality. China's rapid growth is widening the social gap in the distribution of wealth. At some point, either because the government may seek to limit such differences or because of social resentment from below, the regional disparities and the wealth gap could in turn impact on the country's political stability.

The second reason for cautious skepticism regarding the widespread prognoses of China's emergence during the next quarter of a century as a dominating power in global affairs is, indeed, the future of China's politics. The dynamic character of China's nonstatist economic transformation, including its social openness to the rest of the world, is not mutually compatible in the long run with a relatively closed and bureaucratically rigid Communist dictatorship. The proclaimed communism of that dictatorship is progressively less a matter of ideological commitment and more a matter of bureaucratic vested interest. The Chinese political elite remains organized as a self-contained, rigid, disciplined, and monopolistically intolerant hierarchy, still ritualistically proclaiming its fidelity to a dogma that is said to justify its power but that the same elite is no longer implementing socially. At some point, these two dimensions of life will collide head-on, unless Chinese politics begin to adapt gradually to the social imperatives of China's economics.

Thus, the issue of democratization cannot be evaded indefinitely, unless China suddenly makes the same decision it made in the year 1474: to isolate itself from the world, somewhat like contemporary North Korea. To do that, China would have to recall its more than seventy thousand students currently studying in America, expel foreign businessmen, shut down its computers, and tear down satellite dishes from millions of Chinese homes. It would be an act of madness, reminiscent of the Cultural Revolution. Perhaps for a brief moment, in the context of a domestic struggle for power, a dogmatic wing of the ruling but fading Chinese Communist Party might attempt to emulate North Korea, but it could not be more than a brief episode. More likely than not, it would produce economic stagnation and then prompt a political explosion.

In any case, self-isolation would mean the end of any serious Chinese aspirations not only to global power but even to regional primacy. Moreover, the country has too much of a stake in access to the world, and that world, unlike that of 1474, is simply too intrusive to be effectively excluded. There is thus no practical, economically productive, and politically viable alternative to China's continued openness to the world.

Democratization will thus increasingly haunt China. Neither that issue nor the related question of human rights can be evaded for too long. China's future progress, as well as its emergence as a major power, will thus depend to a large degree on how skillfully the ruling Chinese elite handles the two related problems of power succession from the present generation of rulers to a younger team and of coping with the growing tension between the country's economic and political systems.

The Chinese leaders might perhaps succeed in promoting a slow and evolutionary transition to a very limited electoral authoritarianism, in which some low-level political choice is tolerated, and only thereafter move toward more genuine political pluralism, including more emphasis on incipient constitutional rule. Such a controlled transition would be more compatible with the imperatives of the increasingly open economic dynamics of the country than persistence in maintaining exclusive Party monopoly on political power.

To accomplish such controlled democratization, the Chinese political elite will have to be led with extraordinary skill, guided by pragmatic common sense, and stay relatively united and willing to yield some of its monopoly on power (and personal privilege)— while the population at large will have to be both patient and undemanding. That combination of felicitous circumstances may prove difficult to attain. Experience teaches that pressures for democratization from below, either from those who have felt themselves politically suppressed (intellectuals and students) or economically exploited (the new urban labor class and the rural poor), generally tend to outpace the willingness of rulers to yield. At some point, the politically and the socially disaffected in China are likely to join forces in demanding more democracy, freedom of expression, and respect for human rights. That did not happen in Tiananmen Square in 1989, but it might well happen the next time.

Accordingly, it is unlikely that China will be able to avoid a phase of political unrest. Given its size, the reality of growing regional differences, and the legacy of some fifty years of doctrinal dictatorship, such a phase could be disruptive both politically and economically. Even the Chinese leaders themselves seem to expect as much, with internal Communist Party studies undertaken in the early 1990s foreseeing potentially serious political unrest.[1] Some China experts have even prophesied that China might spin into one of its historic cycles of internal fragmentation, thereby halting China's march to greatness altogether. But the probability of such an extreme eventuality is diminished by the twin impacts of mass nationalism and modern communications, both of which work in favor of a unified Chinese state.

There is, finally, a third reason for skepticism regarding the prospects of China's emergence in the course of the next twenty or so years as a truly major—and to some Americans, already menacing—global power. Even if China avoids serious political disruptions and even if it somehow manages to sustain its extraordinarily high rates of economic growth over a quarter of a century—which are both rather big "ifs"—China would still be relatively very poor. Even a tripling of GDP would leave China's population in the lower ranks of the world's nations in per capita income, not to mention

---

[1]"Official Document Anticipates Disorder During the Post-Deng Period," *Cheng Ming* (Hong Kong), February 1, 1995, provides a detailed summary of two analyses prepared for the Party leadership concerning various forms of potential unrest. A Western perspective on the same topic is contained in Richard Baum, "China After Deng: Ten Scenarios in Search of Reality," *China Quarterly* (March 1996).

the actual poverty of a significant portion of its people.[2] Its comparative standing in per capita access to telephones, cars, and computers, let alone consumer goods, would be very low.

To sum up: even by the year 2020, it is quite unlikely even under the best of circumstances that China could become truly competitive in the key dimensions of *global* power. Even so, however, China is well on the way to becoming the preponderant *regional* power in East Asia. It is already geopolitically dominant on the mainland. Its military and economic power dwarfs its immediate neighbors, with the exception of India. It is, therefore, only natural that China will increasingly assert itself regionally, in keeping with the dictates of its history, geography, and economics.

Chinese students of their country's history know that as recently as 1840, China's imperial sway extended throughout Southeast Asia, all the way down to the Strait of Malacca, including Burma, parts of today's Bangladesh as well as Nepal, portions of today's Kazakhstan, all of Mongolia, and the region that today is called the Russian Far Eastern Province, north of where the Amur River flows into the ocean (see map on page 14 in chapter 1). These areas were either under some form of Chinese control or paid tribute to China. Franco-British colonial expansion ejected Chinese influence from Southeast Asia during the years 1885–95, while two treaties imposed by Russia in 1858 and 1864 resulted in territorial losses in the Northeast and Northwest. In 1895, following the Sino-Japanese War, China also lost Taiwan.

It is almost certain that history and geography will make the Chinese increasingly insistent—even emotionally charged—regarding the necessity of the eventual reunification of Taiwan with the mainland. It is also reasonable to assume that China, as its power grows, will make that goal its principal objective during the first decade of the next century, following the economic absorption and political digestion of Hong Kong. Perhaps a peaceful reunification—maybe under a formula of "one nation, several

[2]In the somewhat optimistic report titled "China's Economy Toward the 21st Century" (*Zou xiang 21 shi ji de Zhongguo jinji*), issued in 1996 by the Chinese Institute for Quantitative Economic and Technological Studies, it was estimated that the per capita income in China in 2010 will be approximately $735, or less than $30 higher than the World Bank definition of a low-income country.

systems" (a variant of Deng Xiaoping's 1984 slogan "one country, two systems")—might become appealing to Taiwan and would not be resisted by America, but only if China has been successful in sustaining its economic progress and adopting significant democratizing reforms. Otherwise, even a regionally dominant China is still likely to lack the military means to impose its will, especially in the face of American opposition, in which case the issue is bound to continue galvanizing Chinese nationalism while souring American-Chinese relations.

Geography is also an important factor driving the Chinese interest in making an alliance with Pakistan and establishing a military presence in Burma. In both cases, India is the geostrategic target. Close military cooperation with Pakistan increases India's security dilemmas and limits India's ability to establish itself as the regional hegemon in South Asia and as a geopolitical rival to China. Military cooperation with Burma gains China access to naval facilities on several Burmese offshore islands in the Indian Ocean, thereby also providing some further strategic leverage in Southeast Asia generally and in the Strait of Malacca particularly. And if China were to control the Strait of Malacca and the geostrategic choke point at Singapore, it would control Japan's access to Middle Eastern oil and European markets.

Geography, reinforced by history, also dictates China's interest in Korea. At one time a tributary state, a reunited Korea as an extension of American (and indirectly also of Japanese) influence would be intolerable to China. At the very minimum, China would insist that a reunited Korea be a nonaligned buffer between China and Japan and would also expect that the historically rooted Korean animosity toward Japan would of itself draw Korea into the Chinese sphere of influence. For the time being, however, a divided Korea suits China best, and thus China is likely to favor the continued existence of the North Korean regime.

Economic considerations are also bound to influence the thrust of China's regional ambitions. In that regard, the rapidly growing demand for new energy sources has already made China insistent on a dominant role in any regional exploitation of the seabed deposits of the South China Sea. For the same reason, China is beginning to display an increasing interest in the independence of the energy-rich Central Asian states. In April 1996, China,

Russia, Kazakstan, Kyrgyzstan, and Tajikistan signed a joint border and security agreement; and during President Jiang Zemin's visit to Kazakstan in July of the same year, the Chinese side was quoted as having provided assurances of China's support for "the efforts made by Kazakstan to defend its independence, sovereignty, and territorial integrity." The foregoing clearly signaled China's growing involvement in the geopolitics of Central Asia.

History and economics also conspire to increase the interest of a regionally more powerful China in Russia's Far East. For the first time since China and Russia have come to share a formal border, China is the economically more dynamic and politically stronger party. Seepage into the Russian area by Chinese immigrants and traders has already assumed significant proportions, and China is becoming more active in promoting Northeast Asian economic cooperation that also engages Japan and Korea. In that cooperation, Russia now holds a much weaker card, while the Russian Far East increasingly becomes economically dependent on closer links with China's Manchuria. Similar economic forces are also at work in China's relations with Mongolia, which is no longer a Russian satellite and whose formal independence China has reluctantly recognized.

A Chinese sphere of regional influence is thus in the making. A sphere of influence, however, should not be confused with a zone of exclusive political domination, such as the Soviet Union exercised in Eastern Europe. It is socioeconomically more porous and politically less monopolistic. Nonetheless, it entails a geographic space in which its various states, when formulating their own policies, pay special deference to the interests, views, and anticipated reactions of the regionally predominant power. In brief, a Chinese sphere of influence—perhaps a sphere of deference would be a more accurate formulation—can be defined as one in which the very first question asked in the various capitals regarding any given issue is "What is Beijing's view on this?"

The map that follows traces out the potential range over the next quarter of a century of a regionally dominant China and also of China as a global power, in the event that—despite the internal and external obstacles already noted—China should actually become one. A regionally dominant Greater China, which would mobilize the political support of its enormously rich and economically

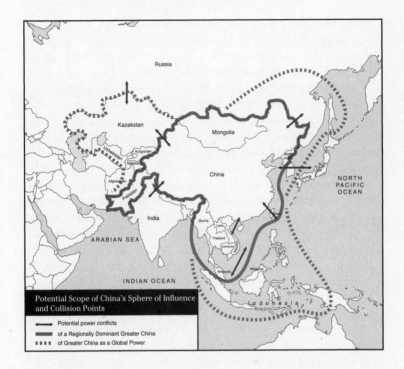

Potential Scope of China's Sphere of Influence and Collision Points

◄────► Potential power conflicts
━━━━ of a Regionally Dominant Greater China
▪▪▪▪ of Greater China as a Global Power

powerful diaspora in Singapore, Bangkok, Kuala Lumpur, Manila, and Jakarta, not to speak of Taiwan and Hong Kong (see footnote below for some startling data)[3] and which would penetrate into both Central Asia and the Russian Far East, would thus approximate in its radius the scope of the Chinese Empire before the onset of its decline some 150 years ago, even expanding its geopolitical range through the alliance with Pakistan. As China rises in power and prestige, the wealthy overseas Chinese are likely to identify themselves more and more with China's aspirations and will thus become a powerful vanguard of China's imperial momentum. The Southeast Asian states may find it prudent to defer to China's polit-

[3]According to *Yazhou Zhoukan* (Asiaweek), September 25, 1994, the aggregate assets of the 500 leading Chinese-owned companies in Southeast Asia totaled about $540 billion. Other estimates are even higher: *International Economy,* November/December 1996, reported that the annual income of the 50 million overseas Chinese was approximately the above

ical sensitivities and economic interests—and they are increasingly doing so.[4] Similarly, the new Central Asian states increasingly view China as a power that has a stake in their independence and in their role as buffers between China and Russia.

The scope of China as a global power would most probably involve a significantly deeper southern bulge, with both Indonesia and the Philippines compelled to adjust to the reality of the Chinese navy as the dominant force in the South China Sea. Such a China might be much more tempted to resolve the issue of Taiwan by force, irrespective of America's attitude. In the West, Uzbekistan, the Central Asian state most determined to resist Russian encroachments on its former imperial domain, might favor a countervailing alliance with China, as might Turkmenistan; and China might also become more assertive in the ethnically divided and thus nationally vulnerable Kazakstan. A China that becomes truly both a political and an economic giant might also project more overt political influence into the Russian Far East, while sponsoring Korea's unification under its aegis (see map on page 167).

But such a bloated China would also be more likely to encounter strong external opposition. The previous map makes it evident that in the West, both Russia and India would have good geopolitical reasons to ally in seeking to push back China's challenge. Cooperation between them would be likely to focus heavily

---

amount and thus roughly equal to the GDP of China's mainland. The overseas Chinese were said to control about 90 percent of Indonesia's economy, 75 percent of Thailand's, 50–60 percent of Malaysia's, and the whole economy in Taiwan, Hong Kong, and Singapore. Concern over this condition even led a former Indonesian ambassador to Japan to warn publicly of a "Chinese economic intervention in the region," which might not only exploit such Chinese presence but which could even lead to Chinese-sponsored "puppet governments" (Saydiman Suryohadiprojo, "How to Deal with China and Taiwan," *Asahi Shimbun* [Tokyo], September 23, 1996).

[4]Symptomatic in that regard was the report published in the Bangkok English-language daily, *The Nation* (March 31, 1997), on the visit to Beijing by the Thai Prime Minister, Chavalit Yongchaiyudh. The purpose of the visit was defined as establishing a firm strategic alliance with "Greater China." The Thai leadership was said to have "recognized China as a superpower that has a global role," and as wishing to serve as "a bridge between China and ASEAN." Singapore has gone even farther in stressing its identification with China.

on Central Asia and Pakistan, whence China would threaten their interests the most. In the south, opposition would be strongest from Vietnam and Indonesia (probably backed by Australia). In the east, America, probably backed by Japan, would react adversely to any Chinese efforts to gain predominance in Korea and to incorporate Taiwan by force, actions that would reduce the American political presence in the Far East to a potentially unstable and solitary perch in Japan.

Ultimately, the probability of either scenario sketched out on the maps fully coming to pass depends not only on how China itself develops but also very much on American conduct and presence. A disengaged America would make the second scenario much more likely, but even the comprehensive emergence of the first would require some American accommodation and self-restraint. The Chinese know this, and hence Chinese policy has to be focused primarily on influencing both American conduct and, especially, the critical American-Japanese connection, with China's other relationships manipulated tactically with that strategic concern in mind.

China's principal objection to America relates less to what America actually does than to what America currently is and where it is. America is seen by China as the world's current hegemon, whose very presence in the region, based on its dominant position in Japan, works to contain China's influence. In the words of a Chinese analyst employed in the research arm of the Chinese Foreign Ministry: "The U.S. strategic aim is to seek hegemony in the whole world and it cannot tolerate the appearance of any big power on the European and Asian continents that will constitute a threat to its leading position."[5] Hence, simply by being what it is and where it is, America becomes China's unintentional adversary rather than its natural ally.

Accordingly, the task of Chinese policy—in keeping with Sun Tsu's ancient strategic wisdom—is to use American power to

[5]Song Yimin. "A Discussion of the Division and Grouping of Forces in the World After the End of the Cold War," *International Studies* (China Institute of International Studies, Beijing) 6–8 (1996):10. That this assessment of America represents the view of China's top leadership is indicated by the fact that a shorter version of the analysis appeared in the mass-circulation official organ of the Party, *Renmin Ribao* (People's Daily), April 29, 1996.

peacefully defeat American hegemony, but without unleashing any latent Japanese regional aspirations. To that end, China's geostrategy must pursue two goals simultaneously, as somewhat obliquely defined in August 1994 by Deng Xiaoping: "First, to oppose hegemonism and power politics and safeguard world peace; second, to build up a new international political and economic order." The first obviously targets the United States and has as its purpose the reduction in American preponderance, while carefully avoiding a military collision that would end China's drive for economic power; the second seeks to revise the distribution of global power, capitalizing on the resentment in some key states against the current global pecking order, in which the United States is perched at the top, supported by Europe (or Germany) in the extreme west of Eurasia and by Japan in the extreme east.

China's second objective prompts Beijing to pursue a regional geostrategy that seeks to avoid any serious conflicts with its immediate neighbors, even while continuing its quest for regional preponderance. A tactical improvement in Sino-Russian relations is particularly timely, especially since Russia is now weaker than China. Accordingly, in April 1997, both countries joined in denouncing "hegemonism" and declaring NATO's expansion "impermissible." However, it is unlikely that China would seriously consider any long-term and comprehensive Russo-Chinese alliance against America. That would work to deepen and widen the scope of the American-Japanese alliance, which China would like to dilute slowly, and it would also isolate China from critically important sources of modern technology and capital.

As in Sino-Russian relations, it suits China to avoid any direct collision with India, even while continuing to sustain its close military cooperation with Pakistan and Burma. A policy of overt antagonism would have the negative effect of complicating China's tactically expedient accommodation with Russia, while also pushing India toward a more cooperative relationship with America. To the extent that India also shares an underlying and somewhat anti-Western predisposition against the existing global "hegemony," a reduction in Sino-Indian tensions is also in keeping with China's broader geostrategic focus.

The same considerations generally apply to China's ongoing relations with Southeast Asia. Even while unilaterally asserting their claims to the South China Sea, the Chinese have simultaneously cultivated Southeast Asian leaders (with the exception of the historically hostile Vietnamese), exploiting the more outspoken anti-Western sentiments (particularly on the issue of Western values and human rights) that in recent years have been voiced by the leaders of Malaysia and Singapore. They have especially welcomed the occasionally strident anti-American rhetoric of Prime Minister Datuk Mahathir of Malaysia, who in a May 1996 forum in Tokyo even publicly questioned the need for the U.S.-Japan Security Treaty, demanding to know the identity of the enemy the alliance is supposed to defend against and asserting that Malaysia does not need allies. The Chinese clearly calculate that their influence in the region will be automatically enhanced by any diminution of America's standing.

In a similar vein, patient pressure appears to be the motif of China's current policy toward Taiwan. While adopting an uncompromising position with regard to Taiwan's international status— to the point of even being willing to deliberately generate international tensions in order to convey China's seriousness on this matter (as in March 1996)—the Chinese leaders presumably realize that for the time being they will continue to lack the power to compel a satisfactory solution. They realize that a premature reliance on force would only serve to precipitate a self-defeating clash with America, while strengthening America's role as the regional guarantor of peace. Moreover, the Chinese themselves acknowledge that how effectively Hong Kong is first absorbed into China will greatly determine the prospects for the emergence of a Greater China.

The accommodation that has been taking place in China's relations with South Korea is also an integral part of the policy of consolidating its flanks in order to be able to concentrate more effectively on the central goal. Given Korean history and public emotions, a Sino-Korean accommodation of itself contributes to a reduction in Japan's potential regional role and prepares the ground for the reemergence of the more traditional relationship between China and (either a reunited or a still-divided) Korea.

Most important, the peaceful enhancement of China's regional standing will facilitate the pursuit of the central objective, which ancient China's strategist Sun Tsu might have formulated as follows: *to dilute American regional power to the point that a diminished America will come to need a regionally dominant China as its ally and eventually even a globally powerful China as its partner.* This goal is to be sought and accomplished in a manner that does not precipitate either a defensive expansion in the scope of the American-Japanese alliance or the regional replacement of America's power by that of Japan.

To attain the central objective, in the short run, China seeks to prevent the consolidation and expansion of American-Japanese security cooperation. China was particularly alarmed at the implied increase in early 1996 in the range of U.S.-Japanese security cooperation from the narrower "Far East" to a wider "Asia-Pacific," perceiving in it not only an immediate threat to China's interests but also the point of departure for an American-dominated Asian system of security aimed at containing China (in which Japan would be the vital linchpin,[6] much as Germany was in NATO during the Cold War). The agreement was generally perceived in Beijing as facilitating Japan's eventual emergence as a major military power, perhaps even capable of relying on force to resolve outstanding economic or maritime disputes on its own. China thus is likely to fan energetically the still strong Asian fears of any significant Japanese military role in the region, in order to restrain America and intimidate Japan.

However, in the longer run, according to China's strategic calculus, American hegemony cannot last. Although some Chinese, especially among the military, tend to view America as China's im-

---

[6]An elaborate examination of America's alleged intent to construct such an anti-China Asian system is contained in Wang Chunyin, "Looking Ahead to Asia-Pacific Security in the Early Twenty-first Century," *Guoji Zhanwang* (World Outlook), February 1996.

Another Chinese commentator argued that the American-Japanese security arrangement has been altered from a "shield of defense" aimed at containing Soviet power to a "spear of attack" pointed at China (Yang Baijiang, "Implications of Japan-U.S. Security Declaration Outlined," *Xiandai Guoji Guanxi* [Contemporary International Relations], June 20, 1996). On January 31, 1997, the authoritative daily organ of the Chinese Communist Party, *Renmin Ribao*, published an article entitled "Strengthening Military Alliance Does Not Conform with Trend of the Times," in which the redefinition of the scope of the U.S.-Japanese military cooperation was denounced as "a dangerous move."

placable foe, the predominant expectation in Beijing is that America will become regionally more isolated because of its excessive reliance on Japan and that consequently America's dependence on Japan will grow even further, but so will American-Japanese contradictions and American fears of Japanese militarism. That will then make it possible for China to play off America and Japan against each other, as China did earlier in the case of the United States and the Soviet Union. In Beijing's view, the time will come when America will realize that—to remain an influential Asia-Pacific power—it has no choice but to turn to its natural partner on the Asian mainland.

JAPAN: NOT REGIONAL BUT INTERNATIONAL

How the American-Japanese relationship evolves is thus a critical dimension in China's geopolitical future. Since the end of the Chinese civil war in 1949, America's policy in the Far East has been based on Japan. At first only the site for the occupying American military, Japan has since become the basis for America's political-military presence in the Asia-Pacific region and America's centrally important global ally, yet also a security protectorate. The emergence of China, however, does pose the question whether—and to what end—the close American-Japanese relationship can endure in the altering regional context. Japan's role in an anti-China alliance would be clear; but what should Japan's role be if China's rise is to be accommodated in some fashion even as it reduces America's primacy in the region?

Like China, Japan is a nation-state with a deeply ingrained sense of its unique character and special status. Its insular history, even its imperial mythology, has predisposed the highly industrious and disciplined Japanese people to see themselves as endowed with a distinctive and superior way of life, which Japan first defended by splendid isolation and then, when the world imposed itself in the nineteenth century, by emulating the European empires in seeking to create one of its own on the Asian mainland. The disaster of World War II then focused the Japanese people on the one-dimensional goal of economic recovery, but it also left them uncertain regarding their country's wider mission.

Current American fears of a dominant China are reminiscent of the relatively recent American paranoia regarding Japan. Japanophobia has now yielded to Sinophobia. A mere decade ago, predictions of Japan's inevitable and imminent appearance as the world's "superstate"—poised not only to dethrone America (even to buy it out!) but to impose some sort of a "Pax Nipponica"—were a veritable cottage industry among American commentators and politicians. But not only among the Americans. The Japanese themselves soon became eager imitators, with a series of best-sellers in Japan propounding the thesis that Japan was destined to prevail in its high-tech rivalry with the United States and that Japan would soon become the center of a global "information empire," while America was allegedly sliding into a decline because of historical fatigue and social self-indulgence.

These facile analyses obscured the degree to which Japan was, and remains, a vulnerable country. It is vulnerable to the slightest disruptions in the orderly global flow of resources and trade, not to mention global stability more generally, and it is beset by surfacing domestic weaknesses—demographic, social, and political. Japan is simultaneously rich, dynamic, and economically powerful, but it is also regionally isolated and politically limited by its security dependence on a powerful ally that happens to be the principal keeper of global stability (on which Japan so depends) as well as Japan's main economic rival.

It is unlikely that Japan's current position—on the one hand, as a globally respected economic powerhouse and, on the other, as a geopolitical extension of American power—will remain acceptable to the new generations of Japanese, no longer traumatized and shamed by the experience of World War II. For reasons of both history and self-esteem, Japan is a country not entirely satisfied with the global status quo, though in a more subdued fashion than China. It feels, with some justification, that it is entitled to formal recognition as a world power but is also aware that the regionally useful (and, to its Asian neighbors, reassuring) security dependence on America inhibits that recognition.

Moreover, China's growing power on the mainland of Asia, along with the prospect that its influence may soon radiate into the maritime regions of economic importance to Japan, intensifies the

Japanese sense of ambiguity regarding the country's geopolitical future. On the one hand, there is in Japan a strong cultural and emotional identification with China as well as a latent sense of a common Asian identity. Some Japanese may also feel that the emergence of a stronger China has the expedient effect of enhancing Japan's importance to the United States as America's regional paramountcy is reduced. On the other hand, for many Japanese, China is the traditional rival, a former enemy, and a potential threat to the stability of the region. That makes the security tie with America more important than ever, even if it increases the resentment of some of the more nationalistic Japanese concerning the irksome restraints on Japan's political and military independence.

There is a superficial similarity between Japan's situation in Eurasia's Far East and Germany's in Eurasia's Far West. Both are the principal regional allies of the United States. Indeed, American power in Europe and Asia is derived directly from the close alliances with these two countries. Both have respectable military establishments, but neither is independent in that regard: Germany is constrained by its military integration into NATO, while Japan is restricted by its own (though American-designed) constitutional limitations and the U.S.-Japan Security Treaty. Both are trade and financial powerhouses, regionally dominant and also preeminent on the global scale. Both can be classified as quasi-global powers, and both chafe at the continuing denial to them of formal recognition through permanent seats on the UN Security Council.

But the differences in their respective geopolitical conditions are pregnant with potentially significant consequences. Germany's actual relationship with NATO places the country on a par with its principal European allies, and under the North Atlantic Treaty, Germany has formal reciprocal defense obligations with the United States. The U.S.-Japan Security Treaty stipulates American obligations to defend Japan, but it does not provide (even if only formally) for the use of the Japanese military in the defense of America. The treaty in effect codifies a protective relationship.

Moreover, Germany, by its proactive membership in the European Union and NATO, is no longer seen as a threat by those neighbors who in the past were victims of its aggression but is viewed instead as a desirable economic and political partner. Some even welcome the potential emergence of a German-led Mitteleuropa, with Germany seen as a benign regional power. That is far from the case with Japan's Asian neighbors, who harbor lingering animosity toward Japan over World War II. A contributing factor to neighborly resentment is the appreciation of the yen, which has not only prompted bitter complaints but has impeded reconciliation with Malaysia, Indonesia, the Philippines, and even China, 30 percent of whose large long-term debts to Japan are in yen.

Japan also has no equivalent in Asia to Germany's France: that is, a genuine and more or less equal regional partner. There is admittedly a strong cultural attraction to China, mingled perhaps with a sense of guilt, but that attraction is politically ambiguous in that neither side trusts the other and neither is prepared to accept the other's regional leadership. Japan also has no equivalent to Germany's Poland: that is, a much weaker but geopolitically important neighbor with whom reconciliation and even cooperation is becoming a reality. Perhaps Korea, especially so after eventual reunification, could become that equivalent, but Japanese-Korean relations are only formally good, with the Korean memories of past domination and the Japanese sense of cultural superiority impeding any genuine social reconciliation.[7] Finally, Japan's relations with Russia have been much cooler than Germany's. Russia still retains the southern Kuril Islands by force, which it seized just before the end of World War II, thereby freezing the Russo-Japanese relationship. In brief, Japan is politically isolated in its region, whereas Germany is not.

In addition, Germany shares with its neighbors both common democratic principles and Europe's broader Christian heritage. It also seeks to identify and even sublimate itself within an entity and a cause larger than itself, namely, that of "Europe." In contrast, there is no comparable "Asia." Indeed, Japan's insular past and even its current democratic system tend to separate it from the rest of the region, in spite of the emergence in recent years of democracy in several Asian countries. Many Asians view Japan not only as nationally selfish but also as overly imitative of the West and reluctant to join them in questioning the West's views

---

[7]*The Japan Digest*, February 25, 1997, reported that, according to a governmental poll, only 36 percent of the Japanese felt friendly toward South Korea.

on human rights and on the importance of individualism. Thus, Japan is perceived as not truly Asian by many Asians, even as the West occasionally wonders to what degree Japan has truly become Western.

In effect, though in Asia, Japan is not comfortably Asian. That condition greatly limits its geostrategic options. A genuinely regional option, that of a regionally preponderant Japan that overshadows China—even if no longer based on Japanese domination but rather on benign Japanese-led regional cooperation—does not seem viable for solid historical, political, and cultural reasons. Furthermore, Japan remains dependent on American military protection and international sponsorship. The abrogation or even the gradual emasculation of the U.S.-Japan Security Treaty would render Japan instantly vulnerable to the disruptions that any serious manifestation of regional or global turmoil might produce. The only alternatives then would be either to accept China's regional predominance or to undertake a massive—and not only costly but also very dangerous—program of military rearmament.

Understandably, many Japanese find their country's present position—simultaneously a quasi-global power and a security protectorate—to be anomalous. But dramatic and viable alternatives to the existing arrangements are not self-evident. If it can be said that China's national goals, notwithstanding the inescapable variety of views among the Chinese strategists on specific aspects, are reasonably clear and the regional thrust of China's geopolitical ambitions relatively predictable, Japan's geostrategic vision tends to be relatively cloudy and the Japanese public mood much more ambiguous.

Most Japanese realize that a strategically significant and abrupt change of course could be dangerous. Can Japan become a regional power in a region where it is still the object of resentment and where China is emerging as the regionally preeminent power? Yet should Japan simply acquiesce in such a Chinese role? Can Japan become a truly comprehensive global power (in all its dimensions) without jeopardizing American support and galvanizing even more regional animosity? And will America, in any case, stay put in Asia, and if it does, how will its reaction to China's growing influence impinge on the priority so far given to the American-Japanese connection? For most of the Cold War, none of these questions ever had to be raised. Today, they have become strategically salient and are propelling an increasingly lively debate in Japan.

Since the 1950s, Japanese foreign policy has been guided by four basic principles promulgated by postwar Prime Minister Shigeru Yoshida. The Yoshida Doctrine postulated that (1) Japan's main goal should be economic development, (2) Japan should be lightly armed and should avoid involvement in international conflicts, (3) Japan should follow the political leadership of and accept military protection from the United States, and (4) Japanese diplomacy should be nonideological and should focus on international cooperation. However, since many Japanese also felt uneasy about the extent of Japan's involvement in the Cold War, the fiction of semineutrality was simultaneously cultivated. Indeed, as late as 1981, Foreign Minister Masayoshi Ito was forced to resign for having permitted the term "alliance" (*domei*) to be used in characterizing U.S.-Japan relations.

That is now all past. Japan was then recovering, China was self-isolated, and Eurasia was polarized. By contrast, Japan's political elite now senses that a rich Japan, economically involved in the world, can no longer define self-enrichment as its central national purpose without provoking international resentment. Further, an economically powerful Japan, especially one that competes with America, cannot simply be an extension of American foreign policy while at the same time avoiding any international political responsibilities. A politically more influential Japan, especially one that seeks global recognition (for example, a permanent seat on the UN Security Council), cannot avoid taking stands on the more critical security or geopolitical issues affecting world peace.

As a result, recent years have seen a proliferation of special studies and reports by a variety of Japanese public and private bodies, as well as a plethora of often controversial books by well-known politicians and professors, outlining new missions for Japan in the post–Cold War era.[8] Many of these have involved

---

[8]For example, the Higuchi Commission, a prime-ministerial advisory board that outlined the "Three Pillars of Japanese Security Policy" in a report issued in the summer of 1994, stressed the primacy of the American-Japanese security ties but also advocated an Asian multilateral security dialogue; the 1994 Ozawa Committee report, "Blueprint for a New Japan";

speculation regarding the durability and desirability of the American-Japanese security alliance and have advocated a more active Japanese diplomacy, especially toward China, or a more energetic Japanese military role in the region. If one were to judge the state of the American-Japanese connection on the basis of the public dialogue, one would be justified in concluding that by the mid-1990s relations between the two countries had entered a crisis stage.

However, on the level of public policy, the seriously discussed recommendations have been, on the whole, relatively sober, measured, and moderate. The extreme options—that of outright pacifism (tinged with an anti-U.S. flavor) or of unilateral and major rearmament (requiring a revision of the Constitution and pursued presumably in defiance of an adverse American and regional reaction)—have won few adherents. The public appeal of pacifism has, if anything, waned in recent years, and unilateralism and militarism have also failed to gain much public support, despite the advocacy of some flamboyant spokesmen. The public at large and certainly the influential business elite viscerally sense that neither option provides a real policy choice and, in fact, could only endanger Japan's well-being.

The politically dominant public discussions have primarily involved differences in emphasis regarding Japan's basic interna-

---

the *Yomiuri Shimbun's* outline for "A Comprehensive Security Policy" of May 1995, advocating among other items the use abroad of the Japanese military for peacekeeping; the April 1996 report of the Japan Association of Corporate Executives (*keizai doyukai*), prepared with the assistance of the Fuji Bank think tank, urging greater symmetry in the American-Japanese defense system; the report entitled "Possibility and Role of a Security System in the Asian-Pacific Region," submitted to the prime minister in June 1996 by the Japan Forum on International Affairs; as well as numerous books and articles published over the last several years, often much more polemical and extreme in their recommendations and more often cited by the Western media than the above-mentioned mostly mainstream reports. For example, in 1996 a book edited by a Japanese general evoked widespread press commentaries when it dared to speculate that under some circumstances the United States might fail to protect Japan and hence Japan should augment its national defense capabilities (see General Yasuhiro Morino, ed., *Next Generation Ground Self-Defense Force* and the commentary on it in "Myths of the U.S. Coming to Our Aid," *Sankei Shimbun,* March 4, 1996).

tional posture, with some secondary variations concerning geopolitical priorities. In broad terms, three major orientations, and perhaps a minor fourth one, can be identified and labeled as follows: the unabashed "America Firsters," the global mercantilists, the proactive realists, and the international visionaries. However, in the final analysis, all four share the same rather general goal and partake of the same central concern: *to exploit the special relationship with the United States in order to gain global recognition for Japan, while avoiding Asian hostility and without prematurely jeopardizing the American security umbrella.*

The first orientation takes as its point of departure the proposition that the maintenance of the existing (and admittedly asymmetrical) American-Japanese relationship should remain the central core of Japan's geostrategy. Its adherents desire, as do most Japanese, greater international recognition for Japan and more equality in the alliance, but it is their cardinal article of faith, as Prime Minister Kiichi Miyazawa put it in January 1993, that "the outlook for the world going into the twenty-first century will largely depend on whether or not Japan and the United States . . . are able to provide coordinated leadership under a shared vision." This viewpoint has been dominant within the internationalist political elite and the foreign policy establishment that has held power over the course of the last two or so decades. On the key geostrategic issues of China's regional role and America's presence in Korea, that leadership has been supportive of the United States, but it also sees its role as a source of restraint on any American propensity to adopt a confrontationist posture toward China. In fact, even this group has become increasingly inclined to emphasize the need for closer Japanese-Chinese relations, ranking them in importance just below the ties with America.

The second orientation does not contest the geostrategic identification of Japan's policy with America's, but it sees Japanese interests as best served by the frank recognition and acceptance of the fact that Japan is primarily an economic power. This outlook is most often associated with the traditionally influential bureaucracy of the MITI (Ministry of International Trade and Industry) and with the country's trading and export business leadership. In this view, Japan's relative demilitarization is an asset worth preserving. With America assuring the security of the country, Japan is free to pursue a policy of global economic engagement, which quietly enhances its global standing.

In an ideal world, the second orientation would be inclined to favor a policy of at least de facto neutralism, with America offsetting China's regional power and thereby protecting Taiwan and South Korea, thus making Japan free to cultivate a closer economic relationship with the mainland and with Southeast Asia. However, given the existing political realities, the global mercantilists accept the American-Japanese alliance as a necessary arrangement, including the relatively modest budgetary outlays for the Japanese armed forces (still not much exceeding 1 percent of the country's GDP), but they are not eager to infuse the alliance with any regionally significant substance.

The third group, the proactive realists, tend to be the new breed of politicians and geopolitical thinkers. They believe that as a rich and successful democracy Japan has both the opportunity and the obligation to make a real difference in the post–Cold War world. By doing so, it can also gain the global recognition to which Japan is entitled as an economic powerhouse that historically ranks among the world's few truly great nations. The appearance of such a more muscular Japanese posture was foreshadowed in the 1980s by Prime Minister Yasuhiro Nakasone, but perhaps the best-known exposition of that perspective was contained in the controversial Ozawa Committee report, published in 1994 and entitled suggestively "Blueprint for a New Japan: The Rethinking of a Nation."

Named after the committee's chairman, Ichiro Ozawa, a rapidly rising centrist political leader, the report advocated both a democratization of the country's hierarchical political culture and a rethinking of Japan's international posture. Urging Japan to become "a normal country," the report recommended the retention of the American-Japanese security connection but also counseled that Japan should abandon its international passivity by becoming actively engaged in global politics, especially by taking the lead in international peacekeeping efforts. To that end, the report recommended that the country's constitutional limitations on the dispatch abroad of Japanese armed forces be lifted.

Left unsaid but implied by the emphasis on "a normal country" was also the notion of a more significant geopolitical emancipation from America's security blanket. The advocates of this viewpoint tended to argue that on matters of global importance, Japan should not hesitate to speak up for Asia, instead of automatically following the American lead. However, they remained characteristically vague on such sensitive matters as the growing regional role of China or the future of Korea, not differing much from their more traditionalist colleagues. Thus, in regard to regional security, they partook of the still strong Japanese inclination to let both matters remain primarily the responsibility of America, with Japan merely exercising a moderating role on any excessive American zeal.

By the second half of the 1990s, this proactive realist orientation was beginning to dominate public thinking and affect the formulation of Japanese foreign policy. In the first half of 1996, the Japanese government started to speak of Japan's "independent diplomacy" (*jishu gaiko*), even though the ever-cautious Japanese Foreign Ministry chose to translate the Japanese phrase as the vaguer (and to America presumably less pointed) term "proactive diplomacy."

The fourth orientation, that of the international visionaries, has been less influential than any of the preceding, but it occasionally serves to infuse the Japanese viewpoint with more idealistic rhetoric. It tends to be associated publicly with outstanding individuals—like Akio Morita of Sony—who personally dramatize the importance to Japan of a demonstrative commitment to morally desirable global goals. Often invoking the notion of "a new global order," the visionaries call on Japan—precisely because it is not burdened by geopolitical responsibilities—to be a global leader in the development and advancement of a truly humane agenda for the world community.

All four orientations are in agreement on one key regional issue: that the emergence of more multilateral Asia-Pacific cooperation is in Japan's interest. Such cooperation can have, over time, three positive effects: it can help to engage (and also subtly to restrain) China; it can help to keep America in Asia, even while gradually reducing its predominance; and it can help to mitigate anti-Japanese resentment and thus increase Japan's influence. Although it is unlikely to create a Japanese sphere of regional influence, it might gain Japan some degree of regional deference, especially in the offshore maritime countries that may be uneasy over China's growing power.

All four viewpoints also agree that a cautious cultivation of China is much to be preferred over any American-led effort toward the direct containment of China. In fact, the notion of an American-led strategy to contain China, or even the idea of an informal balancing coalition confined to the island states of Taiwan, the Philippines, Brunei, and Indonesia, backed by Japan and America, has had no significant appeal for the Japanese foreign policy establishment. In the Japanese perspective, any effort of that sort would not only require an indefinite and major American military presence in both Japan and Korea but—by creating an incendiary geopolitical overlap between Chinese and American-Japanese regional interests (see map on page 184)—would be likely to become a self-fulfilling prophesy of a collision with China.[9] The result would be to inhibit Japan's evolutionary emancipation and threaten the Far East's economic well-being.

By the same token, few favor the opposite: a grand accommodation between Japan and China. The regional consequences of such a classical reversal of alliances would be too unsettling: an American withdrawal from the region as well as the prompt subordination of both Taiwan and Korea to China, leaving Japan at China's mercy. This is not an appealing prospect, save perhaps to a few extremists. With Russia geopolitically marginalized and historically despised, there is thus no alternative to the basic consensus that the link with America remains Japan's central lifeline. Without it, Japan can neither ensure itself a steady supply of oil nor protect itself from a Chinese (and perhaps soon, also a Korean) nuclear bomb. The only real policy issue is how best to manipulate the American connection in order to advance Japanese interests.

Accordingly, the Japanese have gone along with American desires to enhance American-Japanese military cooperation, including the seemingly increased scope from the more specific "Far

[9]Some conservative Japanese have been tempted by the notion of a special Japan-Taiwan connection, and in 1996 a "Japan-Taiwan Parliamentarians' Association" was formed to promote that goal. The Chinese reaction has been predictably hostile.

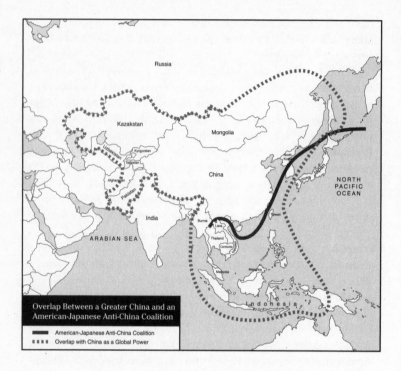

Overlap Between a Greater China and an
American-Japanese Anti-China Coalition

▬▬▬ American-Japanese Anti-China Coalition
▪ ▪ ▪ ▪ Overlap with China as a Global Power

East" to a broader "Asia-Pacific formula." Consistent with this, in early 1996 in its review of the so-called Japan-U.S. defense guidelines, the Japanese government also broadened its reference to the possible use of Japanese defense forces from in "Far East emergencies" to "emergencies in Japan's neighboring regions." Japanese willingness to accommodate America on this matter has also been driven by percolating doubts regarding America's long-term staying power in Asia and by concerns that China's rise—and America's seeming anxiety over it—could at some point in the future still impose on Japan an unacceptable choice: to stand with America against China or without America and allied with China.

For Japan, that fundamental dilemma also contains a historic imperative: since becoming a dominant regional power is not a viable goal and since without a regional base the attainment of truly comprehensive global power is unrealistic, it follows that Japan can best attain the status of a global leader through active involvement in worldwide peacekeeping and economic development. By taking advantage of the American-Japanese military alliance to ensure the stability of the Far East—but without letting it evolve into an anti-Chinese coalition—Japan can safely carve out a distinctive and influential global mission as the power that promotes the emergence of genuinely international and more effectively institutionalized cooperation. Japan could thus become a much more powerful and globally influential equivalent of Canada: a state that is respected for the constructive use of its wealth and power but one that is neither feared nor resented.

AMERICA'S GEOSTRATEGIC ADJUSTMENT

It should be the task of American policy to make certain that Japan pursues such a choice and that China's rise to regional preeminence does not preclude a stable triangular balance of East Asian power. The effort to manage both Japan and China and to maintain a stable three-way interaction that also involves America will severely tax American diplomatic skills and political imagination. Shedding past fixation on the threat allegedly posed by Japan's economic ascension and eschewing fears of Chinese political muscle could help to infuse cool realism into a policy that must be based on careful strategic calculus: *how to channel Japanese energy in the international direction and how to steer Chinese power into a regional accommodation.*

Only in this manner will America be able to forge on the eastern mainland of Eurasia a geopolitically congenial equivalent to Europe's role on the western periphery of Eurasia, that is, a structure of regional power based on shared interests. However, unlike the European case, a democratic bridgehead on the eastern mainland will not soon emerge. Instead, in the Far East the redirected alliance with Japan must also serve as the basis for an American accommodation with a regionally preeminent China.

For America, several important geostrategic conclusions flow from the analysis contained in the preceding two sections of this chapter:

The prevailing wisdom that China is the next global power is breeding paranoia about China and fostering megalomania within

China. Fears of an aggressive and antagonistic China that before long is destined to be the next global power are, at best, premature; and, at worst, they can become a self-fulfilling prophecy. It follows that it would be counterproductive to organize a coalition designed to contain China's rise to global power. That would only ensure that a regionally influential China would be hostile. At the same time, any such effort would strain the American-Japanese relationship, since most Japanese would be likely to oppose such a coalition. Accordingly, the United States should desist from pressing Japan to assume larger defense responsibilities in the Asia-Pacific region. Efforts to that effect will merely hinder the emergence of a stable relationship between Japan and China, while also further isolating Japan in the region.

But precisely because China is in fact not likely to emerge soon as a global power—and because for that very reason it would be unwise to pursue a policy of China's regional containment—it is desirable to treat China as a globally significant player. Drawing China into wider international cooperation and granting it the status it craves can have the effect of dulling the sharper edges of China's national ambitions. An important step in that direction would be to include China in the annual summit of the world's leading countries, the so-called G-7 (Group of Seven), especially since Russia has also been invited to it.

Despite appearances, China does not in fact have grand strategic options. China's continued economic success remains heavily dependent on the inflow of Western capital and technology and on access to foreign markets, and that severely limits China's options. An alliance with an unstable and impoverished Russia would not enhance China's economic or geopolitical prospects (and for Russia it would mean subordination to China). It is thus not a viable geostrategic option, even if it is tactically tempting for both China and Russia to toy with the idea. Chinese aid to Iran and Pakistan is of more immediate regional and geopolitical significance to China, but that also does not provide the point of departure for a serious quest for global power status. An "antihegemonic" coalition could become a last-resort option if China came to feel that its national or regional aspirations were being blocked by the United States (with Japan's support). But it would be a coalition of the poor, who would then be likely to remain collectively poor for quite some time.

A Greater China is emerging as the regionally dominant power. As such, it may attempt to impose itself on its neighbors in a manner that is regionally destabilizing; or it may be satisfied with exercising its influence more indirectly, in keeping with past Chinese imperial history. Whether a hegemonic sphere of influence or a vaguer sphere of deference emerges will depend in part on how brutal and authoritarian the Chinese regime remains and in part also on the manner in which the key outside players, notably America and Japan, react to the emergence of a Greater China. A policy of simple appeasement could encourage a more assertive Chinese posture; but a policy of merely obstructing the emergence of such a China would also be likely to produce a similar outcome. Cautious accommodation on some issues and a precise drawing of the line on others might avoid either extreme.

In any case, in some areas of Eurasia, a Greater China may exercise a geopolitical influence that is compatible with America's grand geostrategic interests in a stable but politically pluralistic Eurasia. For example, China's growing interest in Central Asia inevitably constrains Russia's freedom of action in seeking to achieve any form of political reintegration of the region under Moscow's control. In this connection and as related to the Persian Gulf, China's growing need for energy dictates a common interest with America in maintaining free access to and political stability in the oil-producing regions. Similarly, China's support for Pakistan restrains India's ambitions to subordinate that country and offsets India's inclination to cooperate with Russia in regard to Afghanistan and Central Asia. Finally, Chinese and Japanese involvement in the development of eastern Siberia can likewise help to enhance regional stability. These common interests should be explored through a sustained strategic dialogue.[10]

There are also areas where Chinese ambitions might clash with

[10]In a meeting in 1996 with China's top national security and defense officials, I identified (using occasionally deliberately vague formulations) the following areas of common strategic interest as the basis for such a dialogue: (1) a peaceful Southeast Asia; (2) nonuse of force in the resolution of offshore issues; (3) peaceful reunification of China; (4) stability in Korea; (5) independence of Central Asia; (6) balance between India and Pakistan; (7) an economically dynamic and internationally benign Japan; (8) a stable but not too strong Russia.

American (and also Japanese) interests, especially if these ambitions were to be pursued through historically more familiar strong-arm tactics. This applies particularly to Southeast Asia, Taiwan, and Korea.

Southeast Asia is potentially too rich, geographically too spread out, and simply too big to be easily subordinated by even a powerful China—but it is also too weak and politically too fragmented not to become at least a sphere of deference for China. China's regional influence, abetted by the Chinese financial and economic presence in all of the area's countries, is bound to grow as China's power increases. Much depends on how China applies that power, but it is not self-evident that America has any special interest in opposing it directly or in becoming involved in such issues as the South China Sea dispute. The Chinese have considerable historical experience in subtly managing unequal (or tributary) relationships, and it would certainly be in China's own interest to exercise self-restraint in order to avoid regional fears of Chinese imperialism. That fear could generate a regional anti-Chinese coalition (and some overtones of that are already present in the nascent Indonesian-Australian military cooperation), which would then most likely seek support from the United States, Japan, and Australia.

A Greater China, especially after digesting Hong Kong, will almost certainly seek more energetically to achieve Taiwan's reunification with the mainland. It is important to appreciate the fact that China has never acquiesced in the indefinite separation of Taiwan. Therefore, at some point, that issue could generate a head-on American-Chinese collision. Its consequences for all concerned would be most damaging: China's economic prospects would be set back; America's ties with Japan could become severely strained; and American efforts to create a stable balance of power in eastern Eurasia could be derailed.

Accordingly, it is essential to attain and maintain reciprocally the utmost clarity on this issue. Even if for the foreseeable future China is likely to lack the means to effectively coerce Taiwan, Beijing must understand—and be credibly convinced—that American acquiescence in an attempt at the forcible reintegration of Taiwan, sought by the use of military power, would be so devastating to America's position in the Far East that America simply could not afford to remain militarily passive if Taiwan were unable to protect itself.

In other words, America would have to intervene not for the sake of a separate Taiwan but for the sake of America's geopolitical interests in the Asia-Pacific area. This is an important distinction. The United States does not have, per se, any special interest in a separate Taiwan. In fact, its official position has been, and should remain, that there is only one China. But how China seeks reunification can impinge on vital American interests, and the Chinese have to be clearly aware of that.

The issue of Taiwan also gives America a legitimate reason for raising the human rights question in its dealings with China without justifying the accusation of interference in Chinese domestic affairs. It is perfectly appropriate to reiterate to Beijing that reunification will be accomplished only when China becomes more prosperous and more democratic. Only such a China will be able to attract Taiwan and assimilate it within a Greater China that is also prepared to be a confederation based on the principle of "one country, several systems." In any case, because of Taiwan, it is in China's own interest to enhance respect for human rights, and it is appropriate in that context for America to address the matter.

At the same time, it behooves the United States—in keeping with its promise to China—to abstain from directly or indirectly supporting any international upgrading of Taiwan's status. In the 1990s, some U.S.-Taiwanese official contacts conveyed the impression that the United States was tacitly beginning to treat Taiwan as a separate state, and the Chinese anger over this issue was understandable, as was Chinese resentment of the intensifying effort by Taiwanese officials to gain international recognition for Taiwan's separate status.

The United States should not be shy, therefore, in making it clear that its attitude toward Taiwan will be adversely affected by Taiwanese efforts to alter the long-established and deliberate ambiguities governing the China-Taiwan relationship. Moreover, if China does prosper and does democratize and if its absorption of Hong Kong does not involve a retrogression regarding civil rights, American encouragement of a serious cross-Strait dialogue regarding the terms of an eventual reunification would also help generate pressure for increased democratization within China, while fostering a wider strategic accommodation between the United States and a Greater China.

Korea, the geopolitically pivotal state in Northeast Asia, could again become a source of contention between America and China, and its future will also impact directly on the American-Japanese connection. As long as Korea remains divided and potentially vulnerable to a war between the unstable North and the increasingly rich South, American forces will have to remain on the peninsula. Any unilateral U.S. withdrawal would not only be likely to precipitate a new war but would, in all probability, also signal the end of the American military presence in Japan. It is difficult to conceive of the Japanese continuing to rely on continued U.S. deployment on Japanese soil in the wake of an American abandonment of South Korea. Rapid Japanese rearmament would be the most likely consequence, with broadly destabilizing consequences in the region as a whole.

Korea's reunification, however, would also be likely to pose serious geopolitical dilemmas. If American forces were to remain in a reunified Korea, they would inevitably be viewed by the Chinese as pointed against China. In fact, it is doubtful that the Chinese would acquiesce in reunification under these circumstances. If that reunification were taking place by stages, involving a so-called soft landing, China would obstruct it politically and support those elements in North Korea that remained opposed to reunification. If that reunification were taking place violently, with North Korea "crash landing," even Chinese military intervention could not be precluded. From the Chinese perspective, a reunified Korea would be acceptable only if it is not simultaneously a direct extension of American power (with Japan in the background as its springboard).

However, a reunified Korea without U.S. troops on its soil would be quite likely to gravitate first toward a form of neutrality between China and Japan and then gradually—driven in part by residual but still intense anti-Japanese feelings—toward a Chinese sphere of either politically more assertive influence or somewhat more delicate deference. The issue would then arise as to whether Japan would still be willing to serve as the only Asian base for

American power. At the very least, the issue would be most divisive within Japanese domestic politics. Any resulting retraction in the scope of U.S. military reach in the Far East would in turn make the maintenance of a stable Eurasian balance of power more difficult. These considerations thus enhance the American and Japanese stakes in the Korean status quo (though in each case, for somewhat different reasons), and if that status quo is to be altered, it must occur in very slow stages, preferably in a setting of a deepening American-Chinese regional accommodation.

In the meantime, a true Japanese-Korean reconciliation would contribute significantly to a more stable regional setting for any eventual reunification. The various international complications that could ensue from Korean reintegration would be mitigated by a genuine reconciliation between Japan and Korea, resulting in an increasingly cooperative and binding political relationship between these two countries. The United States could play the critical role in promoting that reconciliation. Many specific steps that were taken to advance first the German-French reconciliation and later that between Germany and Poland (for example, ranging from joint university programs eventually to combined military formations) could be adapted to this case. A comprehensive and regionally stabilizing Japanese-Korean partnership would, in turn, facilitate a continuing American presence in the Far East even perhaps after Korea's unification.

It almost goes without saying that a close political relationship with Japan is in America's global geostrategic interest. But whether Japan is to be America's vassal, rival, or partner depends on the ability of the Americans and Japanese to define more clearly what international goals the countries should seek in common and to demarcate more sharply the dividing line between the U.S. geostrategic mission in the Far East and Japan's aspirations for a global role. For Japan, despite the domestic debates about Japan's foreign policy, the relationship with America still remains the central beacon for its own sense of international direction. A disoriented Japan, lurching toward either rearmament or a separate accommodation with China, would spell the end of the American role in the Asia-Pacific region and would foreclose the emergence of a regionally stable triangular arrangement involving America, Japan, and China. That, in turn, would preclude the shaping of an American-managed political equilibrium throughout Eurasia.

In brief, a disoriented Japan would be like a beached whale: thrashing around helplessly but dangerously. It could destabilize Asia, but it could not create a viable alternative to the needed stabilizing balance among America, Japan, and China. It is only through a close alliance with Japan that America will be able to accommodate China's regional aspirations and constrain its more arbitrary manifestations. Only on that basis can an intricate three-way accommodation—one that involves America's global power, China's regional preeminence, and Japan's international leadership—be contrived.

It follows that in the foreseeable future, reduction of the existing levels of U.S. forces in Japan (and, by extension, in Korea) is not desirable. By the same token, however, any significant increase in the geopolitical scope and the actual magnitude of the Japanese military effort is also undesirable. A significant U.S. withdrawal would most probably prompt a major Japanese armament program in the context of an unsettling strategic disorientation, whereas American pressure on Japan to assume a greater military role can only damage the prospects for regional stability, impede a wider regional accommodation with a Greater China, divert Japan from undertaking a more constructive international mission, and thereby complicate the effort to foster stable geopolitical pluralism throughout Eurasia.

It also follows that Japan—if it is to turn its face to the world and away from Asia—must be given a meaningful incentive and a special status, so that its own national interest is thereby well served. Unlike China, which can seek global power by first becoming a regional power, Japan can gain global influence by eschewing the quest for regional power. But that makes it all the more important for Japan to feel that it is America's special partner in a global vocation that is as politically satisfying as it is economically beneficial. To that end, the United States would do well to consider the adoption of an American-Japanese free trade agreement, thereby creating a common American-Japanese economic space. Such a step, formalizing the growing linkage between the two economies, would provide the geopolitical underpinning both for America's continued presence in the Far East and for Japan's constructive global engagement.[11]

To conclude: For America, Japan should be its vital and foremost partner in the construction of an increasingly cooperative and pervasive system of global cooperation but not primarily its military ally in any regional arrangement designed to contest China's regional preeminence. In effect, Japan should be America's global partner in tackling the new agenda of world affairs. A regionally preeminent China should become America's Far Eastern anchor in the more traditional domain of power politics, helping thereby to foster a Eurasian balance of power, with Greater China in Eurasia's East matching in that respect the role of an enlarging Europe in Eurasia's West.

[11]A strong case for this initiative, pointing out the mutual economic benefits thereof, is made by Kurt Tong, "Revolutionizing America's Japan Policy," *Foreign Policy* (Winter 1996–1997).

CHAPTER 7

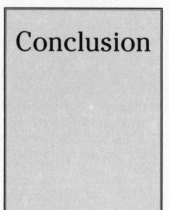

Conclusion

T HE TIME HAS COME for the United States to formulate and prosecute an integrated, comprehensive, and long-term geostrategy for all of Eurasia. This need arises out of the interaction between two fundamental realities: America is now the only global superpower, and Eurasia is the globe's central arena. Hence, what happens to the distribution of power on the Eurasian continent will be of decisive importance to America's global primacy and to America's historical legacy.

American global primacy is unique in its scope and character. It is a hegemony of a new type that reflects many of the features of the American democratic system: it is pluralistic, permeable, and flexible. Attained in the course of less than a century, the principal geopolitical manifestation of that hegemony is America's unprecedented role on the Eurasian landmass, hitherto the point of origin of all previous contenders for global power. America is now Eurasia's arbiter, with no major Eurasian issue soluble without America's participation or contrary to America's interests.

How the United States both manipulates and accommodates the principal geostrategic players on the Eurasian chessboard and how it manages Eurasia's key geopolitical pivots will be critical to the longevity and stability of America's global primacy. In Europe, the key players will continue to be France and Germany, and America's central goal should be to consolidate and expand the existing democratic bridgehead on Eurasia's western periphery. In Eurasia's Far East, China is likely to be increasingly central, and America will not have a political foothold on the Asian mainland unless an American-Chinese geostrategic consensus is successfully nurtured. In the center of Eurasia, the space between an enlarging Europe and a regionally rising China will remain a geopolitical black hole at least until Russia resolves its inner struggle over its postimperial self-definition, while the region to the south of Russia—the Eurasian Balkans—threatens to become a cauldron of ethnic conflict and great-power rivalry.

In that context, for some time to come—for more than a generation—America's status as the world's premier power is unlikely to be contested by any single challenger. No nation-state is likely to match America in the four key dimensions of power (military, economic, technological, and cultural) that cumulatively produce decisive global political clout. Short of a deliberate or unintentional American abdication, the only real alternative to American global leadership in the foreseeable future is international anarchy. In that respect, it is correct to assert that America has become, as President Clinton put it, the world's "indispensable nation."

It is important to stress here both the fact of that indispensability and the actuality of the potential for global anarchy. The disruptive consequences of population explosion, poverty-driven migration, radicalizing urbanization, ethnic and religious hostilities, and the proliferation of weapons of mass destruction would become unmanageable if the existing and underlying nation-state-based framework of even rudimentary geopolitical stability were itself to fragment. Without sustained and directed American involvement, before long the forces of global disorder could come to dominate the world scene. And the possibility of such a fragmentation is inherent in the geopolitical tensions not only of today's Eurasia but of the world more generally.

The resulting risks to global stability are likely to be further increased by the prospect of a more general degradation of the human condition. Particularly in the poorer countries of the world, the demographic explosion and the simultaneous urbanization of these populations are rapidly generating a congestion not only of the disadvantaged but especially of the hundreds of millions of unemployed and increasingly restless young, whose level of frustration is growing at an exponential rate. Modern communications intensify their rupture with traditional authority, while making them increasingly conscious—and resentful—of global inequality and thus more susceptible to extremist mobilization. On the one hand, the rising phenomenon of global migrations, already reaching into the tens of millions, may act as a temporary safety valve, but on the other hand, it is also likely to serve as a vehicle for the transcontinental conveyance of ethnic and social conflicts.

The global stewardship that America has inherited is hence likely to be buffeted by turbulence, tension, and at least sporadic violence. The new and complex international order, shaped by American hegemony and within which "the threat of war is off the table," is likely to be restricted to those parts of the world where American power has been reinforced by democratic sociopolitical systems and by elaborate external multilateral—but also American-dominated—frameworks.

An American geostrategy for Eurasia will thus be competing with the forces of turbulence. In Europe, there are signs that the momentum for integration and enlargement is waning and that traditional European nationalisms may reawaken before long. Large-scale unemployment persists even in the most successful European states, breeding xenophobic reactions that could suddenly cause a lurch in French or German politics toward significant political extremism and inward-oriented chauvinism. Indeed, a genuinely prerevolutionary situation could even be in the making. The historical timetable for Europe, outlined in chapter 3, will be met only if Europe's aspirations for unity are both encouraged and even prodded by the United States.

The uncertainties regarding Russia's future are even greater and the prospects for a positive evolution much more tenuous. It is therefore imperative for America to shape a geopolitical context that is congenial to Russia's assimilation into a larger setting of growing European cooperation and that also fosters the self-reliant independence of its newly sovereign neighbors. Yet the viability of, say, Ukraine or Uzbekistan (not to speak of the ethnically bifurcated Kazakstan) will remain uncertain, especially if American attention becomes diverted by new internal crises in Europe, by a growing gap between Turkey and Europe, or by intensifying hostility in American-Iranian relations.

The potential for an eventual grand accommodation with China could also be aborted by a future crisis over Taiwan; or because internal Chinese political dynamics prompt the emergence of an aggressive and hostile regime; or simply because American-Chinese relations turn sour. China could then become a highly destabilizing force in the world, imposing enormous strains on the American-Japanese relationship and perhaps also generating a disruptive geopolitical disorientation in Japan itself. In that setting, the stability of Southeast Asia would certainly be at risk, and one can only speculate how the confluence of these events would impact on the posture and cohesion of India, a country critical to the stability of South Asia.

These observations serve as a reminder that neither the new global problems that go beyond the scope of the nation-state nor more traditional geopolitical concerns are likely to be resolved, or even contained, if the underlying geopolitical structure of global power begins to crumble. With warning signs on the horizon across Europe and Asia, any successful American policy must focus on Eurasia as a whole and be guided by a geostrategic design.

A GEOSTRATEGY FOR EURASIA

The point of departure for the needed policy has to be hard-nosed recognition of the three unprecedented conditions that currently define the geopolitical state of world affairs: for the first time in history, (1) a single state is a truly global power, (2) a non-Eurasian state is globally the preeminent state, and (3) the globe's central arena, Eurasia, is dominated by a non-Eurasian power.

However, a comprehensive and integrated geostrategy for Eurasia must also be based on recognition of the limits of America's effective power and the inevitable attrition over time of its scope. As noted earlier, the very scale and diversity of Eurasia, as well as the potential power of some of its states, limit the depth of American influence and the degree of control over the course of events. This condition places a premium on geostrategic insight and on the deliberately selective deployment of America's resources on the huge Eurasian chessboard. And since America's unprecedented power is bound to diminish over time, the priority must be to manage the rise of other regional powers in ways that do not threaten America's global primacy.

As in chess, American global planners must think several moves ahead, anticipating possible countermoves. A sustainable geostrategy must therefore distinguish between the short-run perspective (the next five or so years), the middle term (up to twenty or so years), and the long run (beyond twenty years). Moreover, these phases must be viewed not as watertight compartments but as part of a continuum. The first phase must gradually and consistently lead into the second—indeed, be deliberately pointed toward it—and the second must then lead subsequently into the third.

In the short run, it is in America's interest to consolidate and perpetuate the prevailing geopolitical pluralism on the map of Eurasia. That puts a premium on maneuver and manipulation in order to prevent the emergence of a hostile coalition that could eventually seek to challenge America's primacy, not to mention the remote possibility of any one particular state seeking to do so. By the middle term, the foregoing should gradually yield to a greater emphasis on the emergence of increasingly important but strategically compatible partners who, prompted by American leadership, might help to shape a more cooperative trans-Eurasian security system. Eventually, in the much longer run still, the foregoing could phase into a global core of genuinely shared political responsibility.

The most immediate task is to make certain that no state or combination of states gains the capacity to expel the United States from Eurasia or even to diminish significantly its decisive arbitrating role. However, the consolidation of transcontinental geopolitical pluralism should not be viewed as an end in itself but only as a means to achieve the middle-term goal of shaping genuine strategic partnerships in the key regions of Eurasia. It is unlikely that democratic America will wish to be permanently engaged in the difficult, absorbing, and costly task of managing Eurasia by constant manipulation and maneuver, backed by American military resources, in order to prevent regional domination by any one power. The first phase must, therefore, logically and deliberately lead into the second, one in which a benign American hegemony still discourages others from posing a challenge not only by making the costs of the challenge too high but also by not threatening the vital interests of Eurasia's potential regional aspirants.

What that requires specifically, as the middle-term goal, is the fostering of genuine partnerships, predominant among them those with a more united and politically defined Europe and with a regionally preeminent China, as well as with (one hopes) a postimperial and Europe-oriented Russia and, on the southern fringe of Eurasia, with a regionally stabilizing and democratic India. But it will be the success or failure of the effort to forge broader strategic relationships with Europe and China, respectively, that will shape the defining context for Russia's role, either positive or negative.

It follows that a wider Europe and an enlarged NATO will serve well both the short-term and the longer-term goals of U.S. policy. A larger Europe will expand the range of American influence—and, through the admission of new Central European members, also increase in the European councils the number of states with a pro-American proclivity—without simultaneously creating a Europe politically so integrated that it could soon challenge the United States on geopolitical matters of high importance to America elsewhere, particularly in the Middle East. A politically defined Europe is also essential to the progressive assimilation of Russia into a system of global cooperation.

Admittedly, America cannot on its own generate a more united Europe—that is up to the Europeans, especially the French and the Germans—but America can obstruct the emergence of a more united Europe. And that could prove calamitous for stability in Eurasia and thus also for America's own interests. Indeed, unless Europe becomes more united, it is likely to become more disunited again. Accordingly, as stated earlier, it is vital that America work closely with both France and Germany in seeking a Europe that is politically viable, a Europe that remains linked to the United States, and a Europe that widens the scope of the cooperative democratic international system. Making a choice between France and Germany is not the issue. Without either France or Germany, there will be no Europe, and without Europe there will be no trans-Eurasian system.

In practical terms, the foregoing will require gradual accommodation to a shared leadership in NATO, greater acceptance of France's concerns for a European role not only in Africa but also in the Middle East, and continued support for the eastward expansion of the EU, even as the EU becomes a more politically and economically assertive global player.[1] A Transatlantic Free Trade Agreement, already advocated by a number of prominent Atlantic leaders, could also mitigate the risk of growing economic rivalry between a more united EU and the United States. In any case, the EU's eventual success in burying the centuries-old European nationalist antagonisms, with their globally disruptive effects, would be well worth some gradual diminution in America's decisive role as Eurasia's current arbitrator.

The enlargement of NATO and the EU would serve to reinvigorate Europe's own waning sense of a larger vocation, while consolidating, to the benefit of both America and Europe, the democratic gains won through the successful termination of the Cold War. At stake in this effort is nothing less than America's long-range relationship with Europe itself. A new Europe is still taking shape, and if that new Europe is to remain geopolitically a part of the "Euro-Atlantic" space, the expansion of NATO is essential. By the same token, a failure to widen NATO, now that the commitment has been made, would shatter the concept of an expanding Europe and demoralize the Central Europeans. It could even reignite currently dormant or dying Russian geopolitical aspirations in Central Europe.

Indeed, the failure of the American-led effort to expand NATO could reawaken even more ambitious Russian desires. It is not yet evident—and the historical record is strongly to the contrary—that the Russian political elite shares Europe's desire for a strong

---

[1] A number of constructive proposals to that end were advanced at the CSIS (Center for International and Strategic Studies) Conference on America and Europe, held in Brussels in February 1997. They ranged from joint efforts at structural reform, designed to reduce government deficits, to the development of an enhanced European defense industrial base, which would enhance transatlantic defense collaboration and a greater European role in NATO. A useful list of similar and other initiatives, meant to generate a greater European role, is contained in David C. Gompert and F. Stephen Larrabee, eds., *America and Europe: A Partnership for a New Era* (Santa Monica, Calif.: RAND, 1997).

and enduring American political and military presence. Therefore, while the fostering of an increasingly cooperative relationship with Russia is clearly desirable, it is important for America to send a clear message about its global priorities. If a choice has to be made between a larger Euro-Atlantic system and a better relationship with Russia, the former has to rank incomparably higher to America.

For that reason, any accommodation with Russia on the issue of NATO enlargement should not entail an outcome that has the effect of making Russia a de facto decision-making member of the alliance, thereby diluting NATO's special Euro-Atlantic character while simultaneously relegating its newly admitted members to second-class status. That would create opportunities for Russia to resume not only the effort to regain a sphere of influence in Central Europe but to use its presence within NATO to play on any American-European disagreements in order to reduce the American role in European affairs.

It is also crucial that, as Central Europe enters NATO, any new security assurances to Russia regarding the region be truly reciprocal and thus mutually reassuring. Restrictions on the deployment of NATO troops and nuclear weapons on the soil of new members can be an important factor in allaying legitimate Russian concerns, but these should be matched by symmetrical Russian assurances regarding the demilitarization of the potentially strategically menacing salient of Kaliningrad and by limits on major troop deployments near the borders of the prospective new members of NATO and the EU. While all of Russia's newly independent western neighbors are anxious to have a stable and cooperative relationship with Russia, the fact is that they continue to fear it for historically understandable reasons. Hence, the emergence of an equitable NATO/EU accommodation with Russia would be welcomed by all Europeans as a signal that Russia is finally making the much-desired postimperial choice in favor of Europe.

That choice could pave the way for a wider effort to enhance Russia's status and esteem. Formal membership in the G-7, as well as the upgrading of the policy-making machinery of the OSCE (within which a special security committee composed of America, Russia, and several key European countries could be established), would create opportunities for constructive Russian engagement in shaping both the political and security dimensions of Europe. Coupled with ongoing Western financial assistance to Russia, along with the development of much more ambitious schemes for linking Russia more closely to Europe through new highway and railroad networks, the process of giving substance to a Russian choice in favor of Europe could move forward significantly.

Russia's longer-term role in Eurasia will depend largely on the historic choice that Russia has to make, perhaps still in the course of this decade, regarding its own self-definition. Even with Europe and China increasing the radius of their respective regional influence, Russia will remain in charge of the world's largest single piece of real estate. It spans ten time zones and is territorially twice as large as either the United States or China, dwarfing in that regard even an enlarged Europe. Hence, territorial deprivation is not Russia's central problem. Rather, the huge Russia has to face squarely and draw the proper implications from the fact that both Europe and China are already economically more powerful and that China is also threatening to outpace Russia on the road to social modernization.

In these circumstances, it should become more evident to the Russian political elite that Russia's first priority is to modernize itself rather than to engage in a futile effort to regain its former status as a global power. Given the enormous size and diversity of the country, a decentralized political system, based on the free market, would be more likely to unleash the creative potential of both the Russian people and the country's vast natural resources. In turn, such a more decentralized Russia would be less susceptible to imperial mobilization. A loosely confederated Russia—composed of a European Russia, a Siberian Republic, and a Far Eastern Republic—would also find it easier to cultivate closer economic relations with Europe, with the new states of Central Asia, and with the Orient, which would thereby accelerate Russia's own development. Each of the three confederated entities would also be more able to tap local creative potential, stifled for centuries by Moscow's heavy bureaucratic hand.

A clear choice by Russia in favor of the European option over the imperial one will be more likely if America successfully pursues the second imperative strand of its strategy toward Russia: namely, reinforcing the prevailing geopolitical pluralism in the post-Soviet space. Such reinforcement will serve to discourage any imperial temptations. A postimperial and Europe-oriented Russia should actually view American efforts to that end as helpful in consolidating regional stability and in reducing the possibility of conflicts along its new, potentially unstable southern frontiers. But the policy of consolidating geopolitical pluralism should not be conditioned on the existence of a good relationship with Russia. Rather, it is also important insurance in case such a good relationship fails to develop, as it creates impediments to the reemergence of any truly threatening Russian imperial policy.

It follows that political and economic support for the key newly independent states is an integral part of a broader strategy for Eurasia. The consolidation of a sovereign Ukraine, which in the meantime redefines itself as a Central European state and engages in closer integration with Central Europe, is a critically important component of such a policy, as is the fostering of a closer relationship with such strategically pivotal states as Azerbaijan and Uzbekistan, in addition to the more generalized effort to open up Central Asia (in spite of Russian impediments) to the global economy.

Large-scale international investment in an increasingly accessible Caspian–Central Asian region would not only help to consolidate the independence of its new countries but in the long run would also benefit a postimperial and democratic Russia. The tapping of the region's energy and mineral resources would generate prosperity, prompting a greater sense of stability and security in the area, while perhaps also reducing the risks of Balkan-type conflicts. The benefits of accelerated regional development, funded by external investment, would also radiate to the adjoining Russian provinces, which tend to be economically underdeveloped. Moreover, once the region's new ruling elites come to realize that Russia acquiesces in the region's integration into the global economy, they will become less fearful of the political consequences of close economic relations with Russia. In time, a nonimperial Russia could thus gain acceptance as the region's preeminent economic partner, even though no longer its imperial ruler.

To promote a stable and independent southern Caucasus and Central Asia, America must be careful not to alienate Turkey and should explore whether an improvement in American-Iranian relations is feasible. A Turkey that feels that it is an outcast from Europe, which it has been seeking to join, will become a more Islamic Turkey, more likely to veto the enlargement of NATO out of spite and less likely to cooperate with the West in seeking both to stabilize and integrate a secular Central Asia into the world community.

Accordingly, America should use its influence in Europe to encourage Turkey's eventual admission to the EU and should make a point of treating Turkey as a European state—provided internal Turkish politics do not take a dramatic turn in the Islamist direction. Regular consultations with Ankara regarding the future of the Caspian Sea basin and Central Asia would foster in Turkey a sense of strategic partnership with the United States. America should also strongly support Turkish aspirations to have a pipeline from Baku in Azerbaijan to Ceyhan on the Turkish Mediterranean coast serve as major outlet for the Caspian Sea basin energy sources.

In addition, it is not in America's interest to perpetuate American-Iranian hostility. Any eventual reconciliation should be based on the recognition of a mutual strategic interest in stabilizing what currently is a very volatile regional environment for Iran. Admittedly, any such reconciliation must be pursued by both sides and is not a favor granted by one to the other. A strong, even religiously motivated but not fanatically anti-Western Iran is in the U.S. interest, and ultimately even the Iranian political elite may recognize that reality. In the meantime, American long-range interests in Eurasia would be better served by abandoning existing U.S. objections to closer Turkish-Iranian economic cooperation, especially in the construction of new pipelines, and also to the construction of other links between Iran, Azerbaijan, and Turkmenistan. Long-term American participation in the financing of such projects would in fact also be in the American interest.[2]

[2]It is appropriate to quote here the wise advice offered by my colleague at CSIS, Anthony H. Cordesman (in his paper on "The American Threat to the United States," February 1997, p. 16, delivered as a speech to the Army War College), who has warned against the American propensity to demonize issues and even nations. As he put it: "Iran, Iraq, and Libya are cases where the U.S. has taken hostile regimes that pose real, but limited threats and 'demonized' them without developing any workable mid- to long-term end game for its strategy. U.S. planners cannot hope to totally isolate these states, and it makes no sense to treat them as if they were identical 'rogue' or 'terrorist' states. . . . The U.S. lives in a morally gray world and cannot succeed by trying to make it black and white."

India's potential role needs also to be highlighted, although it is currently a relatively passive player on the Eurasian scene. India is contained geopolitically by the Chinese-Pakistani coalition, while a weak Russia cannot offer it the political support once provided by the Soviet Union. However, the survival of its democracy is of importance in that it refutes better than volumes of academic debate the notion that human rights and democracy are purely a parochial Western manifestation. India proves that antidemocratic "Asian values," propagated by spokesmen from Singapore to China, are simply antidemocratic but not necessarily characteristic of Asia. India's failure, by the same token, would be a blow to the prospects for democracy and would remove from the scene a power that contributes to greater balance on the Asian scene, especially given China's rise to geopolitical preeminence. It follows that a progressive engagement of India in discussions pertaining to regional stability, especially regarding the future of Central Asia, is becoming timely, not to mention the promotion of more directly bilateral connections between American and Indian defense communities.

Geopolitical pluralism in Eurasia as a whole will neither be attainable nor stable without a deepening strategic understanding between America and China. It follows that a policy of engaging China in a serious strategic dialogue, eventually perhaps in a three-way effort that involves Japan as well, is the necessary first step in enhancing China's interest in an accommodation with America that reflects the several geopolitical interests (especially in Northeast Asia and in Central Asia) the two countries in fact share in common. It also behooves America to eliminate any uncertainties regarding America's own commitment to the one-China policy, lest the Taiwan issue fester and worsen, especially after China's absorption of Hong Kong. By the same token, it is in China's own interest to make that absorption a successful demonstration of the principle that even a Greater China can tolerate and safeguard increased diversity in its internal political arrangements.

While—as argued earlier in chapters 4 and 6—any would-be Chinese-Russian-Iranian coalition against America is unlikely to jell beyond some occasional tactical posturing, it is important for the United States to deal with China in a fashion that does not drive

Beijing in that direction. In any such "antihegemonic" alliance, China would be the linchpin. It would be the strongest, the most dynamic, and thus the leading component. Such a coalition could only emerge around a disaffected, frustrated, and hostile China. Neither Russia nor Iran has the wherewithal to be the central magnet for such a coalition.

An American-Chinese strategic dialogue regarding the areas that both countries desire to see free of domination by other aspiring hegemons is therefore imperative. But to make progress, the dialogue should be sustained and serious. In the course of such communication, more contentious issues pertaining to Taiwan and even to human rights could then be addressed more persuasively. Indeed, the point can be made quite credibly that the issue of China's internal liberalization is not a purely domestic Chinese affair, since only a democratizing and prosperous China has any prospect of peacefully enticing Taiwan. Any attempt at forcible reunification would not only place the American-Chinese relationship in jeopardy but would inevitably generate adverse consequences for China's capacity to attract foreign capital and sustain its development. China's own aspirations to regional preeminence and global status would thereby be victimized.

Although China is emerging as a regionally dominant power, it is not likely to become a global one for a long time to come (for reasons stated in chapter 6)—and paranoiac fears of China as a global power are breeding megalomania in China, while perhaps also becoming the source of a self-fulfilling prophesy of intensified American-Chinese hostility. Accordingly, China should be neither contained nor propitiated. It should be treated with respect as the world's largest developing state, and—so far at least—a rather successful one. Its geopolitical role not only in the Far East but in Eurasia as a whole is likely to grow as well. Hence, it would make sense to coopt China into the G-7 annual summit of the world's leading countries, especially since Russia's inclusion has widened the summit's focus from economics to politics.

As China becomes more integrated into the world system and hence less able and less inclined to exploit its regional primacy in a politically obtuse fashion, it also follows that a de facto emergence of a Chinese sphere of deference in areas of historic interest to China is likely to be part of the emerging Eurasian structure of geopolitical accommodation. Whether a united Korea will oscillate toward such a sphere depends much on the degree of Japanese-Korean reconciliation (which America should more actively encourage), but in any case, the reunification of Korea without an accommodation with China is unlikely.

A Greater China at some point will inevitably press for a resolution of the issue of Taiwan, but the degree of China's inclusion in an increasingly binding set of international economic and political links may also have a positive impact on the nature of Chinese domestic politics. If China's absorption of Hong Kong proves not to be repressive, Deng's formula for Taiwan of "one country, two systems" can become redefined as "one country, several systems." That might make reunification more acceptable to the parties concerned—which again reinforces the point that without some political evolution of China itself, a peaceful reconstitution of one China will not be possible.

In any case, for historic as well as geopolitical reasons, China should consider America its natural ally. Unlike Japan or Russia, America has never had any territorial designs on China; and, unlike Great Britain, it never humiliated China. Moreover, without a viable strategic consensus with America, China is not likely to be able to keep attracting the massive foreign investment so necessary to its economic growth and thus also to its attainment of regional preeminence. For the same reason, without an American-Chinese strategic accommodation as the eastern anchor of America's involvement in Eurasia, America will not have a geostrategy for mainland Asia; and without a geostrategy for mainland Asia, America will not have a geostrategy for Eurasia. Thus for America, China's regional power, co-opted into a wider framework of international cooperation, can be a vitally important geostrategic asset—in that regard coequally important with Europe and more weighty than Japan—in assuring Eurasia's stability.

However, unlike the European situation, a democratic bridgehead on the eastern mainland will not emerge soon. That makes it all the more important that America's efforts to nurture a deepening strategic relationship with China be based on the unambiguous acknowledgment that a democratic and economically successful Japan is America's premier Pacific and key global partner. Although Japan cannot become a dominant Asian regional power, given the strong regional aversion it evokes, it can become a leading international one. Tokyo can carve out a globally influential role by cooperating closely with the United States regarding what might be called the new agenda of global concerns, while avoiding any futile and potentially counterproductive effort to become a regional power itself. The task of American statesmanship should hence be to steer Japan in that direction. An American-Japanese free trade agreement, creating a common economic space, would fortify the connection and promote the goal, and hence its utility should be jointly examined.

It is through a close political relationship with Japan that America will more safely be able to accommodate China's regional aspirations, while opposing its more arbitrary manifestations. Only on that basis can an intricate three-way accommodation—one that involves America's global power, China's regional preeminence, and Japan's international leadership—be contrived. However, that broad geostrategic accommodation could be undermined by an unwise expansion of American-Japanese military cooperation. Japan's central role should not be that of America's unsinkable aircraft carrier in the Far East, nor should it be America's principal Asian military partner or a potential Asian regional power. Misguided efforts to promote any of the foregoing would serve to cut America off from the Asian mainland, to vitiate the prospects for reaching a strategic consensus with China, and thus to frustrate America's capacity to consolidate stable geopolitical pluralism throughout Eurasia.

A TRANS-EURASIAN SECURITY SYSTEM

The stability of Eurasia's geopolitical pluralism, precluding the appearance of a single dominant power, would be enhanced by the eventual emergence, perhaps sometime early in the next century, of a Trans-Eurasian Security System (TESS). Such a transcontinental security agreement should embrace an expanded NATO—connected by a cooperative charter with Russia—and China as well as Japan (which would still be connected to the United States by the bilateral security treaty). But to get there, NATO must first expand, while engaging Russia in a larger regional framework of security cooperation. In addition, the Americans and Japanese must closely consult and collaborate in setting in motion a triangular political-security dialogue in the Far East that engages China. Three-way American-Japanese-Chinese security talks could eventually involve more Asian participants and later lead to a dialogue between them and the Organization for Security and Cooperation in Europe. In turn, such a dialogue could pave the way for a series of conferences by all European and Asian states, thereby beginning the process of institutionalizing a transcontinental security system.

In time, a more formal structure could begin to take shape, prompting the emergence of a Trans-Eurasian Security System that for the first time would span the entire continent. The shaping of that system—defining its substance and then institutionalizing it—could become the major architectural initiative of the next decade, once the policies outlined earlier have created the necessary preconditions. Such a broad transcontinental security framework could also contain a standing security committee, composed of the major Eurasian entities, in order to enhance TESS's ability to promote effective cooperation on issues critical to global stability. America, Europe, China, Japan, a confederated Russia, and India, as well as perhaps some other countries, might serve together as the core of such a more structured transcontinental system. The eventual emergence of TESS could gradually relieve America of some of its burdens, even while perpetuating its decisive role as Eurasia's stabilizer and arbitrator.

BEYOND THE LAST GLOBAL SUPERPOWER

In the long run, global politics are bound to become increasingly uncongenial to the concentration of hegemonic power in the hands of a single state. Hence, America is not only the first, as well as the only, truly global superpower, but it is also likely to be the very last.

That is so not only because nation-states are gradually becoming increasingly permeable but also because knowledge as power is becoming more diffuse, more shared, and less constrained by national boundaries. Economic power is also likely to become more dispersed. In the years to come, no single power is likely to reach the level of 30 percent or so of the world's GDP that America sustained throughout much of this century, not to speak of the 50 percent at which it crested in 1945. Some estimates suggest that by the end of this decade, America will still account for about 20 percent of global GDP, declining perhaps to about 10–15 percent by 2020 as other powers—Europe, China, Japan—increase their relative share to more or less the American level. But global economic preponderance by a single entity, of the sort that America attained in the course of this century, is unlikely, and that has obviously far-reaching military and political implications.

Moreover, the very multinational and exceptional character of American society has made it easier for America to universalize its hegemony without letting it appear to be a strictly national one. For example, an effort by China to seek global primacy would inevitably be viewed by others as an attempt to impose a national hegemony. To put it very simply, anyone can become an American, but only a Chinese can be Chinese—and that places an additional and significant barrier in the way of any essentially national global hegemony.

Accordingly, once American leadership begins to fade, America's current global predominance is unlikely to be replicated by any single state. Thus, the key question for the future is "What will America bequeath to the world as the enduring legacy of its primacy?"

The answer depends in part on how long that primacy lasts and on how energetically America shapes a framework of key power partnerships that over time can be more formally institutionalized. In fact, the window of historical opportunity for America's constructive exploitation of its global power could prove to be relatively brief, for both domestic and external reasons. A genuinely populist democracy has never before attained international supremacy. The pursuit of power and especially the economic costs and human sacrifice that the exercise of such power often requires are not generally congenial to democratic instincts. Democratization is inimical to imperial mobilization.

Indeed, the critical uncertainty regarding the future may well be whether America might become the first superpower unable or unwilling to wield its power. Might it become an impotent global power? Public opinion polls suggest that only a small minority (13 percent) of Americans favor the proposition that "as the sole remaining superpower, the U.S. should continue to be the preeminent world leader in solving international problems." An overwhelming majority (74 percent) prefer that America "do its fair share in efforts to solve international problems together with other countries."[3]

Moreover, as America becomes an increasingly multicultural society, it may find it more difficult to fashion a consensus on foreign policy issues, except in the circumstances of a truly massive and widely perceived direct external threat. Such a consensus generally existed throughout World War II and even during the Cold War. It was rooted, however, not only in deeply shared democratic values, which the public sensed were being threatened, but also in a cultural and ethnic affinity for the predominantly European victims of hostile totalitarianisms.

In the absence of a comparable external challenge, American society may find it much more difficult to reach agreement regarding foreign policies that cannot be directly related to central beliefs and widely shared cultural-ethnic sympathies and that still require an enduring and sometimes costly imperial engagement. If anything, two extremely varying views on the implications of America's historic victory in the Cold War are likely to be politically more appealing: on the one hand, the view that the end of the Cold War justifies a significant reduction in America's global engagement, irrespective of the consequences for America's global standing; and on the other, the perception that the time has come for genuine international multilateralism, to which America should even yield some of its sovereignty. Both extremes command the loyalty of committed constituencies.

More generally, cultural change in America may also be uncon-

---

[3]"An Emerging Consensus—A Study of American Public Attitudes on America's Role in the World" (College Park: Center for International and Security Studies at the University of Maryland, July 1996). It is noteworthy, but not inconsistent with the foregoing, that studies by the above center, conducted in early 1997 (under principal investigator Steven Kull), also showed a considerable majority in favor of NATO expansion (62 percent in favor, with 27 percent strongly in favor; and only 29 percent against, with 14 percent strongly against).

genial to the sustained exercise abroad of genuinely imperial power. That exercise requires a high degree of doctrinal motivation, intellectual commitment, and patriotic gratification. Yet the dominant culture of the country has become increasingly fixated on mass entertainment that has been heavily dominated by personally hedonistic and socially escapist themes. The cumulative effect has made it increasingly difficult to mobilize the needed political consensus on behalf of sustained, and also occasionally costly, American leadership abroad. Mass communications have been playing a particularly important role in that regard, generating a strong revulsion against any selective use of force that entails even low levels of casualties.

In addition, both America and Western Europe have been finding it difficult to cope with the cultural consequences of social hedonism and the dramatic decline in the centrality of religious-based values in society. (The parallels with the decline of the imperial systems summarized in chapter 1 are striking in that respect.) The resulting cultural crisis has been compounded by the spread of drugs and, especially in America, by its linkage to the racial issue. Lastly, the rate of economic growth is no longer able to keep up with growing material expectations, with the latter stimulated by a culture that places a premium on consumption. It is no exaggeration to state that a sense of historical anxiety, perhaps even of pessimism, is becoming palpable in the more articulate sectors of Western society.

Almost half a century ago, a noted historian, Hans Kohn, having observed the tragic experience of the two world wars and the debilitating consequences of the totalitarian challenge, worried that the West may have become "fatigued and exhausted." Indeed, he feared that

> [t]wentieth century man has become less confident than his nineteenth century ancestor was. He has witnessed the dark powers of history in his own experience. Things which seemed to belong to the past have reappeared: fanatical faith, infallible leaders, slavery and massacres, the uprooting of whole populations, ruthlessness and barbarism.[4]

[4]Hans Kohn. *The Twentieth Century* (New York: 1949), p. 53.

That lack of confidence has been intensified by widespread dis-appointment with the consequences of the end of the Cold War. In-stead of a "new world order" based on consensus and harmony, "things which seemed to belong to the past" have all of a sudden be-come the future. Although ethnic-national conflicts may no longer pose the risk of a central war, they do threaten the peace in signifi-cant parts of the globe. Thus, war is not likely to become obsolete for some time to come. With the more-endowed nations constrained by their own higher technological capacity for self-destruction as well as by self-interest, war may have become a luxury that only the poor peoples of this world can afford. In the foreseeable future, the impoverished two-thirds of humanity may not be motivated by the restraint of the privileged.

It is also noteworthy that international conflicts and acts of terrorism have so far been remarkably devoid of any use of the weapons of mass destruction. How long that self-restraint may hold is inherently unpredictable, but the increasing availability, not only to states but also to organized groups, of the means to inflict massive casualties—by the use of nuclear or bacteriologi-cal weapons—also inevitably increases the probability of their employment.

In brief, America as the world's premier power does face a nar-row window of historical opportunity. The present moment of rela-tive global peace may be short lived. This prospect underlines the urgent need for an American engagement in the world that is delib-erately focused on the enhancement of international geopolitical stability and that is capable of reviving in the West a sense of his-torical optimism. That optimism requires the demonstrated capac-ity to deal simultaneously with internal social and external geopolitical challenges.

However, the rekindling of Western optimism and the universal-ism of the West's values are not exclusively dependent on America and Europe. Japan and India demonstrate that the notions of hu-man rights and the centrality of the democratic experiment can be valid in Asian settings as well, both in highly developed ones and in those that are still only developing. The continued democratic success of Japan and India is, therefore, also of enormous impor-tance in sustaining a more confident perspective regarding the fu-ture political shape of the globe. Indeed, their experience, as well as that of South Korea and Taiwan, suggests that China's continued economic growth, coupled with pressures from outside for change generated by greater international inclusion, might perhaps also lead to the progressive democratization of the Chinese system.

Meeting these challenges is America's burden as well as its unique responsibility. Given the reality of American democracy, an effective response will require generating a public understanding of the continuing importance of American power in shaping a widening framework of stable geopolitical cooperation, one that simultaneously averts global anarchy and successfully defers the emergence of a new power challenge. These two goals—averting global anarchy and impeding the emergence of a power rival—are inseparable from the longer-range definition of the purpose of America's global engagement, namely, that of forging an enduring framework of global geopolitical cooperation.

Unfortunately, to date, efforts to spell out a new central and worldwide objective for the United States, in the wake of the termination of the Cold War, have been one-dimensional. They have failed to link the need to improve the human condition with the imperative of preserving the centrality of American power in world affairs. Several such recent attempts can be identified. During the first two years of the Clinton administration, the advocacy of "assertive multilateralism" did not sufficiently take into account the basic realities of contemporary power. Later on, the alternative emphasis on the notion that America should focus on global "democratic enlargement" did not adequately take into account the continuing importance to America of maintaining global stability or even of promoting some expedient (but regrettably not "democratic") power relationships, as with China.

As the central U.S. priority, more narrowly focused appeals have been even less satisfactory, such as those concentrating on the elimination of prevailing injustice in the global distribution of income, on shaping a special "mature strategic partnership" with Russia, or on containing weapons proliferation. Other alternatives—that America should concentrate on safeguarding the environment or, more narrowly, on combating local wars—have also tended to ignore the central realities of global power. As a result, none of the foregoing formulations have fully addressed the need to create minimal global geopolitical stability as the essential foundation for the simultaneous protraction of American hegemony and the effective aversion of international anarchy.

In brief, the U.S. policy goal must be unapologetically twofold: to perpetuate America's own dominant position for at least a generation and preferably longer still; and to create a geopolitical framework that can absorb the inevitable shocks and strains of social-political change while evolving into the geopolitical core of shared responsibility for peaceful global management. A prolonged phase of gradually expanding cooperation with key Eurasian partners, both stimulated and arbitrated by America, can also help to foster the preconditions for an eventual upgrading of the existing and increasingly antiquated UN structures. A new distribution of responsibilities and privileges can then take into account the changed realities of global power, so drastically different from those of 1945.

These efforts will have the added historical advantage of benefiting from the new web of global linkages that is growing exponentially outside the more traditional nation-state system. That web—woven by multinational corporations, NGOs (nongovernmental organizations, with many of them transnational in character) and scientific communities and reinforced by the Internet—already creates an informal global system that is inherently congenial to more institutionalized and inclusive global cooperation.

In the course of the next several decades, a functioning structure of global cooperation, based on geopolitical realities, could thus emerge and gradually assume the mantle of the world's current "regent," which has for the time being assumed the burden of responsibility for world stability and peace. Geostrategic success in that cause would represent a fitting legacy of America's role as the first, only, and last truly global superpower.

Index